## Praise for *The Challenge of Mod*

"This well-written book should not be ignored. With elegance and determination, Christine Douglass-Williams documents a variety of Muslim reformers, of a wide range of backgrounds and persuasions. These courageous men and women should be as well-known as human rights dissidents Solzhenitsyn, Sakharov, and Havel were during the Cold War. Through a series of probing interviews and careful reflection, Douglass-Williams draws out the nature of reformers' inner struggles and ideals, contrasting them with the beliefs of Islamists. This book is highly recommended for those wishing to learn more about Muslim reformers, and it is a must-read for U.S. policymakers who wish to understand the challenge of Islamism in America and the world today."

> —Ayaan Hirsi Ali, research fellow at the Hoover Institution at Stanford University and Founder of the AHA Foundation

"Incisive and informed, *The Challenge of Modernizing Islam* by Christine Douglass-Williams offers us the powerful insight needed to launch a new conversation about Islam. It fills the mind with deep knowledge and urgent necessity."

> —Edwin Black, author of *IBM and the Holocaust* and *The Farhud*

"My library contains a wall of books about modern Islam. But hardly a one of them covers the topic of this important study by Christine Douglass-Williams....She also helps establish this movement as a serious intellectual endeavor, putting contemporary modernizers on the map as never before, thereby boosting their cause. Given the global threat of Islamism, that is a constructive, indeed a great, achievement."

> —From the Foreword by Daniel Pipes

"*The Challenge of Modernizing Islam* is extraordinary, refreshing, and much needed. The interviews that Christine Douglass-Williams conducts with some of the leading moderate Muslim spokesmen in the United States and Canada are unique in their probing honesty. Douglass-Williams also provides illuminating ways for readers to avoid hazards that have misled numerous analysts of Islam and its prospects for reform. *The Challenge of Modernizing Islam* uniquely equips readers to make an informed and intelligent evaluation of how peaceful the future of non-Muslim countries is likely to be."

—From the Foreword by Robert Spencer

# THE CHALLENGE OF
# MODERNIZING ISLAM

## REFORMERS SPEAK OUT AND THE OBSTACLES THEY FACE

### CHRISTINE DOUGLASS-WILLIAMS
#### WITH A NEW PREFACE BY THE AUTHOR

New York • London

First American edition published in 2017 by Encounter Books,
an activity of Encounter for Culture and Education, Inc.,
a nonprofit, tax exempt corporation.
Encounter Books website address: www.encounterbooks.com

Manufactured in the United States and printed on
acid-free paper. The paper used in this publication meets
the minimum requirements of ANSI/NISO Z39.48-1992
(R 1997) (*Permanence of Paper*).

First paperback edition published in 2019.
Paperback edition ISBN: 978-1-64177-020-0

THE LIBRARY OF CONGRESS HAS CATALOGUED
THE HARDCOVER EDITION AS FOLLOWS:

Names: Douglass-Williams, Christine, author.
Title: The challenge of modernizing Islam : reformers speak out and the
obstacles they face / by Christine Douglass-Williams ; with forewords by
Daniel Pipes and Robert Spencer.
Description: New York : Encounter Books, 2017. |
Includes bibliographical references and index.
Identifiers: LCCN 2017017617 (print) | LCCN 2016058766 (ebook) |
ISBN 9781594039393 (hardcover : alk. paper) | ISBN 9781594039409 (Ebook)
Subjects: LCSH: Reformers—Islamic countries—Interviews. |
Islamic renewal. | Islam and politics.
Classification: LCC BP70 .D69 2017 (ebook) | LCC BP70 (print) |
DDC 297.09/051—dc23
LC record available at https://lccn.loc.gov/2017017617

*Interior page design and composition: BooksByBruce.com*

*This book is dedicated to my joy and my heart,*
*my daughter Natasha Leigh Williams*

# CONTENTS

# PREFACE TO THE PAPERBACK EDITION

July 31, 2018

Since *The Challenge of Modernizing Islam* first appeared, I have been targeted by the Liberal Government of Canada for doing what the Muslims I profile in the book are doing: standing up against Islamic jihad violence, Muslim Brotherhood stratagems, and the oppression that is justified by the Sharia.

On December 19, 2017, I was terminated from the Board of Directors of the Canadian Race Relations Foundation (CRRF) by the Queen's Privy Council, on the advice of the Heritage Minister of Justin Trudeau's government in Canada, Melanie Joly, who was moved to a Tourism portfolio in July 2018 during a cabinet shuffle.

My termination came four months after I received a threatening letter from Joly about my writings on political Islam for the online publication *Jihad Watch,* directed by Robert Spencer and a project of the David Horowitz Freedom Center in California.

I was appointed to the CRRF in 2012 under the Conservative Stephen Harper government, and reappointed in 2015. The CRRF was switched from the Department of Citizenship and Immigration over to the Department of Heritage after Justin Trudeau was elected as Prime Minister of Canada in 2015. Trudeau also immediately shut down the Office of Religious Freedom of which I served as an external advisor. The office, which denounced draconian blasphemy laws globally, was deemed by the Liberals to have favored one religion over another. It was originally dedicated to Shahbaz Bhatti, a Christian who was minister of minorities in Pakistan who openly opposed Pakistan's blasphemy laws and was assassinated for doing so by Islamic extremists.

My role on the CRRF was an active one as I served on the CRRF's Executive Committee, Human Resources Committee, Nominations Committee, and was the Chair of the Investment Committee. Joly made good on her written threat to have me removed as a Director with the CRRF under fabricated accusations of "Islamophobia." My performance had nothing to do with my termination and that fact was reflected in CRRF Chairman Albert Lo's statement to the *Toronto Star*, following my dismissal: "We always appreciated her positive contributions. She's always supportive of positive race relations." Lo added that, "Douglass-Williams has been involved with a number of foundation initiatives involving Muslim issues. I saw quite a number of participants in the Muslim community say they were very warm to her and always positive and friendly."[1]

I personally make a distinction between those Muslims who choose to practice Islam in peace and with respect for the separation from mosque and state, and those with their agenda to usurp democratic constitutions, demand special privileges over other creeds, and attack innocent people as a supremacist entitlement. I make this distinction clear in the pages of this book.

It is odd to be removed from a race-relations foundation for my private work in criticizing the intolerance, supremacism, and range of abuses that are characteristic of political Islam, particularly in light of the fact that Islam is not a race. I was made a public example as Canada marches to the orders of Muslim Brotherhood operatives. Canada's Motion M103 was passed, just as action against my position with the CRRF was unfolding.

On March 23, 2017, Canada passed Motion M103 in Canadian Parliament, a motion that called on the government of Canada to "recognize the need to quell the increasing public climate of hate and fear" and to "condemn Islamophobia and all forms of systemic racism and religious discrimination."[2]

Canadian member of Parliament Iqra Khalid tabled M103, a document that caused division and valid concern about the merits and lack of a definition of the term "Islamophobia," the latter of which the Organization of Islamic Cooperation has dedicated an Islamophobia Observatory to battle "Islamophobia" on a global scale.[3]

The only firm definition of "Islamophobia" which showed up in Canada was contained in an official guidebook published by the

Toronto District School Board (TDSB) that condemned "Islamopho-bia" and defined the term as "fear, prejudice, hatred or dislike directed against Islam or Muslims, or towards Islamic politics or culture."[4] This guidebook was prepared with the support of the National Council of Canadian Muslims, which strongly campaigned for M103.[5]

The Jewish lobby group, B'nai Brith Canada, complained that the reference to "politics" could lead to students or staff being punished for expressing dislike for the Republic of Iran's persecution of LGBTQ people or restrictions placed on women in Saudi Arabia.[6] B'nai Brith also expressed concern that "banning or even discouraging any 'dislike' of 'Islamic politics' would pose a severe problem in combatting the virulent Jew hatred that we have seen emanating from some Muslim institutions in Canada."[7] The TDSB subsequently amended its defini-tion of "Islamophobia" to be in line with the Ontario Human Rights Commission's, which omits the reference to politics, but includes "dread, hatred, hostility towards Islam."[8,9] This implies that those who have a dread for Islamic Sharia practices like wife-beating, female genital mutilation, honor violence, and the inferiority of women will be labeled "Islamophobic."

While delivering testimony before M103 Committee hearings in October 2017, celebrated human rights lawyer David Matas urged members of Parliament "to be careful in their use of the term Islamo-phobia," saying "fear of some elements of Islam is mere prudence."[10]

Iqra Khalid—the face behind M103—has a noteworthy history. She is a former president of the Muslim Brotherhood–linked Mus-lim Student Association (MSA) at York University. MSA chapters are linked to the Muslim World League, which is a Muslim Brotherhood operation funded by the Saudis.[11] The Muslim Student Association is also well-known for its aggressive Boycott, Divestment, and Sanctions drives on campus to demonize and delegitimize the State of Israel, and for its members' intimidation of Jewish students. Behind Khalid's "anti-Islamophobia" initiative were muscular Muslim Brotherhood lobbies.[12]

M103 was built on petition e-411 by Samer Majzoub, who managed a Muslim Brotherhood–linked Montreal high school, and is a leader of the self-described Muslim Brotherhood–linked Muslim Association of Canada (MAC). Majzoub even accused Conservative MPs of "stoking a wave of anti-Muslim sentiment" in opposing M103.[13]

The passage of Motion M103 was a manifestation of the fact that the anti-racism industry has been overshadowed by the "anti-Islamophobia" victimology narrative. The chapter "The Islamophobia Deception" explains this narrative.

As a follow-up to M103—which was described by its proponents as benign and nonbinding—the government of Canada vowed to "take action" against those whom it deems to be exhibiting "Islamophobia."

On June 1, 2018, the Liberal Government released a document titled "Government Response to the Tenth Report of the Standing Committee on Canadian Heritage Entitled: Taking Action Against Systemic Racism and Religious Discrimination Including Islamophobia." The document was signed by Melany Joly and addressed to Julie Dabrusin, Chair of the Standing Committee on Canadian Heritage.[14]

Twenty-three million dollars of taxpayer money was designated by the Liberal Government over two years to provide increased funds for the Multiculturalism Program administered by Canadian Heritage, of which fighting "Islamophobia" is included.[15]

Iqra Khalid held a press conference at the end of June 2018 in which she openly admitted that the National Council of Canadian Muslims (NCCM) and International Relief Fund for the Afflicted and Needy Canada (IRFAN) will be receiving funds from the $23 million. Khalid boldly stated:

> We don't need support as Canadians, we need a foundation and that is what the government is doing with this funding, with these $23 million that will go a long way toward helping organizations like The Boys and Girls Club...NCCM that does a lot of data collecting on hate crimes and pushing that advocacy needle forward in our country or like Islamic Relief...that does not only work within Canada, across Canada but across the world in removing those stereotypes and there are so many more...."[16]

The Council on American Islamic Relations Canada (CAIR-CAN) was renamed NCCM, and the group's connections to the Muslim Brotherhood are described in the chapter "Who Speaks for Muslims." There are also connections between IRFAN and the self-described

Muslim Brotherhood–affiliated Muslim Association of Canada (MAC). IRFAN was designated as a banned terrorist organization by the Conservative Stephen Harper government in 2014.[17]

In 2015, it was uncovered that a RCMP (Royal Canadian Mounted Police) search warrant linked the MAC headquarters in Mississauga (near Toronto) to IRFAN. A Canada Revenue Agency document showed that between 2001 and 2010, MAC provided $296,514 to IRFAN-Canada. Within that period, from 2005 and 2009, "IRFAN-Canada transferred approximately $14.6 million worth of resources to various organizations associated with Hamas," according to the Federal Department of Public Safety.[18]

In the debate surrounding the introduction of Motion M103, its proponents frequently argued that the motion was not law, but a benign motion that would be passed in Parliament for further study by the Heritage Committee. It subsequently proved to be as dangerous as opponents had warned. Now, action against "Islamophobia" has bypassed the legislature to be fully incorporated into a government "action" plan that would affect Canadian society. One of the features of Melanie Joly's document indicated:

> As part of the "Islamophobia" initiative, Canadian citizens will be monitored for compliance: the Public Service Commission of Canada "offers standardized assessment instruments through its Personnel Psychology Center for use by public service organizations." These tests are developed with "diverse groups and are monitored and maintained with diversity in mind."[19]

It has already been established as Iqra Khalid mentioned that the NCCM and IRFAN are groups that the Liberal Government of Canada takes seriously in its partnership to help fight "Islamophobia." According to the NCCM website, the organization also provides education to "government departments, law enforcement officers, media agencies, and private organizations" through workshops and "full day Bootcamps."[20]

The National Council of Canadian Muslims also influenced my termination from the Canadian Race Relations Foundation. According to the *Toronto Star* article "Board member of anti-racism agency fired amid accusations of Islamophobic commentary":

The NCCM expressed concerns and sent a formal letter to the government in October. Executive director Ihsaan Gardee said Douglass-Williams' removal is an "appropriate corrective measure taken by government to address (her) disturbing public record…The removal of Ms. Douglass-Williams is long overdue in light of her known Islamophobic commentary and her public association with purveyors of hateful propaganda, such as Robert Spencer who has long been identified by human rights institutions as a leading figure of the Islamophobia movement in North America," he said in an emailed statement.[21]

As Dr. Sheikh Subhy Mansour, founder of the Quranist sect in Egypt, states of his own experience in the pages ahead of this book:

> I stood against the Saudi influence and suffered…When I came here to the U.S., I had dreams and ideas, because this was America. But when I went to mosque, I found the same people, advocating the same Sharia. I escaped from there and found them here, so I said to myself, what could I do after that? Escape to the moon?

With regard to Muslim Brotherhood organizations on American soil, he warns that they

> exploit the American values of freedom of expression and freedom of religion to brainwash American Muslims to prevent their integration into the American society. They even try to turn them into enemies of their country and their fellow citizens.

It was once impossible to envisage that Canada would become a country where punitive measures would be levied against those who criticized the advance of political Islam, its expansionary ambitions, and the global scourge of jihad and barbaric practices that have entered Western countries. "Anti-islamophobia" Motion M103 and my firing for writing for *Jihad Watch* were wakeup calls.

Whether intentionally or not—and like it or not—I was used by the Trudeau government to send a message to all Canadians that Canada now ascribes to a two-tier system of government, in which the Islamic fiqh is prioritized, and in which European culture has had its day.

My firing manifested the present Canadian government's unfortunate decision not to heed the voices of the moderate and reformist Muslims who are depicted in this book, but rather to do the bidding of Muslim Brotherhood forces that have no interest in protecting and defending the foundational principles of every free society—most importantly, the freedom of speech.

If it is now beyond the parameters of acceptable discourse to oppose jihad terror and Sharia oppression, it will not be only I who will ultimately be targeted by the Canadian government (and other like-minded governments in the West), but other defenders of democracy, including the voices of pluralism and tolerance within Islam as well.

In the pages ahead, the moderates and reformists reveal their commitment to: the separation of mosque and state, pluralism, democracy, their personal faith beliefs, warnings about the malignant and covert nature of stealth jihadists, and their personal travails against Islamism of which I can now identify with. I count it a privilege to be among those who have borne the persecutions in standing up for human rights in the face of political correctness and Islamist intimidation.

# FOREWORD BY DR. DANIEL PIPES

My library contains a wall of books about modern Islam. But hardly a one of them covers the topic of this important study by Christine Douglass-Williams. With all the attention paid to Islamists, who has the time or energy to devote to modernizing Muslims?

Indeed, the paucity of books on anti-Islamist Muslims symbolizes their larger predicament: They are threatened, marginalized, and dismissed as frauds.

Threats come from the Islamists, the advocates of applying Islamic law in its entirety and severity as a means to regain the medieval glory of Islam. Islamists attack modernizers with words and weapons, rightly sensing that these liberal Muslims pose a profound challenge to the current Islamist hegemony. However much they dominate today, Islamist reactionaries fully understand modernity's great appeal, not to speak of its victories over two other modern radical utopian movements, fascism and communism. They know their movement is doomed because Muslims will opt for the benefits of modern life, so they fight modernizers tooth and nail.

The Left marginalizes. One might expect that the many differences between socialism and Islamism would make the two camps enemies. One would be wrong. The intensity of their common hostility toward the liberal order brings them together. Leftists overwhelmingly prefer the Islamist program to the modernizing one and so reject the modernizers, going so far to revile them as anti-Islamic, a truly choice insult.

The anti-Islamic Right dismisses. Ironically, it endorses the Islamist claim that Islamists alone are true Muslims, while waving away the modernizers as outliers, fabulists, and frauds. The anti-Islamic Right does so despite sharing the same enemy with modernizing Muslims—the Islamists. Instead of joining forces, it perversely keeps its distance from them, muttering about their *taqiyya* (dissimulation), finding only fault with their analysis, and lobbing colorful slurs at their leaders.

Thus do modernizing Muslims face the problems of establishing current credibility and future potential. Islamists dominate the news with their carnage and cultural aggression; Leftists turn reality on its head, and the anti-Islam types fumble on. Worse, as these detractors flail away at them, modernizers have few opportunities to respond, what with the establishment (what I call the 6 P's: politicians, press, police, prosecutors, professors, and priests) studiously ignoring them. As a result, the public hardly knows an effort to modernize Islam exists and few respect its small but hardy band of leaders. How many of you have heard of the Council on American–Islamic Relations (CAIR)? And how many the Center for Islamic Pluralism (CIP)?

Here, Christine Douglass-Williams, a Canadian journalist and civil rights activist, enters the picture. She took the time to find eight leading North American modernizers and gave them the opportunity to present themselves and their views. Each has a distinctive outlook.

- Ahmed Subhy Mansour founded a new and flexible school of thought, the Koranists.
- Shireen Qudosi challenges the near-worship of Muhammad and wrestles with problematic Koranic passages.
- Jalal Zuberi reveals the Islamists' textual rigidity and celebrates pluralism.
- Tawfik Hamid highlights the Islamists' deceit and their intent to conquer the West.
- Qanta Ahmed rejects Islamic law and argues for Muslims to live as modern citizens.
- Zuhdi Jasser exposes the Islamists' narrative of victimology and emphasizes the need for patriotism.
- Raheel Raza focuses on immigration's mutual demands, arguing that the West must stand by its values, which Muslims must adapt to.

After laying out these interestingly divergent viewpoints, Douglass-Williams devotes the second half of her book to their commonalities. She focuses on the modernizers' efforts to: create an alternative vision to the Islamist one; re-interpret the Koran and other problematic Islamic texts; respond to accusations of "Islamophobia" directed against them; formulate a humane position on Israel; and challenge the Islamist hegemony.

Her careful analysis shows how the modernizing Islamic movement benefits from the freedoms found in the United States and Canada (as opposed to the intellectual repression found in every Muslim-majority country). She also helps establish this movement as a serious intellectual endeavor, putting contemporary modernizers on the map as never before, thereby boosting their cause. Given the global threat of Islamism, that is a constructive, indeed a great, achievement.

DR. PIPES (DANIELPIPES.ORG, @DANIELPIPES) IS AN AMERICAN HISTORIAN, president of the Middle East Forum, author of 16 books, named among Harvard's 100 most influential living graduates, and a member of the Council on Foreign Relations.

# FOREWORD BY ROBERT SPENCER

"This day I have perfected for you your religion and completed my favor upon you and have approved for you Islam as religion."

So says Allah in the Qur'an (5:3), in words that have vexed Islamic reformers and would-be reformers throughout the history of the religion. Traditional and mainstream Islamic theology holds that Islam is perfect, bestowed from above by the supreme being, and hence not only is reform unnecessary, it is heresy that makes the reformer worthy of death if he departs from anything Islamic authorities believe to be divinely revealed.

On the other hand, the cognitive dissonance created by having to believe that the one and only God mandates death for apostasy (Bukhari 6922), stoning for adultery (Bukhari 6829), and amputation of the hand for theft (Qur'an 5:38), and sanctions the sexual enslavement of infidel women (Qur'an 4:3, 4:24, 23:1–6, 33:50, 70:30), the devaluation of a woman's testimony (Qur'an 2:282) and inheritance rights (Qur'an 4:11), and above all, warfare against and the subjugation of non-Muslims (Qur'an 9:29), has led, particularly in modern times, to attempts by believing Muslims to reconcile Islamic morality with contemporary perspectives and mores.

These attempts are fraught with peril. As Christine Douglass-Williams notes in this book, "Mahmoud Muhammad Taha, a Sudanese Muslim theologian who argued that the Meccan passages," which are generally more peaceful, "should take precedence over the Medinan," which call for warfare against non-Muslims, "instead of the reverse, was executed in 1985 by the Sudanese government for heresy and apostasy." Some of those profiled in this book know these perils firsthand: "Sheikh Subhy Mansour recounted, 'If these Muslim Brotherhood people had the chance, they would have killed me according to their punishment for apostasy, plus they claim I'll go to hell.'" Tawfik Hamid noted, "The reformists were killed throughout history, including those who rejected the Sunnah."

Death threats aren't the only dangers either. Europe and North America are full of Muslim spokesmen who present themselves as moderate, Westernized reformers, but are actually just the opposite. Foremost among these is Tariq Ramadan, the grandson of Muslim Brotherhood founder Hassan al-Banna, who has been widely hailed as the "Muslim Martin Luther" but has likewise been accused by French journalist Caroline Fourest, who has published a book-length study of Ramadan's sly duplicity, *Brother Tariq*, of "remaining scrupulously faithful to the strategy mapped out by his grandfather, a strategy of advance stage by stage" toward the imposition of Islamic law in the West.[1]

Douglass-Williams notes this duplicity: "In an example of the distinction to be made between moderates and crypto-moderates, after the brutal riots following the release of the Danish cartoons insulting to Muhammad in 2006, Tariq Ramadan, the Swiss-born theologian and grandson of the founder of the Muslim Brotherhood, Ramadan explained that the reaction of his co-religionists was 'a principle of faith…that God and the prophets never be represented.'" One of her interview subjects, Salim Mansur, observes dryly that "non-Muslims went to the wrong Muslim for an understanding of the faith."

The dominant presence of duplicitous pseudo-reformers, such as Ramadan, considerably muddies the waters. This confusion couldn't possibly come at a worse time, when the governments of the West are doing nothing less than staking the very futures of their nations not only upon the existence of Muslim moderates and reformers, but upon their eventual victory within the Islamic community. This gamble has been made despite the fact that there is no general agreement either inside the Muslim community or outside it, of what "Islamic moderation" actually means, and what "Islamic reform" would really look like.

Against this backdrop, *The Challenge of Modernizing Islam* is extraordinary, refreshing, and much needed in numerous ways. The interviews that Christine Douglass-Williams conducts with some of the leading moderate Muslim spokesmen in the United States and Canada are unique in their probing honesty. While most interviewers from all points of the political spectrum generally are so happy and honored to be in the presence of a Muslim who repudiates Jihad terror that they serve up only softball questions and are content with vague generalities in response, in this book Douglass-Williams asks the questions that need to be asked, and yet are asked only infrequently: How do you explain the various Qur'an verses that call for violence, or are misogynistic or problematic in other ways? How do you propose to convince the vast majority of your co-religionists of the correctness of your position? How is reform possible when the mainstream schools of Islamic jurisprudence mandate death for heresy and apostasy?

The answers vary from thought provoking and searchingly honest to cagey and deflective. And that in itself is illuminating. Not every person interviewed in this book is in agreement with every other, and not every attentive and informed reader will come away from these pages convinced that every person here interviewed is being in every instance entirely forthright. Many believe that the resistance to the global Jihad in all its forms has no legitimacy, or cannot be successful, if Muslim reformers are not on board with it. I do not share that view, but the need for Islamic reform is undeniable, and the people here interviewed are among its foremost exponents in the West. We owe them a fair hearing as much as they owe us honest answers to the questions posed here.

In the second half of the book, Douglass-Williams offers a probing analysis of what her interview subjects told her, and provides illuminating ways for readers to navigate through the thickets and avoid hazards that have captured and misled numerous analysts of Islam and prospects for reform. One of the cardinal services she provides here is the drawing of distinctions in numerous areas where crucial differences and delineations have long been obscured, often deliberately. Her discussions of Islam versus Islamism and Islamic moderation versus Islamic reform are a welcome antidote to the sloppy thinking and cant that dominate the public discourse today. Her examination of problematic Islamic texts is all the more welcome for being even rarer. Her discussions of the controversial and manipulative concept of "Islamophobia" and its relationship to the problems of genuine Islamic reform, and to the role of Israel and how it can help distinguish genuine Islamic reformers from pretenders, are the crown and centerpiece of the book, and examples of the kind of searching analysis that is all too often absent from the public square today, and for that all the more needed.

*The Challenge of Modernizing Islam* is, therefore, an extremely illuminating book, and not always in the ways that its interview subjects may have intended. That is, as is said these days, not a bug, but a feature. It's crucial today that genuine reformers be distinguished from insincere deceivers, and naïve idealists from those with genuine plans. Here is a solid beginning in that effort. This book should be read while bearing in mind how the governments of the West are assuming that their newly accepted Muslim refugees will sooner or later accept the values and mores of the secular West and settle down to become loyal and productive citizens, and how the recent experience of European countries, particularly Sweden, Germany, and France, as well as the United Kingdom, offers abundant reason for concern that this may not be the case.

That same tension between high hopes and harsh realities runs through these interviews, and doubtless through the souls of many of the interviewees. For better or worse, however, any chance for Western countries, as well as non-Muslim countries in the Far East and elsewhere, to enjoy a peaceful future now depends, courtesy of a series of decisions our political leaders have made, upon the victory of Islamic reform. *The Challenge of Modernizing Islam* uniquely equips readers to make an informed and intelligent evaluation of how peaceful the future of non-Muslim countries is likely to be.

ROBERT SPENCER IS THE DIRECTOR OF *Jihad Watch*, a program of the David Horowitz Freedom Center, and the author of sixteen books, including the *New York Times* bestsellers *The Politically Incorrect Guide to Islam (and the Crusades)* and *The Truth About Muhammad*. Spencer has led seminars on Islam and Jihad for the FBI, the United States Central Command, United States Army Command and General Staff College, the US Army's Asymmetric Warfare Group, the Joint Terrorism Task Force (JTTF), the Justice Department's Anti-Terrorism Advisory Council, and the US intelligence community.

# PART ONE

# INTRODUCTION

## A CASE FOR A MODERATE ISLAM

American writer Daniel Greenfield argues, "Moderate Islam is a difficult faith. To believe in it you have to disregard over a thousand years of recorded history, theology, demographics and just about everything that predates 1965. You have to ignore the bearded men chopping off heads because they don't represent the majority of Muslims. Neither does Muhammad, who did his own fair share of head chopping."[1]

Is Greenfield correct that moderate Islam is solely a fantasy? Judaism has long abandoned stonings and conquests; Christianity has renounced forced conversions and slavery; but is Islam, one of the three great Abrahamic religions, tied to the strictures of 1,400 years ago with no possibility of change or evolution?

I will argue—with the help of many Muslim intellectuals, authors, and activists interviewed for this book—that it is possible for Islam to reform and to modernize. In all faiths, humans are the instruments of religious practice and can choose what they accept and what they reject regarding the letter of their faith. Islam is no exception.

To advance the views that Muslims must be violent to be true to their faith and that Islam cannot be reformed because violent passages are embedded in the Koran, Islam's holy book, offers no solutions. It does not address the fact that in the twenty-first century, Islam is one of the world's largest religions, with nearly 1.6 billion adherents that are not going to disappear from the earth, and ignores the evidence that human development and ideological evolution are historical phenomena. Islamic scholar and historian Bernard Lewis wrote, eleven years prior to 9/11, "Islam has brought comfort and peace of mind to countless millions of men and women," and notes that "the Muslim world is far from unanimous in its rejection of the West."[2]

Not all Muslims are Islamists or supremacists who seek to conquer the world and establish a global caliphate, nor advocates of such conquest. Every immigrant group faces the trials of cultural integration, but Islamists exploit such challenges to fuel hatred among their brethren. Today, many mosques that serve immigrant Muslim communities in the West are instructing their congregations to hate infidels and ultimately conquer their lands. These messages are rooted in indoctrination by radical and powerful Muslim leaders who strive to keep their followers in the Dark Ages to control them and discourage them from questioning and seeking answers about their faith.

The decline of the Ottoman Empire and the expansion of European colonialism produced the reactionary Pan-Islamism movement, which was intended to "shore up the ramparts against economic and ideological penetration."[3] Consequently, post–Ottoman states experienced one failure after another, and many today hold rigidly to Islam in their quest for Islamic awakening and resurgence.[4]

In 1928, Egyptian schoolteacher Hassan al-Banna formed the Muslim Brotherhood, which "targeted the Western-educated elite's fumbling attempts to indigenize modernity."[5] In exploiting the widespread political disillusionment that permeated the Islamic world after the 1924 abolition of the Islamic Caliphate by Turkish leader Kemal Atatürk, al-Banna's paradigm married an indigenous religious conservatism with political activism that would restore the "lapsed fortunes" of the Islamic world.[6]

This gave rise to the Puritanical Salafist movement, a traditionalist reform movement which aimed to avenge past failures and encouraged "ancestor worship"; that is, it indoctrinated Muslims with a modernity-phobia, along with the message that the texts of the Koran and Sunnah constituted the "official closed corpus."[7] This fundamentalist veto was derived from historic Muslim luminaries such as the nineth-century jurist Ahmad ibn Hanbal, also known as the Imam of Baghdad, who decreed that "whoever involves themselves in any theological rhetoric is not counted amongst the Ahl us-Sunnah, even if by that he arrives at the Sunnah, until he abandons debating and surrenders to the texts."[8] The Ahl us-Sunnah are the "People of the

Accepted Practice," the Sunnah being the practices that are accept-able as per the Koran and Muhammad's example in the Hadiths, the recorded sayings of the prophet.

Apart from the incongruity of an immutable decree in addressing textual authenticity, Muslim Moroccan scholar and reformist Said Nachid states a strong case against the overriding infallibility of the Koranic text. He argues for the mutability of the text, in that there are many variations in recording oral traditions, uncertainties about preserving the original wordings of oral traditions, and incomplete, scattered, and dispersed verses of the Koran left by Muhammad, as most were preserved orally and at a time before written Arabic was standardized.[9] By the time of the third Caliph Uthman, whose empire expanded into Fars in 650 (modern day Iran), modern day reform-ist and scholar Hasan Mohsen Ramadan contends that some of the Koranic verses were interpreted arbitrarily or by consensus, weaving together Muhammad's life events with that of events from the Torah.[10] Jordanian Arab scholar Shaker al-Nabulsi further notes that the Koran has been distorted by Gulf region Arab scholars to reflect an Arab bravado in which the literalism of the text is the central axis, thus ren-dering human intellect, ethical judgments, and experience meaningless or inferior to the text, while marginalizing discourse and spawning a culture of violence and backwardness—a condition exploited by Muslim leaders and clerics today for hefty monetary gain and power, and aided by authorities as central as Egypt's Al-Azhar University.[11]

Muslim reformists are adamant that every text must be subject to new interpretations that adapt to modernity. Like all other religions, Islam is not static, any more than humans are static, despite how Salaf-ists would have it.

Islamic scholar Dr. Daniel Pipes contends that the believer can take what he wants from the Koran. Just as committed National Socialists comprised only a small percentage of Germans, yet Nazism nonethe-less proliferated as a despotic menace until confronted, Islamism needs to be systematically confronted on Western soil, and reformation sup-ported globally.

Throughout history, mass disenchantment, human unpredictability, and zeal for progress have yielded notable surprises. The eruption of the Arab Spring demonstrated a profound dissatisfaction among the populace in the Muslim world. Despite its failure, as overthrown tyrants were generally replaced by more brutal Islamists, the Arab Spring triggered unforeseen evolutions that continue to cause upheavals and expanding turf wars, with unpredictable outcomes.[12]

The 1979 Iranian Revolution was also a surprise, and today, though radical clerics rule the regime, the discontent of the Iranian people is widely known. Now "a wide chasm has opened between what Iranian citizens profess" under religious dictatorship and what they do, which is a reason for the high walls in private homes, according to Fouad Ajami, Professor of Middle Eastern Studies at John Hopkins University.[13] The ideological dissonance within Iran was most apparent when protestors—emboldened by the Arab Spring—took to the streets for a second time in the space of a week, on February 20, 2011, but were squelched in a brutal crackdown by security forces. Iran's supreme leader, Ayatollah Ali Khamenei, declared that the Arab Spring would result in a win for Islamist clerics: "The enemies try to say that the popular movements in Egypt, Tunisia, and other nations are un-Islamic, but certainly these popular movements are Islamic and must be consolidated."[14] Yet Khamenei later revealed his unease in warning the Arab world "not to allow Western powers and Israel to 'confiscate'" the region's pro-reform uprisings.[15] Even Khamenei recognized that alternative voices who seek "reform" toward the puritanical days of Muhammad undermine the narrative of theocratic tyranny. As violent turf wars erupt in Muslim countries today, the hope of accelerating Islamic reform toward modernity lies in education and the will of the people, who are now exposed to the Internet and social media, and who are fed up with the oppression and backwardness of their leaders.

Author and political scientist Dr. Salim Mansur indicated that he views "the convulsions going on in the Muslim world as the convulsions of a civilization that is going through the process of implosion as a way of coming to terms with the reality around them." Sheikh Subhy Mansour, a former professor at Cairo's Al-Azhar University, was thrown out of that renowned institution for his moderate interpretation of Islam, and was subsequently imprisoned and later exiled from Egypt under Hosni Mubarak's rule in 2002. Mansur arrived in America as a political refugee and relates an early experience: "When I came here to the US, I had dreams and ideas because this was America. But when I went to mosque, I found the same people, advocating the same Sharia. I decided one day while in Boston to take the chance and go to the mosque and pray. When I went to a room in the upper floor, I was so scared when I started to read the newsletters in Arabic. It talked about taking America and taking Jews." Mansour continues his fight in this war for democratic freedoms with a seasoned resolve, stating, "I learn from human experience. Once people are awakened, know the difference between slavery and freedom, and get rid of fear, they will come face to face with the soldiers of dictatorship and succeed." Shiekh Mansour also pointed out that it is his fanatic enemies who have inspired him as a Muslim reformer.

How long a Muslim reformation might take is uncertain, but history offers many surprises, such as the collapse of the Soviet Union, which political analysts failed to foresee. Senator Daniel Patrick Moynihan was one who wrote in 1979 "that the Soviet Union would break up."[16] He was a vociferous critic of the CIA for overestimating the strength of the Soviets, and subsequently introduced a bill to abolish the agency and place intelligence under the mandate of the Secretary of State.[17]

Ayaan Hirsi Ali, a well-known Somali-born activist and former Dutch politician who has rejected the possibility of the emergence of a moderate Islam, has more recently stated, "Both Christianity and Judaism have had their eras of reform. I would argue that the time has come for a Muslim Reformation."[18] She followed up with a book entitled *Heretic* wherein she asserts, "ordinary Muslims are ready for change."[19] According to reformist Dr. Zuhdi Jasser, "normative Islam is what comes out of Al-Azhar University and Saudi schools, which is the majority of what is being taught. It needs tons of reform." With the explosion of global information about Islam since 9/11, fueled by the Internet, Islam is embroiled in a turf war between ruling Muslim despots, backward clerics who seek to "reform" Islam back to the barbaric seventh century, and those who seek to reform Islam to modernity. The West ought to support the latter in its efforts to evolve.

Understanding the difference between Muslims who practice their faith personally, from Islamists who thrive toward a political Islam and to impose their ideologies globally, is the fundamental goal of this endeavor. It is imperative for citizens and authorities in the West to understand this differentiation, as Islamists seek to infiltrate through the vast numbers of Muslims immigrating to the West. Dr. Salim Mansur warns that Westerners "should not be nonchalant about Western values and see them as natural and God-given. People have fought and died for values like gender and race equity, free speech, and the fragile notion of freedom. Such a notion does not exist around the world but has emerged in Western civilization."

It is unrealistic to implement policies that ban Muslim immigration, to deport Muslims already living in the West, or stop every penny crossing our borders from Salafist-funding states in the Middle East, but we can limit the influence of Islamism by asking questions, and to immunize ourselves with knowledge and open dialogue. This book will provide a foundation to ask valid questions.

For the purposes of this book, the word "moderate" means a form of Islam that accepts pluralism and is compatible with modernity and Western democracy. It does not mean that a Muslim can openly rebuke the tactics of the Islamic State (formerly the Islamic State of Iraq and Syria, or ISIS) while stealthily advocating Sharia law globally, and then be deemed a moderate. The media often reports stories of Muslims who condemn the brutality of ISIS and al Qaeda as un-Islamic, but upon further research, many of these so-called moderates have ties to Islamist organizations and are on record advocating Sharia law globally. When close to 100 Muslims in Edmonton, Alberta, Canada, visited the Alberta legislature to pray for the families of the victims of terror attacks in Ottawa and near Montreal in October 2014, accolades went out across the country for this show of solidarity with Canada.[20] Edmonton Imam Bassam Fares was quoted as saying, "When these types of attacks happen, we all, as Canadians, stand against them....We want to offer our condolences, and show our solidarity with these families." Fares's words sounded sincere, but Fares is an Executive Director of the Muslim Association of Canada (MAC), one of the only Muslim organizations in the world to openly admit its origins and ties with the Muslim Brotherhood.[21]

The Islamist group CAIR, the Council on American–Islamic Relations, based in Washington, D.C., and created as an "organization that challenges stereotypes of Islam and Muslims," publicly condemned the "barbaric murder" of US aid worker Peter Kassig by ISIS and joined national and local Muslim scholars and leaders in Washington, D.C., to release an open letter signed by more than 120 international scholars of Islam and Muslim leaders. The letter purported to refute the ideology of ISIS and urged supporters of the terror group to repent and "return to the religion of mercy."[22] CAIR's Communications Director, Ibrahim Hooper, once said, "We are similar to a Muslim NAACP and our stated mission is 'to enhance understanding of Islam, encourage dialogue, protect civil liberties, empower American Muslims, and build coalitions that promote justice and mutual understanding.'"[23] CAIR, however, was designated an "unindicted co-conspirator" linked to Hamas in the largest terrorist financing trial in the history of the United States, the Holy Land Foundation Trial, along with other prominent Muslim organizations that claim to represent the interests of American Muslims.[24] Even the United Arab Emirates formally listed CAIR as a terrorist organization because of its "incitement" and "funding," according to UAE foreign minister Abdullah bin Zayed Al Nahyan.[25]

Westerners applaud "peaceful" Islamists for their gestures of conviviality and national solidarity and embrace them in the name of tolerance and diversity, without realizing that these crypto-moderates are well versed in playing Westerners for fools. To advocate a "peaceful" and stealth replacement of Western democratic constitutions with Sharia law in any form is not moderate; it is a brand of ideological warfare, the end goal of conquest is no different from that of violent Jihadists, but much more difficult to identify.

Professor Bernard Lewis noted, "With the Barbarians in Rome and the Mongols in Iraq, what made it possible [conquest] was that things were going badly wrong within the society so that it was no longer able to offer effective resistance."[26] What is currently going awry in the West is a lack of resolve in defending our constitutional freedoms against the scourge of Islamism, which seeks conquest and domination. It appears that Western institutions, authorities, and analysts are fearful of being branded racists and Islamophobes; this fear obstructs a clear focus on policy solutions. It is the influential moderates featured in this book, who are working as citizens of the West to actively engage in facilitating such "effective resistance" through education, and are sounding an alarm against Islamist strategies.

## THE JOURNEY OF REFORM

In preparing for face-to-face interviews with influential moderate Muslims in the United States and Canada, I found myself confronted by intense questions from non-Muslims. The most frequently asked question was: How is it that moderate Muslims, particularly devout practitioners, call themselves Muslims and modern at the same time, when the Koran calls for violent Jihad, "holy war," the subjugation of women, and much more that is deeply at variance with modernity? I was often reminded that these moderates are not accepted as Muslims by their more fervent co-religionists, who claim "so-called moderate Muslims are not Muslims at all."

The individuals I have interviewed here have formulated responses in ingenious and important ways. My purpose is to better understand and advance the efforts of those who choose to practice Islam in keeping with Western constitutions. I refer to them as "moderates," differentiated from crypto-moderates who appear as genuine, but under further scrutiny support and advance political Islam and global Sharia law.

There are also moderates who prefer to be deemed "reformers" because they believe that there are problematic texts in the Koran that need to be reinterpreted in a fashion that is consistent with modernity, and that it is not sufficient to simply ignore such texts in today's world. In this book, both moderates and reformers explain their contrasting and complementary approaches to the problematic aspects of Islam in the complex, diverse Muslim communities of the twenty-first century.

The tenets of public Sharia law are rejected by every moderate (and reformist) voice featured in these pages; ironically, they defend our freedoms against Islamists more actively than many Westerners, who are phobic about being branded racists. Moderates are unafraid to confront Islamists, unlike reticent Western leaders and media that display paranoia about being called Islamophobes and have thus become unwitting accessories to the Islamist agenda. A different kind of "Islamophobia" has gripped the West: an irrational fear and refusal to criticize Islam when justified. Islamists who subscribe to literal interpretations of Koranic texts are proficient at deploying charges of racism to silence their critics. They exploit Western fears and ignorance about their

religion to assert their authority in defining how the Muslim populace should be treated, while moving our democracies, and our very
civilization, closer to the edge of a cliff.

Genuine moderates are sharply criticized by those who reject
them as Muslims, while also facing criticism from those who chant:
"Where are the moderate voices?" These steadfast defenders of
our freedoms are routinely outshouted by Islamists and Islamist
organizations that claim to be the voice of the mainstream Muslim
majority. Abdur-Rahman Muhammad, a former member of the
International Institute for Islamic Thought (IIIT), emphasized the
importance of the US government moving to "stop legitimizing
groups" like CAIR, the Muslim Public Affairs Council (MPAC), and
the Islamic Society of North America (ISNA), which he described
as a "fifth column" in the United States.[27] His warning is applicable
to every Western country.

It is imperative to question any ideology that is backward, barbaric,
and inconsistent with modernity, human rights, and Western constitutions, particularly one that has seeped virtually unnoticed across borders
through immigration. It is the duty of Western authorities to protect
their citizens from such threats. Every moderate interviewed in this
project asserts that there are verses in the Koran that have no place in
the modern world, and that Islam, like any religion, should be open to
scrutiny, criticism, and discussion by believers and non-believers. These
individuals strongly believe in freedom of speech and know the tricks
of the Islamists firsthand. We need to work with them to thwart the
aspirations of Islamists, and to support their endeavors to modernize
their faith.

As an observer, journalist, and interviewer, I came to know many
of these moderate Muslims on a personal level. I have been to some
of their homes, attended their events, and have listened to them speak
and pray at an Iftar dinner, the meal eaten by Muslims after sunset
during the month of Ramadan. I am witness to the determination of
many devout, practicing Muslims who publicly and ardently defend
peace and Western constitutional freedoms. They are driven by a vehement love for freedom and a desire to see the advancement of human
rights—which many Westerners take for granted.

In interviewing the moderates, I became familiar with the demonization and even death threats that many of them face from their Islamist co-religionists, and the obstacles created by many Westerners who categorized them as either disingenuous, ineffectual in confronting the tsunami of Islamism we face, or who, like Wahhabis, rejected them outright as Muslims. Most evident among the moderates was the self-sacrifice and personal toll that their missions entailed. I have found their zeal and sense of purpose greatly inspiring.

Dr. Salim Mansur stated that Islam is not monolithic, but Islamists are trying to create a monolithic Islam, and their efforts are "now tied with petrodollars." Dr. Mansur states that a prominent characteristic of Muslim reformers is that they are "completely at home in the West—culturally, intellectually, philosophically, and politically"—because Islam to them "is a personal faith, just as to Christians."

I passed many hours with Dr. Zuhdi Jasser, meeting at his private practice in Arizona. He had, as Christians say, a "pastoral" air about him, one of kindness, humility, and caring for the wider community in which he lived. I spent some time waiting for him as he attended to an elderly patient, long after office hours. He stated in his interview: "I think a pious Muslim should be a reformer, and that is what I tell my family daily who deals with the stress of what I am doing. I tell them that this is my piety; life is very short and we must think of what legacy we will leave. The core of my relationship with God is accepting the challenges that he gives me. We are challenged in different ways, either with illness, financial issues, or whatever it is. For me, it is the challenge of dealing with political Islam and Islamism as the greatest threat to civilization in the twenty-first century."

I am fortunate to live in the area with the largest concentration of active moderates in the West: the Greater Toronto Area (also known as the GTA). According to Dr. Daniel Pipes, Canada has the most active anti-Islamist Muslim community in North America, an advantage that offers the potential to export the message of moderate Islam to other Western countries.[28] Today there are Muslims in the United States who are quietly putting together a reformed version of the Koran, reinterpreting the most problematic verses. Muslims from the Muslim Canadian Congress, headed by Tarek Fatah, first whetted my appetite to explore this issue following 9/11. Raheel Raza, who is interviewed in this book, was with this group before establishing the Council for Muslims Facing Tomorrow to counter extremism in Canada, particularly among youth.[29] Raheel described for me an experience that encouraged her as a reformer when she led the first mixed-gender prayer, stating, "All hell broke loose all over the world, and my family disowned me. Today it is acceptable. There are imams who have issued fatwas to say that it is not against Islam for a woman to lead prayers; so change comes through many different phases."

In this book, you may find opinions that you disagree with, but the intentions of the genuine moderates are revealed in their commitment to the principle of separation of mosque and state, and the promotion of a modernized Islam that allows for a plurality of views. They serve as fellow partners in protecting our freedoms in the West in opposing and exposing Islamists. I wish them every success.

Part One provides intriguing views, personal faith journeys, and mission statements of prominent moderate Muslims in a collection of interviews with leaders and reformers living in the United States and Canada, who are dedicated to upholding the tenets of democracy, and who practice their personal faith in peace and privacy. They range from the secular to the devout, yet every one of them rejects the extreme fundamentalism that Islamists seek to impose upon the West, and asserts the need to protect our governments from such anti-democratic intrusions. You will hear varying viewpoints with regards to their faith as they address questions about how a devout Muslim can choose the path of peace. They will warn about the aspirations of Islamists who seek to impose Sharia law in Western democracies. They understand what drives this obsessive quest for supremacy and the deceptions that Islamists employ.

The more Islamists are emboldened, the more aggressive they will become, since "peaceful" Islamists are in agreement with their violent co-religionists, except in their strategies for conquest, which is slow, patient, and insidious. These stealth antagonists are not easily recognized because they live and work among us; they are often our colleagues and neighbors. They may secretly uphold and indirectly support (ideologically and financially) al Qaeda, its affiliates, and offshoots of the Muslim Brotherhood, which include Hamas, waging covert ideological warfare. Crypto-moderates are proficient at using an array of deceptions, notably a canny manipulation of the media to present themselves as the voices and advocates of mainstream Muslims, but these stealth Islamists cannot easily fool their fellow moderate co-religionists, who share their stories in this book.

Part Two brings perspective to the interviews in Part One, providing examples of how the Islamist Project is already well-established, and the methods used by Islamists to infiltrate North America through their manipulation of our constitutions, our naivety, hospitality, multiculturalism, dialogue, and the fear of being branded racists and Islamophobes.

The chapters of Part Two are as follows:

## Islam and Islamism

This chapter highlights important distinctions between Islam and Islamism. It is often argued that there is no distinction between the words "Islamism" and "Islam," because Islam is inherently political. Nonetheless, there are prominent Muslims who do not espouse the politicization of Islam that has come to be known as Islamism; in fact, they condemn it. It is critical for Westerners to understand the enemy we face globally and within our gates—both stealth and violent—and it is equally important to know how to identify our Muslim allies who are well equipped to assist in this fight against the spread of Islamism.

## Moderates and Reformists

Westerners often use the terms "reformist" and "moderate" interchangeably, but there are important nuances. All the interviewees in this book are moderates, but not all wish to be specified or identified as reformists, the latter of whom are adamant that every text must be subject to new interpretations which are consistent with modernity. Moderates generally focus on the Meccan, or first part of the Koran, that is based upon a body of teachings that is generally consistent with peace and modernity.

In addition, Salafists and Wahhabists use the same word "reform" to refer to a puritanical "reform" of Islam emptying it of "innovation" (bid'a, a major sin in traditional Islam) and taking it back to the seventh century. The terms "reform" and "moderate" are used in this book in accordance with Western concepts and standards, which will be explained in Chapter One, not with those of Salafists and Wahhabists.

## Problematic Texts in the Koran

Emphasis is upon the ubiquitousness of problematic Koranic texts in this context. Most—if not all—the moderates in this book reject the Sunnah and the Hadiths, but they were questioned about how problematic texts influence their beliefs in the Koran. Indeed, this chapter includes mention of the Hadiths, but the emphasis is on the Koran that advocates and/or calls for violence; however, the texts of the Hadiths that signify or allude to Muhammad taking a prepubescent girl as a wife, which create division and conflict among Muslims and Westerners alike, will be addressed. For this reason, such texts will be referred to as "problematic texts," with an overview of how moderate Muslims contend with them as part of their personal faith. It will be noted that there are virtually "two Korans"; the earlier portion of the Muslim holy book, was, according to Islamic tradition, received by Muhammad in Mecca during the first twelve years of his prophetic career. There, the most peaceful texts of the Koran were formulated, and Christians and Jews were engaged with tolerance. The second part of the Koran is the product of Muhammad's period of residence at Medina, in the latter half of his prophetic career, when Muhammad became a military conqueror and engaged in war with the Jews, Christians, and pagan Arabs; hence the genesis of the problematic texts.

## The "Islamophobia" Deception

Islamists are proficient at influencing Western democracies by deploying the victimhood narrative. The word "Islamophobia" is now misused so frequently that when Westerners merely question Islam, or its role in terrorism, they risk being accused of victimizing Muslims and being branded as "Islamophobes" or "racists." This victimology subterfuge, carefully manipulated by Islamists, was created with the intent to beat down critics.[30] It has served as a brilliant tool to intimidate and subjugate the infidels of the West.

## The Israel Factor

The majority of moderates who were interviewed in this book pointed out the belief that an individual's attitude toward Israel is a significant factor in determining Islamist sympathies. Although one does not have to be a Muslim to dispute Israel's right to exist, this chapter will explore the historic and current sentiments among Islamists toward the Jewish people, who are erroneously portrayed as antagonists to peace. Dr. Robert Wistrich, Neuburger Professor of European and Jewish history at the Hebrew University of Jerusalem and the head of the University's Vidal Sassoon International Center for the Study of Anti-Semitism, has referred to Muslim anti-Semites as a clear and present danger where this anti-Semitic virus "has taken root in the body politic of Islam to an unprecedented degree."[31] Bernard Lewis notes that "classical anti-Semitism is an essential part of Arab intellectual life…almost as much as happened in Nazi Germany."[32]

## Who Speaks for Muslims?

Besides CAIR, there are other prominent Muslim organizations like the Islamic Society of North America (ISNA), the Islamic Circle of North America (ICNA), and the North American Islamic Trust (NAIT) that present themselves as benign Muslim advocacy groups; but many of these organizations were designated to be "unindicted co-conspirators" in the Holy Land Foundation (HLF) Trial, in which HLF founders were convicted of funneling more than $12 million to Hamas, a Palestinian, Wahhabist entity that espouses violence, and is an offshoot of the Muslim Brotherhood.

Islamists and Islamist groups recognize two types of abode: Dar al-Harb (the House of War) or Dar al-Islam (the House of Islam) where their political goal is to bring non-Islamic territory (the House of War) under Islamic Sharia. This chapter shows them as they are: Islamist groups tied to the Muslim Brotherhood and other terrorist entities that share a common goal of global conquest while cleverly posing as Muslim proponents of diversity and friends of intercultural dialogue. They also function as watchdogs set to stifle our democratic freedoms, particularly the freedom of speech, using lawfare to advance their cause, while demanding unreasonable accommodations. The Muslim Brotherhood Plan for North America will be addressed, as well as the Islamist Project, which will reveal how Muslim advocacy groups that appear harmless have found an effective way to penetrate and destroy the West from within, through "civilizational Jihad," which is a stealth form of Jihad using the strategy of a fifth column to infiltrate and overthrow.

## CHAPTER ONE

# DR. ZUHDI JASSER

### Medical Doctor, Reformist, Founder of American Islamic Forum for Democracy

D R. ZUHDI JASSER IS A MEDICAL DOCTOR who practices in Phoenix, Arizona, specializing in internal medicine and nuclear cardiology. He is also Past President of the Arizona Medical Association. Dr. Jasser served for 11 years as a medical officer, achieving the rank of Lieutenant Commander in the United States Navy.[1]

He is the Founder and President of the American Islamic Forum for Democracy, which started after 9/11 to "provide an American Muslim voice advocating for the preservation of the founding principles of the United States Constitution, liberty and freedom, through the separation of mosque and state."[2]

Dr. Jasser's parents fled to America in the mid 1960s to escape the oppressive Baath regime of Syria. Zuhdi is now a recognized reformist and leader in "the fight to shake the hold that the Muslim Brotherhood and their network of American Islamist organizations and mosques seek to exert on organized Islam in America."[3] He has been featured in a wide range of media, including the *Wall Street Journal*, the *Washington Times*, the *New York Post*, the Dallas Morning News, CNN, CBS, Fox News Channel, MSNBC, and the BBC, as well as many nationally syndicated radio programs.[4]

Dr. Jasser regularly briefs members of the House and Senate congressional anti-terror caucuses on the threat of political Islam, and was appointed to the United States Commission on International Religious Freedom.[5]

# INTERVIEW WITH DR. ZUHDI JASSER

**CHRISTINE:** Who influenced or inspired your mission as a reformist?

**DR. JASSER:** My grandfather influenced me, as did my father. My grandfather was a politician in Syria and a newspaper editorialist. My mother's father was a Sharia court judge, so I had the blessings of an educated family on these issues. There are also public figures, and there is much I disagree with them about, but they were influential to me: Alija Izetbegovic, the President of Bosnia, had political and foreign policy issues I disagree with, but he wrote *Islam Between East and West,* where he talked about the human soul only being realized when you live in freedom without the government getting involved. He said he never felt more Muslim than when he was in solitary confinement under Tito, so he didn't need government to be Muslim. You don't need freedom to be a Muslim. It's a personal relationship between you and God. He said the less freedom you have, the only solace you have is God. So government is really about human rights, and the ability to choose to accept or reject God.

Muhammad Sa'id al-Ashmawi, an Egyptian Supreme Court justice, has a book of his writings called *Against Islamic Extremism.* He was advocating for Islamic law when a case suddenly came before him where he was asked to dissolve a marriage between a Muslim woman and a Muslim man who converted to Christianity. Under Muslim law, a Muslim woman cannot be married to a non-Muslim man, but a Muslim man could marry a non-Muslim woman. When al-Ashmawi was asked to dissolve the marriage, he fought the government against it.

Abdolkarim Soroush wrote *Reason, Freedom, and Democracy in Islam.* Although I disagree with him about Israel, his book deals with separation of mosque and state.

Also, a lot of the Sufi thinkers, like Sufi poet and mystic Jalalu'ddin Rumi and other spiritual writings, have affected my relationship with God.

## ISLAMISM

**CHRISTINE:** How would you define an Islamist?

**DR. JASSER:**  An Islamist is one that believes in the movement or ideology of Islamism. The term "Islamism" is interchangeable with the term "political Islam." It is a comprehensive ideology in which the individual believes that the social, political, legal, and every aspect of society should be dominated by his—or their—interpretation of Islam. Islamists see faith as not just a personal journey, but also a theo-political construct.

Islamists believe in government being driven by Islamic law, that science should be Islamicized, and in the Islamization of knowledge. For example, the International Institute of Islamic Thought has written many books about the Islamization of knowledge. As an anti-Islamist, that does not make sense. I don't see how that relates to my relationship with God. Certainly God teaches me through the Koran to be knowledgeable and educated, but to say that a faith has a monopoly on the best approach is anathema to me, so Islamists have a supremacist project that says other faiths are inferior to theirs. Therefore government and everything in society should be ruled by Islamic law and dominated by an Islamic approach.

Non-Islamists believe that faith is personal, that Islam does not have a monopoly on a communication with God, and that society should be run by reason. Another important thing about Islamism is Sharia law, which Islamists believe should be interpreted by scholars. There are jurists in Islam who come to their conclusions based on scriptural exegesis. This means that they follow certain traditions or historic precedents, which lead to a conclusion on what Sharia should be. This is not based on reason. For instance, an Islamist would determine that alcohol should be prohibited by rules of government. A non-Islamist believes that faith should determine the choice of whether or not a person should drink. I do not drink personally, in accordance with the teachings of my faith for various reasons, but it is incumbent that society gives me that choice, so that I could demonstrate to God that I believe in his law and have an ability to choose or not choose his law. There is no need for government to be involved in that decision, as long as there are no victims of crime. If your goal is to get people not to drink, you can do it through education and other means, but not through the law. This example shows the difference between an Islamist and non-Islamist.

**CHRISTINE:** Is there a litmus test to differentiate an Islamist from a moderate like yourself?

**DR. JASSER:** There are a few litmus tests. Most important is the separation of mosque and state. Do you believe a constitution should be based on reason, or Sharia and the Islamic State? Islamists will answer, "As a minority we follow the laws of the land." Secondly, I would ask them the question: "If Muslims were 99 percent of society, should they form their constitution based on the Koran?" They would answer, "It is up to them and they should vote."

So the question is whether a Muslim believes that the same rules should apply whether Muslims are a majority or a minority. This is also a litmus test. As an example, groups that will refer you to a moderate imam telling his congregants that they should enroll in the military or homeland security as followers of the laws of this land that protects us, is great; but there is more to watch for. Looking at history at the time of Islam, there was an area that was Muslim majority ruled, Dar al-Islam, and the area of war, Dar al-Harb. Everything that wasn't under Muslim majority rule of the Islamic empire from the seventh century to 1450 was regarded as the area of war, so once they got into Europe, that was an area considered of "harb," or of war. It means once you have a majority, you have a different set of rules. If Muslims believe in a certain kind of government, then they should believe in it whether they are one percent of the population or 99 percent.

Another point: Do Islamists and non-Islamists say the same thing at home and publicly? Or do they say the same things inside the mosques in Arabic as they say in English? That's a way to tell them apart.

Something else important to note is groups which are focused heavily on proving their personal Muslim rights and focused on victimology. The question to ask is, are they here to learn about America or American principles, or are they here to teach Americans about Islam?

The Islamists want to do dawah. Dawah in Arabic is education, they say, but it is actually evangelism. It's an effort to spread Islam and convert people to it. Dawah can also be a benign concept. By being nice, humble, courteous, compassionate, you can interpret that as dawah, but the Brotherhood's interpretation of dawah is empowering yourself politically and sociologically to create movements that effect change and turn people into Muslims. If a Muslim believes dawah is a political movement and should be spread to change populations, that is another sign of Islamism.

The time of trying to spread Islam is done. To me, when Islam was first starting at the time of the prophet Muhammad, it would have died had there not been some spread of the faith. Now that it's a quarter of the world's population, there is absolutely no need to do door-to-door evangelism.

Society has already shown that the only societies that work are those based on Western constitutions, where rules and laws are based on reason that separates mosque and state or church and state.

Another litmus test regards the State of Israel. This is a key litmus test. Even though to me, the Palestinian–Israeli issue is not an Islamic one, the geopolitics of the Palestinians, and their inability to recognize a country everyone else in the world recognizes, and their own actions and terrorism makes it a significant issue, as it has been used globally by the Brotherhood as a lightning rod for the Islamist movement. The Islamist Wahhabi from India, Imam Dr. Zakir Naik, who runs Peace TV and has millions of followers, uses the Israeli issue all the time to bring people in. Most non-Islamists stay away from this issue because it's not one of Islam, and support Israel when it comes to its national security.

Another key indicator is the treatment of women as a litmus test and whether they believe women should have equal rights to government, to the presidency, and leadership in mosques.

**CHRISTINE:** Islamist groups and lobbies have gained significant ground in the US and other Western nations. Is there any identifiable strategy that enables such successes?

**DR. JASSER:** I think their formula is in the huge head start they had. As immigrants came to the West and felt foreign, there was an initial sense —as with most immigrants—of wanting to stay together. This includes Italians, Germans and the Jewish community, etc. This fits directly into the Islamist paradigm. Political Islam is based on the collectivism of the faith group.

My own exposure to political Islam happened in 1985, when I was a freshman at the University of Wisconsin, Milwaukee. All of a sudden I found out that the mosque wasn't just about learning the Koran and spirituality, but Friday sermons became about Afghanistan, American imperialism, the CIA infiltration into the Mujahideen, anti-Americanism and politics. I wondered why the imam was bringing this into the mosque, since I thought religion was supposed to be about God, morals, and family values.

I quickly realized that most of the mosques—and even the Muslim Student Associations that I went to—were anti-Israeli and that they used Muslim collectivism to effectuate their political agendas. They carried baggage that accumulated from their families and from dictatorships that taught them that there was no free speech. The Islamic Centers were made into anti-American, anti-Jewish, and anti-Israeli centers. Their baggage was what the Islamists wanted and was fueled by Saudi Arabia's petrodollars that funded their groups.

So to further answer your question of why these groups grow so much here, one is the tribal mindset and the second is their fuel. For example, the World Assembly of Muslim Youth group formed the Muslim Student Association, who in turn formed the Islamic Society of North America (ISNA). The Saudis then helped form the North American Islamic Trust (NAIT), and all of these groups that were listed as part of the Holy Land Foundation were also listed in the Holy Land trial as unindicted co-conspirators and front groups of the Muslim Brotherhood Movement. The Muslim Brotherhood has said that in the West they have a unique opportunity. It frustrates me as a Muslim.

ISNA constantly tries to put forth that Zuhdi is outside the Muslim community; that Zuhdi is part of the Western landscape. They can do that because Muslims are one percent of the population in America and Americans don't know the dynamics and diversity of the Muslim community, so they assume that these Islamists—who are all about Islamic collectivism—must be saying what Muslims really think. Americans don't do enough research.

When Islamists say they represent the Muslim community, and that ISNA has a convention of 50 thousand people and that Zuhdi is just one person who may have a few hundred Muslim members, my response to them is that the non-Islamists have had no reason to collectivize themselves. Non-Islamists belong to their Republican or Democratic parties, to their medical associations, their bar associations, media groups, chambers of commerce, and their faith is personal to them. This is why it is so hard for me. There are about 3 million Muslims in America, but how many are actually members of Islamic groups? And the vast majority of members are apathetic to political activism of Muslims, so Islamists are hoping that Americans will never put two and two together and realize Muslims have a diversity in their mindset.

**CHRISTINE:** Are Islamists purposely exploiting new immigrants?

**DR. JASSER:** Islamists completely exploit the sense of minority and fear. It's intimidating to live in a free system; you're not used to English as a second language. Islamists play into "us versus them." They want Muslims to feel separated and like victims. It has happened across Europe, where Muslims live in ghettos separated from mainstream society. This way, Muslims are controlled by Islamist leaders. Part of the thing that reformists and anti-Islamists do poorly is in providing immigration services to point immigrants in the right direction. If you look at immigrant groups overall in America, they start liberal and move toward conservatism. That's because liberals co-op minority groups into their party by representing themselves as the champion of the oppressed, that America is anti-immigrant, so it follows that the only way to protect yourself as an immigrant is joining a leftist party or the Democratic party. It is a bill of goods.

**CHRISTINE:** How are Islamists exploiting Western lack of knowledge at the political level?

**DR. JASSER:** One of the biggest areas of neglect or ignorance in the West has been to equate democracy with elections. The word democracy does not appear in the US Constitution or in the American Declaration of Independence for a reason. When Iraqis had their vote, it was a great achievement after Saddam Hussein, and we see that Hamas was elected with the West Bank and Gaza.

A Pew poll came out that talked about political Islam really thriving in many of these countries; so they were linking Islam to democracy, and the Brotherhood right now is basing its goals on saying democracy means elections. I spoke about this at the Oslo Freedom Forum, that

Muslim majority countries in the last hundred years have gotten into the rut of saying that life has two choices: Islamic theocracy or secular fascism, where the latter is equated to a dictatorship, like those under Hosni Mubarak, Muammar Gaddafi, Saddam Hussein, which they also equate to Western secularism, that they say are godless societies. Islamic theocracies, like the Saudi Arabian government, has its own relationship with the Wahhabis and their legal system. Similarly, the Iranian theocrats had a merger of the clerics and the government, and then there was the Taliban. Those are all examples of theocracy and there has been no third pathway.

**CHRISTINE:** How will this third pathway that you suggest manifest and function?

**DR. JASSER:** I think the only way to win this war of ideas is to give Muslim populations in these countries a third pathway, which is liberty and the separation of mosque and state, because that choice has not existed.

Western society to my family was very much compatible to our faith because my grandfather was educated in London. My father was also educated in London and went back to Syria, and after the French pulled out, they tried to bring in Western democracy, and I view Western democracy as defined as classic liberalism, in which individual rights have protection. Our Bill of Rights, the First Amendment, and the Establishment Clause make our country work in America. These are ideas that if we don't get into the Muslim consciousness, we will lose to political Islam or Islamism. We have to start to teach that democracy is about individual rights and equal access to government, which is blind to faith, gender, and ethnicity.

Islamists will talk about diversity, but it's actually ethnic, not religious. They don't believe in different interpretations of the Koran. Women must wear the hijab, for example. Moderation means that we tolerate all kinds of diversity, including rejections of Islam and apostasy from Islam. Until that happens, Muslims are not going to absorb the Bill of Rights. Universal humanitarian principles take precedence over any singular interpretation of a faith.

**CHRISTINE:** Can you address the divisions among Islamists globally and how these divisions impact Western understanding?

**DR. JASSER:** There are some differences abroad. Of the world's 1.6 billion Muslims, about 50 percent want Islam in politics. Among the violent ones, you have secular fascists, like the late Saddam Hussein, who will murder. You also have the al Qaeda and bin Laden types that will do anything possible to create the dominance of Islamism. Then there are the Erdogans of the world. The Brotherhood would be upset with the bin Laden type because he outed what their goals were.

After 9/11, you had everybody in the world asking what the heck was going on. You had 19 hijackers attack the most powerful country in the world, that cost them half a million dollars. It ended up costing us in response over a trillion dollars, including Afghanistan, Iraq, etc.

The Brotherhood was starting to disavow terrorism in some areas, while trying to make themselves legitimate. They are still trying to legitimize themselves. A debate we want to have is one to prove to Muslims that this is not what we want, but we cannot force Muslims. I think that's why Turkey went the way it did. Secularism in Turkey forced Islamists underground over years, and when you force these movements underground, they flourish. Having to debate publicly with Islamists, you can start to teach Muslims that Islamism is the wrong way.

By forcing them underground, Turkey allowed them to thrive in their victimization mantras. The Brotherhood also thrived in Egypt under Mubarak's thumb by saying they were attacked, killed, imprisoned, and that all that they wanted was political activity and to form a Muslim party. They came across as victims and nobody looked at their ideology.

When they come to power, they are all about theocracy. People don't see that before. If you take an inside look at how the Muslim Brotherhood runs itself, they are not big on women's rights internally, but they say something different to Western media and publicly.

**CHRISTINE:** You are saying, Dr. Jasser, that peaceful Islamist leaders and al Qaeda are fundamentally one in the same? That the Turkish leader Erdogan, for example, and the late bin Laden have the same goals?

**DR. JASSER:** If you say that their goals are Islamic law, Sharia in government, and creating an Islamic state, then they are one in the same, but the way that Islamic state would end up looking and acting would be different. Bin Laden types would act more like dictators, despots, and there would be no parliament. Erdogan uses Western language, so there would be some separation of powers, a parliament, and elections. He would try to create some legitimacy, but still be driven by wanting to Islamize everything. Erdogan is peaceful in his means along the adage "You can't get people with vinegar, but with honey." It's an "evangelical Islamic thing."

Once this type gets into power, they take it one step further and let people believe they are giving them choices, but they slowly take away choices through non-violence. In Turkey, non-Muslims lost certain parts of the government to the military, and this is where Islamists are very dangerous, because their construct of society purports democracy, but it is not a democracy. A non-Muslim could never be leader, as an example. Like in an oligarchy where only the clerics rule, they will purport that non-Muslims are as sheep, and only an Islamic scholar in Sharia or someone with a similar designation could qualify to make statements about Islam and Sharia or even legitimately vote and decide.

The only positive thing about Turkey is discussion about reforming the Hadith. But what they are practicing now is political Islam, presenting Islam in a way that will confuse the West as they adhere to voting and show an appearance of democracy.

## ISLAMIC REFORM

**CHRISTINE: What is your most essential vision as a reformer?**

**DR. JASSER:** As a reformer, I would like to see a time in which Islam is not a threat to national security and in no way conflicts with societies like America, which is based on the Constitution and on the Establishment Clause. If that goal can become normative Islam so that people stop seeing my ideas as a sort of mutation, I think that would be a sign of success.

**CHRISTINE: The notion of Islamic reform has been contentious. How would you explain the concept of reform and its necessity?**

**DR. JASSER:** I once stayed away from that term when we first started the American Islamic Forum for Democracy in 2003. From 2007, I have been using it repeatedly. It took a while to warm up to the word reform.

Let me start by giving an example: Many Muslims like to compare domestic violence against their women to domestic violence against women in America. While Muslims don't have a monopoly on domestic violence, when Muzzammil Hassan—who founded Bridges TV, the first American Muslim network broadcast in English—beheaded his wife, they compared it to domestic violence in America and intentionally ignored the theological underpinnings of what motivates such people. This is not my version of Islam, but it is one important version of Islam.

Normative Islam is what comes out of Al-Azhar University and Saudi schools, which is the majority of what is being taught. It needs tons of reform, as it involves being anti-women, cutting of limbs, killing people that leave Islam, oppression of minorities, etc.

When Muslims say I'm exaggerating, I say show me the book, *Reliance of The Traveller*, which is the fourteenth-century Shafi'i Islamic law book, and I can show you a page that says to kill a Muslim if he leaves Islam. Now show me a book that says this is all wrong from a Western classic liberalist perspective in a way that forms a new school of thought. This is needed and has not been done. There are books on reform and reformist scholars that have shaped my thinking but have not formed a new school of thought, but this is needed.

There used to be four thousand schools of thought in Islam. The Sufis have a number of schools that have been modernized, but the Islamic state concept needs to be put into the dustbin of history, and the only way you can do that is through reform. I think it is complete denial to say Islam could come out of the Islamic state concept without reform.

I'm not saying we should change the Arabic text. I think this is where some reformers get into trouble, thinking the only thing that keeps us Muslim is that we agree on the Arabic text of the Koran, but one can take some of the passages of the Koran and say that it applied to the seventh century. For instance, although the Koran referred to the Jewish tribe of Banu Qurayza, it only applied to that tribe, not to every Jew. But that's what the Wahhibis do, they translate and transport one specific interpretation into everything else, and in a very malignant way, versus a more moderate way.

**CHRISTINE:** One of the stumbling blocks of the concept of reform is the question of "which reform?" That is, is one trying to reform back to the early days of Muhammad or is the goal to reform Islam into an ideology that is consistent with modernity and democracy?

**DR. JASSER:** Wahhabi reform is one of the biggest, confusing aspects of Islamic history. Abdul Wahhab from Saudi Arabia in the late 1800s presented himself as a fundamentalist reformer that was tired of all the foreign inventions called bid'as that were coming into Islam, into prayers and tombs. Sufis were especially attacked. The Wahhabis wanted to bring back Salaf, which was the Salafi tradition of bringing everything back to exactly the way it was under the prophet Muhammad. They felt that the people had strayed and needed to return to what their interpretation was about the prophet Muhammad, but that was no more reform than as Adolf Hitler was to the German people.

To me, reform is taking the American experiment. We are Americans who happen to be Muslim, and not Muslims who demand to be American. Islamist groups are in the victim mindset, making demands about rights, about being American in the form of "You're going to give us what we want and we will not change what we are." My family and others have adopted American values. I am American by virtue of living here happily with my family, accepting civil court marriages, accepting the way we did our will and testament without needing an Islamic court. I work with men and women. My wife drives every day, and she chooses to not wear a hijab. All of these are examples that we have reformed.

I love the way I live, which means I have reformed my faith and done it intellectually. That to me is an example of reform that is happening in practice on the grassroots level. But at the leadership level with the imams, clerics, organizations, no one is touching that, so there is need of change. We need to build alternative organizations and do it from an indigenous and domestic point of view. We don't need funding that is influenced by foreign entanglements and foreign movements like the Muslim Brotherhood and their Salafi friends in Saudi Arabia.

**CHRISTINE: What is the success of the reform movement so far, Zuhdi, in your estimation?**

**DR. JASSER:** I'm on the inside, so from my perspective I think it's doing well compared to the resources we have versus what the Islamists have. Our grade is a D-minus by comparison, but yet relatively speaking an A-plus for the reformers. Our US administration has been missing in action.

**CHRISTINE: Can a pious Muslim be a reformer?**

**DR. JASSER:** I think a pious Muslim should be a reformer, and that is what I tell my family daily, who deals with the stress of what I am doing. I tell them that this is my piety and life is very short, so we must think of what legacy we will leave. And to me, the core of my relationship with God is accepting the challenges that he gives me. We are challenged in different ways, either with illness, financial issues, or whatever it is. For me, the challenge of dealing with political Islam, and Islamism, as the greatest threat to civilization in the twenty-first century, is a challenge I have to take and is part of my piety.

**CHRISTINE: Looking back historically, is there a time when you saw the beginnings of a moderate reformist movement or is the last decade or so the first we are seeing of it?**

**DR. JASSER:** I think that ultimately there are a lot of books written, like Bernard Lewis's *The Crisis of Islam*. His book summarizes the struggles in reform and what went wrong in Muslim majority countries. The Islamic majority countries were on a trajectory. From the time of the Prophet Muhammad, they were headed in a trajectory as Europe was headed, and even at the time of the Dark Ages, the Jewish community and their scholars came to the Islamic world because they were more persecuted in Europe than they were in Islamic areas, but that does not mean that the Muslim world was like America. Jews were still second-class citizens, and they did not have equal rights. Then something happened in the thirteenth, fourteenth, and fifteenth centuries, and ultimately the Ottomans solidified an era that stopped ijtihad, which I define as the critical interpretation of scripture in light of modern day.

We now need a grassroots movement to reopen questions and questioning of authority, a top-down movement from imams to reopen ijtihad. It is not going to happen from me. I can build an organization that would separate mosque and state and get the clerics out of government. However, the building of new schools of Islamic thought that is compatible with American-type systems of government is going to have to come from my children and other kids raised in this type of society that love it and then learn Islam. As for the children that learn Islam first, like in the Middle East, it's very hard to get them into this kind of mindset, because there has been no example like this in Islamic history.

**CHRISTINE:** Are you suggesting that this kind of Islamic reform has to start in a Western-type scenario?

**DR. JASSER:** I think so. I call myself a Jeffersonian type of Muslim, as my ideas came out of reading Jefferson's papers on religious freedom and also James Madison's arguments that he had with George Mason and others. That's how I became an American patriot. I have also read the writings of a Moroccan poet who was a secularist who believed in separation of mosque and state. I have read Abdolkarim Soroush, who has a book called *Reason, Freedom, and Democracy in Islam* where it seems like he has absorbed the ideas of John Locke. If we took the work of Jefferson, Locke, Frédéric Bastiat, and classical liberal thinkers and translated into Arabic all the languages that Muslims speak and fed it into the Middle East, that would effect change.

You talk to families of reformers overseas and see that there is no ability for them to build institutions based on critical thinking, because the governments are so oppressive. For example, Pakistan is a secular government, but it's an Islamic state where the madrassas have flourished. There is a bizarre toxic relationship in most of these countries between radical Islam and the secular fascists. It's like two major mafia families in a neighborhood where everybody else who is different either disappears or is dead. Take Saudi Arabia as an example: The monarchies have had a toxic relationship with the Wahhabis and the moderate women and anti-Islamists have disappeared.

**CHRISTINE: How do you empower the desire to follow the non-Islamist path?**

**DR. JASSER:** You need two prongs to this: a think tank aspect to create a body of knowledge to allow imams and clerics to look at Sharia and the vision to see where you can reform it without divorcing Muslims from scripture and without divorcing yourself from the example of the prophet Muhammad. In other words, you need to tangle intellectually with the Islamists.

One of the problems I have is with people saying Muhammad was a pedophile and that he beheaded people after battle. You cannot reform a faith by saying its founder was an immoral person. You can take examples of that intellectually to investigate and separate history and religion. For example, in the passage that says, "Kill them where you find them," some people say that refers to Christians and infidels. It refers to a pagan tribe that had violated a treaty and it allowed war against them. If after the Taliban had declared war on America and were beheading our troops, and General Petraeus told his troops to kill the Taliban where you find them, this would not be immoral. There are cases of just war and you don't denigrate the character of Muhammad to bring about reform. This is one of the ways you empower regular Muslims; you show them that they don't have to divorce themselves from their faith to become strong, patriotic Americans.

Secondly, you protect reformers and give them venues. As an example, I took a position against an international entity, a huge fund that I was concerned was doing charity work that would funnel its funds to terrorist groups. I got threatened with libel in London, which is lawfare. There is a lot of intimidation, and we need to give reformers platforms where we don't feel threatened.

A third way to empower a non-Islamist path regards fuel. That is, no petrodollars. We will not win this war without the help for us to establish institutes. This is not just a Muslim problem. Muslims don't largely understand the Establishment Clause, the separation of church and state.

Non-Muslims can help by building a network with like-minded groups and individuals, provide forums, and train local media to not fear religion. We need to break down walls of political correctness. Our Founding Fathers talked a lot about religion leading up to the Establishment Clause, but along the way those skills disappeared. No one wants to talk now about religion except in the context of victimization.

The Nidal Hasan report came out of the Pentagon. We spent a lot of money on a 78-page review on Hasan. Nowhere were the words "Muslim" or "Islam" found in that report. For a country like ours that produces admirals and generals to produce a report like Hasan's where those words were avoided, you're not helping reformists. Instead, they are listening to Islamist groups. In 2007, Attorney General Gonzales put out a memo to the Department of Justice, saying to not use the words "Jihad" and "Islamist" because it empowers the bin Ladens of the world. Non-Muslims could help reformers by opening up the field to public discussion between Muslims and lead panels of different Muslims, as well as encourage debates for Americans to see that the problem is within the House of Islam. It isn't between Islam and the West, and it isn't about how Muslims are treated that leads to terrorism. All of these excuses are diverting.

The best metaphor is AA. Muslims need a twelve-step process like alcoholics, and they are stuck in the first stage, which is denial. Islamists don't want to acknowledge that al Qaeda is a natural offshoot of their ideology. The non-Islamists escaped the Middle East and don't want to deal with al Qaeda, saying that it is a crime problem, not a Muslim problem, so we need to get past denial and realize that the toxin, or alcohol, is Islamism. Islamists cannot identify with this country. In their souls is a natural allegiance to their faith.

When the youth and young adults get older, it's hard to make them into non-Islamists. We need to educate the younger. The older is difficult to reform. We need to reform the younger, have them write poetry and literature on why they live in the West and what makes them want to be here and not back in their Islamic state. It's a huge struggle and there is no information war right now. No one is advocating for Western society among Muslims. They aren't watching Fox and CNN. They're watching Al Jazeera, their own websites, and absorbing their own literature.

Islamists don't want diversity in mosques. They focus on victimology and hate crimes against them. We want to expose that. The American Islamic Forum for Democracy has been distributing flyers about faith and American patriotism in mosques across the country, and if they resist, we go to the media and show them the fliers, asking, what's harmful about it? We make efforts to expose Islamists.

## PROBLEMATIC KORANIC TEXTS AND ISLAMIST IDEOLOGIES

**CHRISTINE:** This notion of inferiority of non-Muslims, women, races, is this a battle you still grapple with on Western soil since it was ingrained?

**DR. JASSER:** That's a great question. It cuts to the core and there are a couple key elements. One is the concept of religion and exclusivity. You could be an exclusivist without being a supremacist. Some faiths believe unless someone is saved you could go to hell. That's exclusivist. To not separate mosque and state and to implement Islamic law, that is supremacist. Muslims get offended when I point to the ISNA as based on Islamic supremacy, but when you have the head of that organization explaining a passage that men are allowed to beat their wives as long as their elbow doesn't leave their hip, which is a common Islamist interpretation of the passage, that is absurd and it is not moderate. It is medieval and it is supremacist. You have to go through these areas of reform: equality of women, the separation of mosque and state, the recognition that other faiths have access to God and to heaven, and that ultimately we are equal at the table of world religions.

**CHRISTINE:** Looking at Muhammad and accusations of him being a pedophile with regards to Aisha, how do you reckon with this?

**DR. JASSER:** First of all, these questions are legitimate. I have had to reconcile these things. It's also important to recognize how to clarify history. We have enough trouble trying to figure out what happened in Afghanistan, let alone in the times when the prophet Muhammad demanded that certain tribes be beheaded. On the issue of Muhammad being a pedophile, I'm a physician, and the word "pedophile" is a psychiatric term that refers to the pathology of men that have a predilection for sexual contact with children. It is definitely part of history that he was married to Aisha when she was nine. Many Muslims believe that marriage was not consummated for many years after that, and we could debate that it was 15, 18, but I just do not believe it was consummated at the age of nine. Am I deluded? All I can tell you is that is what I was taught.

Some of those marriages were political, some preventing war, some related to a situation he was in. The closest wife Muhammad had was Khadijah, who was older than him and was a businesswoman that was very active in society and fought in some battles. She was an independent example of women. For Muslim reformers, we need to find the aspects of history that allow us to instill in our children and transfer to them an example of the prophet that is consistent with today's society, one that promotes equal rights for women. Even in America, child marriage, especially in the South, was an issue for years, until society decided it was forbidden, and the reforms happened in the West, so this is not something that is particular to Islam. Women's rights movements in the West were active and brought change.

**CHRISTINE:** What about the other problematic texts such as those advocating violence in the Koran or Jihad by the Sword?

**DR. JASSER:** Muslims agree the Koranic texts are only called the Koran when in Arabic. Once you translate it, it becomes a human interpretation from that original language that we believe was transmitted. Most of the translations that exist today have been fueled by the Saudi petrodollars and include interpretations that are very supremacist.

Let me give you a couple of examples I have on my website, *Which Islam and Whose Islam.* In that series, I go through the Passage of the Sword, and I talk about an interpretation that could be modernized out of that passage. What I learned was that passage does not talk about non–Muslims specifically. It talks about infidels, but it does not apply to all people who are not Muslims, but a specific tribe that violated a treaty. According to the passage, there was a peaceful existence between the Muslims and the pagans, where Muslims had the opportunity to go to Mecca and do their pilgrimage each year. In the third or fourth year of that treaty, the pagans attacked a caravan of Muslims on their way. Some of the versions say the Muslims started it. We can't prove what happened. All I can say is that if a version of Islam is taught to our children that tells them that they were attacked, then that violates the treaty and allows them to defend themselves. That became the Passage of the Sword, which legitimized Just War, which does not translate into a barbaric passage.

In another passage about beating your wife, some translations say, "strike." In the English version, one can see it as, "go on strike," which means to stop and separate. But there is one passage that is difficult for me, and that is the cutting of hands because that is pretty clear. I prefer to see it as a metaphor, because I can't believe God can say that. Literalists take everything black and white.

In the area of polygamy, there was a time where a man would benefit from having more than one wife for whatever historic reason, but in modern times I would not apply that any more than I would want my wife to be married to more than one husband. We have evolved from that now, and there is no need for a man to marry more than one wife.

**CHRISTINE:** Is there a need for a revised and reformed Koran?

**DR. JASSER:** There is a need for new interpretations of the Koran and translations, but I would be against anyone trying to remove Arabic script. Every faith has a fabric that holds it together. Some have explained that if you start taking out Arabic passages, it's like pulling a thread out of a basket weave.

## DETERMINING THE FUTURE OF ISLAM

**CHRISTINE:** In your opinion, what countries are the most important in determining the future of Islam?

**DR. JASSER:** The USA, because we have the ability to form institutions and the knowledge and skills in campaigning with a war of ideas that no other country has. For example, you had a successful campaign of "someone" who came out on a message of hope and change, and overnight with a trillion dollars spent, so why can't we change the Islamic consciousness with a campaign, with the right language?

Secondly, it might be Indonesia, as it had problems with radical Islam and corruption, but the penetration of Sufism into their society has stood the test of time in separating nationalism from Islamism. But yet they are still not winning yet. Eighty percent of Muslims in Indonesia believe Islam should play a role in politics, according to a Pew poll, so they are losing the war of ideas, but there is hope.

As for Saudi Arabia, you can't divorce the importance of that country. There are petrodollars, and if they ended up reforming, they could quickly change the world and the global Islamic situation more than anywhere else.

Iraq is another where diversity is abundant, despite the terrorism and exodus of Christians. There are seeds of change that need the right influences from abroad.

In Iran, we saw the revolution in 2008. A positive aspect in Iran is the energy of the youth and university students that want change. The West is falling short because it has a form of ADD. We fail to help those who persistently need help. We need to talk about these issues like Iran week after week, as we do domestic policy.

**CHRISTINE: There are other countries that I would like your opinion on, Zuhdi, regarding the future of Islam. Let's start with Turkey.**

**DR. JASSER:** Turkey is sliding in the wrong direction. The government claims to be moderate, but it's taking away secular protections and empowering the Islamist parties. The fate of Turkey and its direction will depend on this whole war of ideas and whether the West and America decide to engage political Islam or not.

The Pew poll also showed that in all of these countries, there is huge linkage between Islam and politics, and their assessment is a binary choice; i.e., either Islam or secular fascism, so they need the third choice, which is Western liberty achieved through a war of ideas. If you look back at the Soviets during the Cold War, we never fired a bullet against the Soviets, but the Cold War was won by the use of mediums like radio and think tanks built that extolled capitalism over socialism, and socialism was proven to be a failure. The Iron Curtain fell and the

Berlin Wall fell. We have done nothing in the war of ideas and should; most Muslims don't want theocracy. They know it's a failure like in Iran, and Iranians don't want theocracy.

My prediction over the next decade is that Turkey will become more Islamist, and then there will be a curve back, as we wake up to global information and start to turn back. So we need to engage them and find Muslim thinkers in Turkey to engage reformers. We need to lift them up and say we as Americans and Westerners will lift up those we think support universal human rights and stand against political Islam. Under Obama, it has been called mutual respect, mutual interest, but what is that? We need to engage an ideological war, and I think Turkey will be at the forefront of that.

**CHRISTINE:** What about Iran's importance to the future of Islam?

**DR. JASSER:** The next step is that the Green Revolution has shown that given the right ideas and tools, they will flourish. You will have demonstrations, as there is a huge thirst for a movement to change that government. We need to identify leaders, work underground, and openly say that we will not continue to cater to the Islamist regime there, and ultimately we will work with those who defend women's rights. We will also work with the Baha'is, who are under oppression and make open statements that will defend such groups and help reformists that will work to defend these groups.

We need an open strategy concerning Iran. All we hear is about their nuclear weapons. Yes, that is a huge concern, but that is a symptom. Why do they want to obtain such weapons? Why do they hate Israel and are so anti-Semitic? Remember, that was one of the litmus tests for Islamism, and until you treat the core disease, these are symptoms; that is, terrorism and desire for nuclear armaments.

We need a strategy and a long-term policy to help reformers in Iran. We cannot walk away. We have to rebuild American credibility. Part of the American loss of credibility is because such countries see us as short-term thinkers that help one or two movements for a short time and then walk away. They saw what happened to the Shia community in Iraq and to some of the reformers there that we initially helped after the Gulf War and then got decimated by Saddam Hussein a few years later. We went back and changed that government, but we pulled away again. We keep demonstrating that the American people don't have a stomach for long-term engagement. I don't think you're going to be able to build a long-term relationship without their trust, which will develop when they see us defending Iran's minorities and defending the reform groups, so I think Iran is a place to look at the universities and the youth movements, and most of those will end up being on our side.

**CHRISTINE:** What about the influence of Pakistan?

**DR. JASSER:** Pakistan is the one country that I don't have a solution for. It is such a tribal and illiterate place. Military governments have had to deal with the devil with empowered radical ideas. The Balkanization of various parts of Pakistan has happened. Islamists have been losing elections, but look at how Minister of Minorities Shahbaz Bhatti was assassinated for fighting against blasphemy laws. Bhutto too. Such people have a short life expectancy in Pakistan. Our troops weren't in that country. They were in Afghanistan, yet our success in Afghanistan was dependent on what happened in Pakistan. The solution is to raise think tanks and solution-oriented programs that can effectuate change. So there needs to be schools based on liberty-based programs of reform. I think this will be the longest society to accomplish reform.

**CHRISTINE:** Saudi Arabia?

**DR. JASSER:** That will be difficult. I don't think the tribal monarchy there has ever been shown to be willing to relinquish control in history. It will have to be like South Africa where what happened ultimately is that apartheid ended and they let go. We helped Kuwait to get Saddam Hussein out. That was a tribal monarchy, and it still hasn't changed since we left it in 1991. That concerns me.

We have a credibility problem. The world sees us hugging King Abdullah and being tolerant because we don't want to see gas prices go up, but the way they treat women, Christians, non-Muslims, and moderates, it makes it difficult to say we are about freedom and liberty. We need to examine the concept that the enemy of my enemy is my friend. That is not always the case. Yes, Saudi Arabia has been working with us against al Qaeda, but they created that monster. A lot of the ideas that were established by bin Laden are still being spread by leaders in Saudi Arabia.

All of these programs in Saudi Arabia for deprogramming terrorists tell them that violence is not the way. It does not tell them that their core Islamist Salafi ideas are wrong, and that will never happen because the group Assembly of Muslim Jurists of America, which is AMJ online, issues fatwas to American Muslims every day telling them not to serve in Homeland Security and not to vote. These ideas are coming out of Saudi Arabia. They want Americans to protect their soil against Iran and its nuclear weapons, yet when it comes to Sunni Islam, they don't want reform. Yet getting Saudi Arabia to change will be our best return on investment that will propagate to the entire Muslim world.

**CHRISTINE: What message do you have for Islamists who brainwash their following against modernity and democratic institutions into feeling a level of allegiance to their doctrine that is worth dying for?**

**DR. JASSER:** My response to Islamists is that you have no trust for this country, so by living here you are living a lie and should go back to your Muslim majority country.

Growing up, I never heard the word "home" used to describe Syria. My parents felt a loyalty to America the moment they stepped off the plane. This was their country; they adopted it as theirs. My father instilled in me the desire to want to join the military and serve; yet even royal families like princes educated in Harvard or Georgetown, they get the degree and still don't adopt Western values. They return home the same, because they don't want to lose power and billions in oil. Patriotism to Islamists has a crest and a star on the flag.

## CHAPTER TWO

# RAHEEL RAZA

### Founder of Muslims Facing Tomorrow, Journalist, Activist

RAHEEL RAZA IS A PUBLIC SPEAKER for interfaith and intercultural diversity, documentary filmmaker, freelance journalist, and author of *Their Jihad...Not My Jihad*. She is also President of the moderate organization, Council for Muslims Facing Tomorrow. She began writing at a young age because she grew up in a culture where women were supposed to "be seen and not heard."[1] In promoting cultural and religious diversity in multicultural Canada and beyond the borders, she has appeared in print, television, and radio to discuss diversity, harmony, and interfaith. In a presentation to Canadian Members of Parliament and international diplomats at the House of Commons, Raza received a standing ovation for her speech called "Celebrating our Differences."[2]

Raheel is an outspoken advocate for Islamic reform and a critic of Islamists. In an unabashed query in one of her articles, she presents the challenge: "So now, my co-religionists, there are some pressing questions we must ask because our faith as practiced today doesn't embrace humanity, modernity, music, arts, or literature. What we have to see is whether the reformists, academics, and scholars can pull this faith into the twenty-first century to co-exist with others, or will the militant swords cut the hands that hold the pen?"

In questioning the widespread global violence being practiced globally by Muslims that include the massacres of Christians, Islamist death squads, and Muslim on Muslim violence, she asks volubly: "Is it because 'Cyber Mullahs,' 'Hadeeth Hurlers,' and 'Qu'ran Thumpers' are invoking their interpretation of the Qu'ran and insisting that armed Jihad is valid and needed today, while we say it is time to make it obsolete? Is it because there are verses in the Qu'ran that can be, and have been, used to justify violence against non-Muslims? If this is the situation, then it is time for us to lift our heads out of the sand, and understand that the enemy is within."[3]

To those who argue about whether or not Islam is a religion of peace, Raheel does not shy away from offering an answer: "Platitudes about Islam being a faith of peace are not credible anymore. Islam is only as good as the way its followers practice it, and if they have created killing fields in the name of Islam, then Islam will be recognized by the silence of those who did not speak out when their faith was being massacred to massacre humanity."[4]

Raheel has been an inspiration to me personally, as she was a regular guest on the daytime live, open line show I hosted, *On the Line*.

## INTERVIEW WITH RAHEEL RAZA

**CHRISTINE: What motivated you to become a reformer?**

**RAHEEL:** By default of being in Canada and having the freedom for the first time in my life to learn what my faith was about, and knowing what Islamists are practicing is not it. 9/11 spurred me on, and the thought that my children and grandchildren will become innocent victims of someone else's actions if I don't stand up and do something. This is the country that has given me my voice and the right as a woman to stand up and speak. I can now tell these horrible men to back off, even though I feel the hostility. It comes with hate, with death threats, and a lot of challenges, but I have the support of my family. My husband is my biggest supporter.

**CHRISTINE: Who inspired your work as a reformer?**

**RAHEEL:** I read the books of every Muslim woman author I could get my hands on, including Dr. Amina Wadud, who is an African American convert to Islam. Her work gave me hope that for every verse in the Koran, there are possibilities about how it could be interpreted. She was a professor at Virginia University and authored a book called *Qur'an and*

*Woman.* I read her book over 14 years ago, and that was the first time I saw a different perspective. She took every verse in the Koran that related to women and provided different ways of interpretation. She knows Arabic, jurisprudence, and Sharia, and the different ways it could be interpreted. Koran reformists are not changing the words of the Koran, because Muslims believe it is the word of God. They are instead giving options of other ways it could be translated and interpreted to be more compassionate, humane, and merciful. If you understand the persona of God to have these attributes, then you will translate his words the same way. In such a translation, there is no place for violence.

## THE INFLUENCE OF ISLAMISTS

**CHRISTINE:** How can one recognize an Islamist from that of a moderate Muslim like yourself?

**RAHEEL:** An Islamist is someone who uses political ideology to further a goal. Islamists have no interest in the spiritual message of the faith. They have sidelined it and have often not even read the spiritual message of the Koran to understand about compassion, mercy, humanity, and the relationship of Islam with other faiths. They are only interested in furthering their goal of political Islam and turning everyone into a Muslim, which has been taught to them by their leaders. Essentially, one of the philosophies of Islamism is to establish a kind of Islamic Caliphate wherever they live, regardless of whether it is a Muslim country or non-Muslim country.

Their goal is to enforce Sharia law globally and take women back to the Dark Ages. Essentially, they believe that the only good Muslim is a seventh-century Muslim.

**CHRISTINE:** The late Osama bin Laden and members of al Qaeda are straightforward Islamists, but what about leaders such as Recep Tayyip Erdogan and theorists such as Tariq Ramadan, who appear to be "moderate"? Can they all be lumped together as Islamists?

**RAHEEL:** Essentially their goals are the same, to establish Sharia, but their methods differ. One is a civilized veneer, the other is a crude one.

Among Islamists, there are many who are Westernized in their dress, who are very suave, very sophisticated, and highly educated but the issue is the ideology. They have been brainwashed with the ideology of the Jamaat-e-Islami or the Muslim Brotherhood, and their goal is to impose Islam on the entire world. Their philosophies are written in the manifesto of the Muslim Brotherhood, so it's no big secret. It's an anti-West, anti-women, anti-freedom ideology.

**CHRISTINE:** How can average Western citizens tell the difference between an Islamist living among them and a true moderate Muslim?

**RAHEEL:** Islamists are well-versed in the ways of the West. Many are also highly technological and are capable of using an array of facades, but you can ask them basic questions. One is about the separation of mosque and state. Secondly, do they believe that Israel has a right to exist? Ninety-nine percent of Islamists thrive on a very anti-West and anti-Israel policy. I see these as extremely important and intertwined with the whole ideology of hate that they perpetuate.

**CHRISTINE:** How is the Palestinian–Israeli issue manipulated by Islamists?

**RAHEEL:** It is absolutely manipulated by Islamists. The uneducated village guy in Pakistan will burn his shirt and give his life for Palestine, and if you ask him where it is on the map, he has no clue. It is used as an instant political firestorm anytime. When I speak about women's rights in Islam, they will try to derail me by bringing in the Palestinian–Israeli issue. I have caught on to their trick.

Anywhere you go in universities, the Muslim Student Associations, which are very radicalized, instantly throw you off target by speaking about the Palestinian–Israeli issue. It is huge bait, and people fall for it. The Palestinian issue is political, not religious, so they should not bring it into an Islamic conversation.

**CHRISTINE:** For new Muslim immigrants, particularly youth, how do you recommend dealing with the alienation they feel, especially with the threat of Islamist influence?

**RAHEEL:** Every immigrant community feels a sense of alienation. Muslims are not unique in this. It is very important for the elders of the families and the larger support systems within a given community to help build the confidence of these young people. I had two boys, and I have never imposed our faith, nationality, or identity on them. I brought them up as Muslim Canadians and to be proud to be brown, to take pride in who they are, and not try to be anything else.

What is happening in the Muslim community is that its leaders who appear "holier than thou" are trying to make Muslims into better Muslims, rather than better citizens of their host countries. An entire identity crisis has been created in some of the immigrant Muslim communities because of the new immigrants coming in who experience a vacuum and settlement problems. But these new immigrants, to be active participants in their own settlement and integration, also need to reach out. Settlement, integration, and adaptation into new cultures is a two-way street. It cannot be left only to the host society.

Our youth are very confused. They come here, feel alienated, and then they fall into the trap of the Muslim leadership in the mosques that starts telling them that this is not really their land, they will never belong here, that these people are infidels, and they are not part of your faith.

Canada steps out of its way to help immigrants. There are abundant programs in place, but the immigrants also need to be ready to change and to stop slamming everything they don't like. They need to find ways to make it work for themselves and for the new country of their settlement.

A lot depends on how children are brought up. If children are brought up hating people who are different, believing they do not belong to this land, and they don't owe any loyalty to it, then they can be entitled and just take all the rights, all the benefits, and have no responsibilities. Young people then become double-minded, as they have not been taught that with rights comes responsibilities. It's a balancing act that is very important.

**CHRISTINE:** How far-reaching is the impact of the type of message being taught to youths by Islamists?

**RAHEEL:** It has a major effect on them, even for the youth who were born here. The question about home-grown radicalism comes up and is queried by Westerners repeatedly: How could kids that were born and brought up here be a home-grown terrorist? What Westerners need to understand is that it has nothing to do with their physical birth here. It is the ideology and how children are being brought up from day one. They are brought up with a sense of arrogance and superiority—which unfortunately is very much a part of the extremist Muslim ethos, and they internalize the idea that they are the chosen ones, are right, and everyone else is wrong. The victim ideology is also taught so that if someone criticizes you, then they are being Islamophobic. This is what Muslims are teaching the children so that when they grow up, it is evident in their final structure.

**CHRISTINE: Can you elaborate further on the ideological aspect of the brainwashing process of Muslim youth?**

**RAHEEL:** Sadly and unfortunately, the spiritual message of the Muslim faith has been distorted beyond comprehension. When I ask the youth how much they know about the Koran, they don't know because they have never read it themselves. They only follow and listen to what the Muslim authorities in their lives have been telling them. For the leaders, it's all about power, control, and patriarchy. This brainwashing takes place at a very young age, so you find a whole generation of young people who have grown up with a set of ideologies that teach hatred toward others, intolerance of others, disrespect toward others, and that could easily transform into violence. When you put in a foundation of hate, it is easy to take that step of violence.

**CHRISTINE: How can one expect a shift in tide toward the reformist movement, given the magnitude of this aggressive strain of Islamism that is confronting us today?**

**RAHEEL:** There have been thirty years of brainwashing of the Wahhabi ideology going on, which was exported on the back of petrodollars and the Muslim Brotherhood. But we have already sunk to the lowest of the lows. I go to Pakistan every year, and I don't think they can sink any lower. I am an eternal optimist and I still believe that change can still come.

**CHRISTINE:** Have Islamists infiltrated our Western institutions?

**RAHEEL:** Yes, they have, and most of them have done it in very insidious ways. Unfortunately, we moderates have been warning the government for a long time that this is going on, but we are often dismissed as hatemongers, trouble-makers, and shit disturbers, so they don't listen. I have traveled across universities in the UK to speak about hate speech on campuses. Very often, young Muslim students approached me arrogantly, with hostility and wanting to trick me, but I do my homework, and they have no clue about what the Koran said about following the laws of the land. They ask me to show them where it is. This is why I advocate that reform has to come from within, because we reformists have to fight them on the misinformation they have been given.

They have been told that the Koran says they must hate Jews and Christians, and it does not say so. They have been told that the niqab is in the Koran. I have to show them it is not—modesty, yes—but not the head covering and not the face covering. As I learn more and more about their ideology, I can rebut them about the faith on their own grounds. I tell them that my faith is not for show like many people do, but that my relationship with God is between me and God. It is difficult for them to call me racist or Islamophobic. At worst, they say I am not a Muslim at all.

The moderates and the reformists who are fighting this ideology don't have the kind of financing, support, and time structure as these leaders. Wahhabi leaders are organized and have infiltrated into areas in the West where decisions are made like in government and policy-making. Unfortunately, Western governments are half asleep. Go back 30 years and look at the Muslim Brotherhood manifesto. Everything becomes as clear as daylight. The manifesto instructs to first make friends with them, then infiltrate into places where policy is made, and that is exactly what they have done.

**CHRISTINE:** Western governments are at a loss on how to deal with Islamism on home soil. If they try to call it out, they are deemed racists and/or Islamophobes,

**giving Islamists an advantage. In your opinion, how do we stem this problem, short of curbing Muslim immigration, which many, such as Dutch parliamentarian Geert Wilders, propose?**

**RAHEEL:** I will begin answering this question with another: How many Muslims have actually sat down and read the Charter of Rights and Freedoms in Canada? They need to do this, and they need to understand that this is in sync with our Islamic values. But before they come to a country like Canada, and that includes other Western countries, the Canadian government needs to put out material that says clearly that you are not coming to the Islamic Republic of Canada. You're coming to a country that was built on a Judeo–Christian ethos, where you need to have a certain set of values of freedom and democracy. These are not against our Islamic values. It does not have to be a constant battle. It is workable, provided that the majority of moderate Muslims make an effort to bring about change.

It is human nature to make demands of whatever you can get, but if the host country is not even giving you any guidelines on what to expect, then everybody does what they want and multiculturalism becomes a dirty word. In a multicultural society we need to respect diversity. It's not about individual groups forcing change. Even with Muslims, we have Muslims from 60 different parts of the world. We are very diverse, and if we respect where we live and the laws of the land then we can live as one big happy family. We may have our differences, but we learn to respect those differences.

## PROBLEMATIC ISLAMIC TEXTS AND SHARIA IDEOLOGIES

**CHRISTINE:** What are the most problematic Koranic verses that need reform in your view?

**RAHEEL:** Armed Jihad, the verse about striking a woman, and violent texts. The problem is that the Koran has been reinterpreted to read in a very different way, but these reinterpretations are not acceptable yet. Muslims have not arrived at the point where they are even willing to accept that there needs to be a reform in the understanding.

**CHRISTINE:** The history of Islam is littered with violence and brutal conquests and backed by the Koran. Can you validate those?

**RAHEEL:** I read and understand that the history of Islam is based on conquests and violence, but there is the spiritual message also which is important to me. I have also read and reread many translations of the Koran. A lot of conservative and orthodox Muslims have never read anything critical of Islam, but I felt a need to do that. It is also important for us to know how people view it from the outside. I often tell people that even though Islam is a choice to me, it does not have to be the choice for them. Everybody does not have to love Islam and Muslims, as long as I understand why I am Muslim and do not expect to impose it on anyone else.

**CHRISTINE:** Does Muhammad serve as a model consistent with today's values?

**RAHEEL:** In terms of the modeling of ethical values, absolutely, because the ethics he supported are universal, not time-bound. He is an example in how he lived his life. But we are to recognize that his life is in the context of the seventh century, otherwise we would be riding camels now, but I think that Islam and the Koran are flexible enough to adapt to time and place, because what it's teaching us is about ethical and moral boundaries, which are accepted across the board. All faiths teach about being good to people, about not lying and stealing, and those transcend time and place, so definitely for me he is a model I can look up to.

**CHRISTINE:** Internationally, there is the Universal Declaration of Human Rights, but in 1990, the Cairo Declaration of Human Rights was adopted by the Organization of Islamic Cooperation (OIC). The Cairo Declaration is based on Sharia law, and for the OIC, it trumps the UN declaration. Can the two declarations be possibly reconciled?

**RAHEEL:** You cannot reconcile the two. The OIC is a huge problem. I've been to Geneva. I've been to the Human Rights Commission there. The OIC is the biggest problem. They are very powerful and large in number, and believe there are no human rights aberrations in Muslim countries.

**CHRISTINE:** Hold on, Raheel, no human rights aberrations in Muslim countries? Even given the inferior status of women which includes honor killings, stonings, and acid attacks; and that black slavery is still in existence; the severe persecution of Christians; the murder of "apostates"; and the calls to kill infidels?

**RAHEEL:** I'm on record for having told off the Pakistani ambassador—the Secretary-General of the OIC—because he said there is so much victimization of Muslims in Western countries, and I asked him: "What the heck are you talking about? In Pakistan, they are killing Christians en masse every other day and people are not even allowed to demonstrate in the streets, but you are talking about human rights violations against Muslims." So the hypocrisy of this world that they live in is very hard, and for them the most difficult thing about this was the fact that I, as a woman, spoke out against him. He got up and left the room, and he is on video as having left the room as I was speaking. So this is an example of how hard it is to stand up and speak out.

**CHRISTINE:** But how does one reconcile such views like yours with those Muslims who want to fully live out the Koran, with its call for violent Jihad and verses that depict women as inferior?

**RAHEEL:** You can, because Islam is not just reading the Koran. It is reading about the life of the prophet and the historical background of Islam. Muhammad was happy about doing housework and marrying a woman that he worked for. Very soon after the death of the prophet, all of that went by the wayside, because patriarchy, ego, and power set in. It is not difficult to reconcile the Koran with Western values, as long as we pick up the spiritual message. When I decided I wanted to speak out for Muslim women, I first had to see whether or not Islam gave me that freedom, because when I grew up I was used to being told "you're a second-class citizen," that women should be seen and not heard, and "you speak too much."

That was my childhood. So when I came to Canada, I had the freedom, and I reread my history and understood the Koran. I read between the lines and discovered how powerful it was in terms of the rights it gave me as a woman. It gave me the rights 1,400 years ago to vote, to ask for a hand in marriage, to keep my maiden name in marriage, and that I don't have to give my earned wages to the running of the family unless I wanted to. And these were the rights of women at that time, where in modern times, women were only given rights to vote in the 1900s. Yet these women's rights have never been practiced, and no one tells Muslims. I had to find out for myself, since the leadership won't tell us. They want to push it under the table. For example, the Koran speaks about people of other faiths, so it's the biggest lie that the Koran says that Jews and Christians are infidels. There are passages that discuss problems with the Jewish community, but they are historical.

None of this knowledge is given out there, because it's easy to grip people, especially youth, who have this hatred for the US because they "occupy" certain lands. When I started speaking to youth and women, I filled myself with knowledge, the biggest weapon of mass instruction. There has to be a whole different way that Islam is taught, and that's the starting point.

**CHRISTINE: You are a progressive, modernized woman Muslim leader, but there are a lot of Muslim women saying in Western society that they want to be left alone to practice their faith, which for some includes wearing the hijab and even the niqab. Many among this group even state that whatever you call subservient, they call being subservient to Allah, and they don't have a problem with that. How do you reply to them?**

**RAHEEL:** It is very hard. The largest hostility comes from these women who have been brainwashed to believe this. This has been the Muslim girl's brainwashing, and it starts from very young. They genuinely believe it, because they were educated to believe it. But what is taught can be untaught.

I know Muslim women who automatically wear a headscarf until we talk, until the Muslim prayer issue comes up, and then the issues are discussed and debated. I say, don't take my word for it; go and read the Koran for yourself. One of the women did, and she discovered that she did not have to wear her scarf, so she took it off against great resistance from the community, but she said she did it because of the knowledge that came to light. Logically, how can being closer to God be connected to a head covering?

This is where the spiritual aspect comes in: To me, God is in my heart. For Islamists and those who are brainwashed, they argue because they are taught to argue. When knowledge is lacking and women are not given the freedom to learn the faith themselves, the imam will tell them what he wants them to do and not to do. One of the best things about Islam is the fact that there is no priesthood. We as individuals are supposed to read it, understand it, and implement it in our own lives. There is a huge problem of ignorance, lack of knowledge, and there needs to be enlightenment.

## THE WORK CUT OUT FOR REFORMISTS

**CHRISTINE: Define a Muslim reformer.**

**RAHEEL:** Someone who has taken the Koran and interpreted it to suit his or her personal life in today's world. A reformed Muslim essentially understands that there are issues and practices in the glory days of Islam that are not suitable for this time and place. For example, if you took the laws in the United States from even 100 years ago and said you wanted to put them into practice today, they don't work. Similarly, Sharia was put into a place at a certain time and it was supposed to grow with time, but it remained stagnant, and it stinks right now.

Nowhere in the world is Sharia practiced with compassion, mercy, and gender equality. Reformed Muslims are those who could live in the West and respect the practices of democracy, freedom of speech, separation of church and state, and they do not feel they have to impose their spiritual practices in the public sphere. So I am able to live as an observant practicing Muslim in this wonderful country, Canada, far more freely than I can do in Pakistan, because I have that equality as a woman here. When we take out human rights from the mix, we are left with nothing but a political ideology that will use violence to fulfill its goals.

**CHRISTINE: Can one be a pious Muslim and a reformer at the same time?**

**RAHEEL:** To answer this question, it depends on what you mean by the word pious. Pious has been misused by our mullahs and religious leadership. For them, piousness would be to pray five times a day, go for

Hajj, do all the practices of the faith, and yet you are unkind to your neighbor. So to me, being pious translates into whatever I do for my spiritual satisfaction in my relationship with the Creator. My faith is my personal connection with the Creator, and it is seen in my relationship with my neighbor, my co-worker, the people in the street, through my compassion and my respect for other people. If there are none of these and you are praying five times a day and slamming people of other faiths, to me that's not pious. There is a big difference in how Islamists and the radical Muslim leadership define piety, and how I define and respect piety.

**CHRISTINE:   What is the ultimate goal of reformists?**

**RAHEEL:** To live the spiritual message of our faith and to bring about the change within the faith. For us, Canada is where we are, and we try to create an atmosphere where our children and grandchildren can grow up to be caring, respectful Muslims, but at the same time believe in the separation of mosque and state, where they can live as Western Muslims and feel proud of their identity. I want my children and grandchildren to be able to stand up proud and say that they are Canadian Muslims and have respect for everyone else. For me personally, being a reformer also means gender equality, including in places of worship.

A second important goal of reformers is the relationship and respect for people of other faiths. We live in a pluralistic society. You want to celebrate pluralism and differences. It's a simple ethos. Equal rights and respect for those of other faiths are a problem for Islamists. In fact, the sooner women shut up, the better it is for them.

**CHRISTINE:   There are few Muslims like you, Raheel, who are willing to speak out despite the personal cost. Westerners ask: "Where are the voices of the so-called moderates?" How do you answer this question?**

**RAHEEL:** Muslims who are sitting on the fence need to wake up and smell the coffee. It's been said good people want to sit at home and read a book. That's true, but these good Muslims need to speak out, and this is the biggest challenge, because they have been told by the religious leadership that there is no need for reform. Personally, I don't have a problem with the message of the faith, but it has been misinterpreted, misunderstood, and passed on in the most horrible ways, so obviously it needs to reform. We need to reform how women are treated, Sharia, the Hadiths, and the understanding of the violent passages of the Koran, because there are violent passages in every scripture. With Christians and Jews, they have determined it is not applicable at this time. It's the same with the idea of armed Jihad; it is not applicable today. But they use the pulpit to perpetuate their own political views and their egos. They are not delivering the message that needs to be heard in the mosques and places of worship, so that job falls on us moderates, and it is a big challenge.

**CHRISTINE:  What is your hope in a reform movement?**

**RAHEEL:** Let me give you an example of where my hope in the reform movement is: Ten years ago in Canada, where there are freedoms and equality for women, I led the first mixed-gender prayer. All hell broke loose all over the world, and my family disowned me. Today it is acceptable. There are imams who have issued fatwas to say that it is not against Islam for a woman to lead prayers, so change comes through many different phases. Today, there are people in the United States who are putting together a reformed version of the Koran. They have reinterpreted the verses.

Dr. Tawfik Hamid, who is a reformer, says the change has to come from within. I believe that the way the Koran is taught needs to be changed. Some people say there is no need to reform the Koran, but I have attended reform conferences and they are brilliant. My hope is in those people who believe in the Muslim faith like I do, and also believe in reform and change, those who thrive and believe that we can live in sync with Western values and practice and deliver the message that it is not at odds with our own values.

**CHRISTINE:  What practical suggestions can you provide for the reform movement to advance?**

**RAHEEL:** It has to be recognized that this is still the beginning of the reform. It is happening, but will take some time. There need to be round tables—think tanks of like-minded people from across the world.

The kind of democracy that may come in the Middle East may not be a Western democracy, but as long as it implements human rights, values, and freedoms, we have won half the battle. Their style of democracy would have to fit into their psyche, in accordance with their Middle Eastern culture. It does not have to be our style of democracy.

It is just beginning, and in every movement you will find yahoos who are along for the ride, but I have learned to dissect things, to see who the people are, to see where their funding is coming from. There are always wolves in sheep's clothing. There are people whose funding is coming directly from Saudi Arabia and they call themselves moderate, progressive Muslims. If someone wants to check where my funding is coming from, I have no problem with that.

Hearings and inquiries are very acceptable and crucially important. We need to know where funding is coming from and where the agenda is coming from. For example, all funding from Saudi Arabia should be stopped and all ties cut. You have the choice of half of Canada and other Western countries being radicalized or you have the choice of making some hard decisions. Why can't schools and mosques be funded by Muslims living in the West? Set up local institutions and train the imams locally, so that they understand Canadian values.

We all need to work together, to sit with the Christians and ask, how did the reformation work for you? For example, we don't have a Martin Luther, and if you take his example, he never criticized the Bible. He criticized how it was being practiced. He criticized the institution of the church. So when we criticize the institution of the mosque, we are not going against Islam. Reformers are doing it for the faith. We feel it has been hijacked by Wahhabis and we want it back.

## CONSIDERING REFORM OVERSEAS

**CHRISTINE:** Do you see any global hope of any majority Muslim countries actually helping the reform movement?

**RAHEEL:** Yes, there are people in Indonesia and Malaysia where there has been feudalism and where different faiths live together and have not been affected in the same way by Wahhabi ideology, although the Wahhabis have been pumping a lot of money into those countries. The Balkans practiced a very Westernized version of Islam. We don't hear about such places often, where Islam is practiced in a very egalitarian and pluralistic way, but we need to take these examples. Islam is practiced in parts of Africa culturally as though it were an African tribe. Ordinary Arab Muslims will never accept this.

The Arabization of Islam has also been a huge problem, with people asserting that you cannot be a true Muslim unless you are Arabic. The message of the Koran was originally in Arabic because it was sent through the Arab people, who, by the way, have not changed in 1,400 years, but it has been translated in many languages. When Muslims traveled throughout the world, they adopted the cultures of those lands, and this is the beauty of the faith, which is what we should do while keeping our own identity as Muslims.

There is hope in this particular kind of revolution taking place in the Middle East, because freedoms, pluralism, and democracy cannot be kept away from young people anymore because of the Internet, Facebook, and social media. Once you have tasted freedom, you cannot ever go back to that oppression. I have been in Canada for over two decades, and as much as I would like to live in the oil-rich kingdoms of Dubai, I could never do it, because I have tasted freedom and so have my children.

When and if there is a backlash against Muslims, if you ask my children who they are, in their loyalty, they will say Canadian, but they just happen to be Muslim. They have been brought up with a strong sense of identity. Why should they have to suffer because of the garbage of these Islamists who have ruined our faith and turned it into something twisted and ugly, which is not how it was meant to be? It angers me and I fight this battle for the sake of my grandchildren.

**CHRISTINE:  Do you believe that the future direction of Islam will come from the Middle East or a Muslim majority country? Or by Muslims living in the West?**

**RAHEEL:** North America, because we have the freedom to bring about reform, to educate ourselves, to study, to meet, speak, discuss, and debate. My reform came because I came to Canada. I never forget that I was a product of that same culture, but when I came abroad, I was able to question why was it that I was not allowed to speak out. Does Islam not give me the rights? Does the religion make women subservient?

And I reformed my entire understanding of my faith before I went out to speak. In my humble opinion, it is here the reform will come.

**CHRISTINE: I would like to hear your opinion on the evolution of Islam in various other countries abroad. Let's start with your country of birth, Pakistan.**

**RAHEEL:** Very troubling. I am originally from Pakistan, and am very troubled about its future. I see a downward spiral. Well-educated, reform-minded, progressive women have started wearing the niqab. The whole Wahhabi ideology engulfs them because of funding from Saudi Arabia which influences Pakistan, a country with high illiteracy that is prone to radicalization.

When you have economic problems in a village with total ignorance about the faith and these Islamists come and offer to build madrassas and educate your children, you accept. These children are then educated into the Wahhabi ideology. So in other words, their mercenaries are preying on economic issues. The anti-Western ideology also plays a major role, and it permeates the entire culture in Pakistan. Everything is the fault of the US or Israel, and it never stops, so if I say I support the existence of Israel, which is part of the whole reform idea, then I am a Zionist agent, or that I and other reformists are moderates, then we are not regarded as Muslims.

But they cannot say this, because no one has the right to stand up and say that another is not a Muslim. I am a Muslim because I say I am.

The Muslim Brotherhood is not as problematic in Pakistan as is the Jamaat-e-Islami. The funding that the Saudis are giving to Pakistan's Jamaat-e-Islami, Wahhabi ideology, the Taliban, the training of al Qaeda in Pakistan, is far more than anything coming out of the Muslim Brotherhood right now.

**CHRISTINE: Turkey?**

**RAHEEL:** Turkey is problematic. It was going in a positive direction until the Islamist party came in and the army was the only secular organization that was left, but I still see hope in that Turkey is very Westernized in thinking. Think about the Balkans, who said to the Wahhabis, "No, we don't need you, we don't need your free Korans, to set up madrassas." So those who have been able to understand the Wahhabi ideologies and say no to them, that is where there will be success and change. One must understand the Wahhabi ideology, reject it, and fight it.

**CHRISTINE: Saudi Arabia?**

**RAHEEL:** Saudi Arabia is the biggest funder of Islamic radicals, and no one challenges them, because the West is beholden to them for the price of oil. But the West is in bed with them and has sold its soul for the price of oil. The only solution to that is for the West to get its own resources and say no to Saudi Arabia.

**CHRISTINE: What about Iran?**

**RAHEEL:** The Shia lobby is in Iran. The Sunni lobby is in Saudi Arabia, and the battle for turf is fought out in Pakistan.

**CHRISTINE: How do the reformists deal with the Hadiths of which many Muslims reject?**

**RAHEEL:** The Hadiths are very problematic when it comes to reform, because a lot of the Hadiths are not validated and verified. Our guideline on how to approach the Hadiths is that if you look at the Hadiths and it goes against human rights, human values, values of ethics and morals, then you throw it out, because it cannot be accepted. It is simple, even though Islamists have made it so complicated, and they sometimes use the Hadiths instead of the Koran, giving it more importance. There are scholars under the table in Turkey who have been looking at the Hadiths and have been getting rid of those that are not acceptable, so it is the matter of sitting down and using intellect and knowledge to sift through the Hadiths and discard the unacceptable.

## CHAPTER THREE

# SHEIKH DR. AHMED SUBHY MANSOUR

## Founder of Egypt's Koranist Sect

Dr. Ahmed Subhy Mansour is an Islamic scholar, founder of the Koranic movement in Egypt, and President of the International Quranic Center. From 1980 to 1987, he served as Professor of Muslim History in the College of Arabic Language at Al-Azhar University in Cairo.

Dr. Mansour's Koranic movement holds that the Hadith is an unreliable source, and that the Koran is comprehensive and sufficient in itself. Mansour was fired from Al-Azhar University for his beliefs, arrested twice, and imprisoned for two months in 1987, along with 64 of his colleagues. He was subsequently exiled from Egypt and now lives in the United States, where he has been a visiting fellow at the National Endowment for Democracy and Harvard Law School's Human Rights Program. He was also a visiting fellow at the US Commission on International Religious Freedom and the Woodrow Wilson International Center for Scholars. Sheikh Mansour is the author of 24 books and approximately 500 articles in Arabic.[1]

Dr. Mansour has stated that Koranists "want to convince the Islamic world to accept the Universal Declaration of Human Rights as Islamic laws" in accordance with what he believes is "the real core of Islam." As a visionary and reformist, he says that by "doing so, these resolutions could be the main source of legislation in Muslim countries instead of Islamic jurisprudence, which actually means fanatical Wahhabi legislations."[2]

# INTERVIEW WITH SHEIKH DR. AHMED SUBHY MANSOUR

## THE STRUGGLE OF EGYPT'S KORANIST FOUNDER

**CHRISTINE:** Please provide some historic background about the relationship between Egypt and Saudi Arabia, and also Al-Azhar University's influence.

**SHEIKH MANSOUR:** I graduated from Al-Azhar University, the biggest seminary in the Muslim world that controls religious life of Arab and Sunni Muslims even in America and Canada, because many imams come from Al-Azhar. Al-Azhar is influential by its money.

The current Saudi state was established during 1901 to 1932 by Abdel Aziz, the father of the current Saudi kings. Abdel Aziz established his state by his tough Wahhabi fanatic soldiers named Ikhwan, which means "Brothers." The Ikhwan then revolted against Abdel Aziz, but he defeated them in 1929 and 1930. Abdel Aziz wanted to create an alterative Ikhwan in Egypt to take over Egypt and to convert Egyptian Muslims from Sufism to Wahhabism for his new state to survive. But Egypt was inspired by the Western secular culture, and had its new school of religious reform led by Sheikh Muhammad Abduh [who lived] between 1849 and 1905, who struggled to reform Al-Azhar and was against Sufism and Wahhabism. His successor was the Syrian Sheikh Rashid Reda, who was bribed by Abdel Aziz to orchestrate many Wahhabi organizations. Al Ikhwan Al Muslimeen, or Muslim Brotherhood, was one of them.

The Egyptian Muslim Brothers succeeded in infiltrating the Egyptian society and others in the Arab world. Their greatest success was in infiltrating the Egyptian army and its Free Officers, who took over Egypt in 1952 by the leadership of Gamal Abdel Nasser. The Muslim Brothers was the alliance of Nasser. Afterward they tried to assassinate him, but he got rid of them. Some of them escaped to the Saudi Kingdom and were welcomed there. Nasser made the first step in changing Al-Azhar and had his own political ideology of Arab Nationalism to face Wahhabism. Nasser was defeated, and his successor Anwar Sadat allied Egypt to the Saudi Kingdom and placed the Egyptian education, media, and mosques in the hands of Wahhabis.

**CHRISTINE:** Actually, Sadat only came to power on Nasser's death.

**SHEIKH MANSOUR:** The Egyptian military regime needs Muslim Brothers as an excuse to be in power, and needs the Saudi money for its corruption, so Wahhabism has become the practical religion in Egypt since the time of Mubarak. Since the 1980s, Egyptians were brainwashed to believe in Wahhabism as the real Islam. In this climate, I have established the Koranic trend to face Wahhabism from within Islam and to revive the abandoned Islamic values of freedom of religion, freedom of speech and thought, justice, tolerance, human brotherhood and dignity, and human rights and democracy.

**CHRISTINE:** Sheikh Mansour, given your vital leadership in modern-day reform and your founding of the Koranist sect in Egypt, please detail your difficult historical path to reform, and your experience at Al-Azhar University in Egypt.

**SHEIKH MANSOUR:** I stood against the Saudi influence and suffered. Establishing the Koranic intellectual trend is a story of agony and a severe peaceful struggle against Al-Azhar and the dictators of Egypt and the Saudi regime. My struggle and persecution began inside Al-Azhar. Al-Azhar is like the Vatican for the Catholics. It is the leading seminary for more than one billion Muslims. It was built in the same year that Cairo itself was built, in 972 CE. The Egyptian military regime benefits from the name of Al-Azhar and its influence inside and outside of Egypt. In spite of its respectable famous name, Al-Azhar is a stagnant bog of ignorance and traditional ideas that belong to the Dark Ages but are still alive.

I was the youngest pupil that joined Al-Azhar primary school in 1960. In 1973, I got my B.A. in Muslim History and was appointed lecturer in the Department of Muslim History. In 1975, I got my honors M.A. at Al-Azhar in Muslim History and became an assistant teacher and lecturer there. My dissertation for my PhD degree was the effect of Sufism in Egypt during the Mamelukes era: 1250–1517 CE. In that time, Al-Azhar was under the Sufi control, and its Grand Imam was Dr. Abdel Halim Mahmoud, the most famous Sheikh for four decades. He was a fanatic Sufi scholar who believed in Sufism as the real version of Islam. So my dissertation was refused, and they asked me to change my writing to praise Sufism instead of criticizing it. I refused, saying I get all my references from the original Sufi texts and their history in that time, and they are the same texts that are well known inside Al-Azhar, but I analyzed them in the light of the Koran. This was my first stage of persecution, which lasted from 1975 to 1980. Finally, we had a compromise to delete and omit two thirds of my dissertation, and in October 1980, I got my PhD Degree from Al-Azhar in Muslim History with the highest honors, and became Assistant Professor of Muslim History in 1981.

During this first stage of persecution between 1977 and 1980, I was a moderate Sunni scholar, while the fanatic Sunni Wahhabists were struggling against the Sufi influence inside Al-Azhar. So I was their promising leader, and we worked together in 1984 and 1985 in destroying the Sufi influence in Al-Azhar.

**CHRISTINE: As a result of this struggle emerged your greater zeal for reform and subsequently the founding of the Koranist sect. Explain what evolved after destroying the Sufi influence at Al-Azhar.**

**SHEIKH MANSOUR:** In 1982 to 1985, I was the Managing Editor of the Wahhabi magazine, *Al-Huda Al-Nabawy*. I had thousands of partisans among the moderate Sunni scholars in that time. Many of them become Koranists with me after I had to leave this organization in 1986.

I used my scholarship in reforming the Sunni religion in the light of the Koran, as I did in Sufism. Inside Al-Azhar, I wrote a book that exposed the true history of the most famous Sufi saint in Egypt, who died seven centuries ago. This book proves that Al Sayed Al Badawi was not a saint, or Sufi, although most Muslim Egyptians still idolize him. Rather, he was a terrorist disguised as a saint to plot against the Egyptian regime. Al Sayed Al Badawi used religion to deceive the people and take over Egypt. When he failed, he continued under that cover to protect his life. After his death, his followers took their revenge by destroying all the Egyptian Coptic churches at once. Egyptian Muslims thought God was punishing the Christians.

The book investigates that event, proving that the followers of Al Badawi were criminals. Fearful that teenagers were being taught terrorist ideology and that bloodshed would ensue, the book concluded with a call for a review and revision of Muslim traditions. No one listened.

Bloodshed between the regime and the religious extremists began in 1992. This book is now published on our website.

It has been unusual for scholars to discuss the actual religious life of Muslims, in the present or in their history. Objective historical or sociological research is dangerous, because it elucidates the gap between Islam as it is mentioned in the Koran and religious practices of Muslims. This book was the first step in establishing rules of research to encourage scholars to tackle Muslim history objectively, and proves that Egypt has "Egyptized" Islam. Egyptians recast their old religious traditions in Arabic under the title of Islam, but these traditions had nothing to do with the Islam of the Prophet Muhammad. This book also proves that all Egyptians, Muslims, and Christians share the same rituals with different names, and all of these religious observances grew out of ancient Egyptian civilization.

This book discusses frankly the weaknesses of the Muslim states in the Middle Ages: dictatorships, corruption, and wars between Muslim states. This book analyzes the struggle between the Abbasid Sunni Empire and the secret Shiite organizations. It was banned because it makes some comparisons between that old religious political struggle and the recent clash between the Arab states and their religious oppositions. The book shows that contradiction and calls for reform in Muslim states to get rid of the Abbasid tradition, which has nothing to do with Islam as put forth in the Koran.

It was the most dangerous book in that time. It proves the human nature of the prophet Muhammad, and the contradiction between his presentation in the Koran and the images of him fabricated by Muslim fanatics. Using the Koranic verses, it demonstrates that the prophet Muhammad was not infallible, that he was not the master of the prophets, and he will not intercede on behalf of Muslims on the Day of Judgment, as Muslims believe according to the human-made Muslim religions.

**CHRISTINE:** Given the influence of this book and its adverse effects upon the cause of the fanatical leaders, what was the consequence for you and your cause for reform?

**SHEIKH MANSOUR:** Because of what I suffered, my salary was confiscated and I was accused of being an enemy of Islam. I was tried in Al-

Azhar canonical court and expelled on March 17, 1987. Because of this hard struggle and painful persecution, Koranists have become controversial in the Muslim world. Reading our writings makes thousands of Egyptians convert to the Koranic trend. Working in America, enjoying freedom of speech and having our *Ahl AlQuran* website since 2006 makes the Koranist numbers increase rapidly. God bless America.

Our family in Egypt suffered two more waves of arrest in 2007 and in 2009. Our writings that exposed the sacred secret side of Sunni Wahhabi tradition encouraged other scholars to abandon Sunnah, partially or totally. So the Koranic trend has different levels: We deny all the sayings of the Hadith and we respect the freedom of religion for every human being.

I came to the United States to continue my struggle, and I started the International Quranic Center to bring in open-minded Muslims.

**CHRISTINE:** You said you stood against the Saudi influence and suffered. Can you please discuss more about this influence?

**SHEIK MANSOUR:** Hassan al-Banna was a Saudi agent who founded the Muslim Brotherhood in 1928. In 1949, he was assassinated. He established fifty thousand branches of Muslim Brothers in Egypt, and an international organization of Muslim Brothers in Europe. He also established, inside the Egyptian Army, the Organization of the Free Officers, with the leadership and help of Gamal Abdel Nasser, who was of the Muslim Brothers. Then on July 23, 1952, there was an Egyptian Revolution, which Nasser led. The Free Officers played a big role in Egyptian nationalism and independence from Britain.

In 1994, I wrote about reform to the Egyptian Constitution. In the second article in the constitution, there was a part that says Islam is a religion of the state. My reform was published in Egypt and said the principle of Islamic Sharia is a resource of legislation. My reform does not talk about the Sharia answer, but the Sharia principle. But the Muslim Brothers ignore the word principle and talk about Sharia itself. But Sharia itself is not defined, because which one would you choose? In my belief, the Universal Declaration of Human Rights in the UN is the best example of Islam.

**CHRISTINE:** Who inspired your work as a peaceful Koranist?

**SHEIKH MANSOUR:** My enemies inspired my work. I began my life as a Sunni, but as a Sunni whose brain was working, so I wanted to understand. My father was a very good man and a Sheikh also, but a poor one and very intellectual. I inherited most of my books from him. He was against corruption, so he stayed at home. I asked, why is he not famous like other people who were considered a saint in our village? These people were not good, so I said to myself, if Islam is this, it is a wrong religion, because it should go with good values like my father. I said something was wrong in Islam itself or with Muslims. So this was a new beginning for me.

I was raised as a Sunni, and so studied Sunni Islam and realized they were against Islam. The "good" Sheikhs at the time persecuted me. There was a desperation in me, because if you are an intellectual, you want to have answers, but instead of answers, you will be persecuted. You have to be inspired to learn what the truth is, so I owe these people my guidance and inspiration because of persecution.

**CHRISTINE:** How do Koranists differ from the other main Islamic sects?

**SHEIKH MANSOUR:** The Koranist does not represent a new religion, but is there to reform what people fabricated about the Koran. Muhammad himself is ordered to follow the message of Abraham, as Abraham and his sons are the fathers of all the Arabs.

The central message of Abraham is to believe in God alone and to be a good human and uphold peace, justice, freedom of speech, and freedom of belief, the belief that God will judge all people according to their faith and behavior in this life. No one has the power to interfere with your relationship with God. As long as you are peaceful, you are a brother or sister. And no one has the right to interfere with another's religion, because in the end you will be judged by God and God alone. This is the message of the Koran.

The conflict comes with the view that Islam is from "us" and the kafir is not from "us." That is why it is justified in conquering other people, to occupy their land and establish this mighty empire in the Middle East.

What they call Sharia is written to justify this thinking and make a new fabrication of Islam, so when you read the Sharia translation, kafir means "you," and accordingly you should be killed, but in the Koran you do not kill innocent people.

If you look at the Koran from the point of view of tradition, you will be a fanatic, because it is according to the Sunnis.

The main Muslim sects are Sunni, Shia, and the Sufis. The biggest among them is a combination of the moderate Sunni and Sufis together, which comprise more than a billion and hundreds of millions, respectively. The silent majority believe in praying and going to Mecca. People operate according to their sect. The pure Sunni are very fanatic. The Shia are fanatic when they come to power. The Sufis are very peaceful people. When you go to the fanatic Sunni Muslims, they have four schools: the Shafi'i, the Hanbali, the Maliki, and the Hanifi. The most fanatic are Hanbali. Within the Hanbali are the Wahhabis. Stemming from Wahhabism are the Muslim Brothers, Jamaa Islamia, Hamas, and the Jihadists.

According to its own terminology, the Koran is one of human rights, peace, and democracy. There is a difference between Islamic democracy and Muslim tyranny.

## "FANATICS" CONTROLLING THE WEST

**CHRISTINE:** Explain why you use the word "fanatics" instead of Islamists.

**SHEIKH MANSOUR:** I worked for the US Commission on International Religious Freedom for a year between 2009 and 2010. I wrote my book for them: *Religious Freedom Between Islam and Fanatic Muslims: Addressing Muslim Mentality for Reforming Muslims from Within Islam.* I use the term "fanatic" because I am against the term "Islamist." These people are not Muslims who don't honor freedom of religion, but they are fanatics who claim the name of Islam to do whatever they want to do and to deceive the Muslim silent majority. These fanatics are against the religion of Islam in faith, Sharia jurisprudence, and even in morals and ethics.

Western civilization is actually the nearest to the real forgotten abandoned Islamic values of freedom, justice, tolerance, human dignity, and human rights.

Calling those Wahhabi fanatics "Islamist" gives them the support they need in their claim to have Islam on their side in their war against non-Muslims and the West, and in deceiving the Muslim communities in the West and in the US. Proving the contradiction between them and the religion of Islam exposes them as the real enemy to Islam and helps in undeceiving the majority of the Muslim masses. This is the cause of our Islamic peaceful war of ideas against those Jihadists.

**CHRISTINE:** What are the characteristics to look for in these "fanatics" residing on our soil who call themselves democratic and friends to the West?

**SHEIKH MANSOUR:** They use Islam for their own benefits and they want to bring in their fanatic Sharia law, where it is against a Muslim woman to marry a Jew or a Christian or anyone outside of their religion. Jihad means killing the non-Muslims just because they are not like them.

In the real religion of Islam, if you read the Arabic Koran according to its unique terminology, every peaceful human is a respectable Muslim, regardless of faith and religion. Islam means to believe in and worship the Almighty alone, who is the only one who will judge all the people in the Day of Judgment. So we are ordered in the Koran to live in peace in this world, leaving our religious differences to be solved by our Creator in the Last Day.

This is the key of our war of ideas, in exposing the hypocrites who claim themselves to be moderate Muslims while they consider other decent peaceful people to be kafirs just because they have another religion or another faith.

According to the real abandoned Islam, it is permissible for the Muslim woman to marry any peaceful man regardless of his religion, as long as he is a peaceful man. We in the International Quranic Center encourage and perform this kind of marriage in the name of Islam, to revive this Islamic Sharia, while those hypocrites deny it.

**CHRISTINE:** You had a significant incident reminiscent of your experience in Egypt in a Boston mosque that should serve as a warning to "fanatical" activity on American soil. Please explain.

**SHEIKH MANSOUR:** When I came here to the US, I had dreams and ideas, because this was America. But when I went to mosque, I found the same people, advocating the same Sharia. I escaped from there and found them here, so I said to myself, what could I do after that? Escape to the Moon?

When I finished serving as a visiting fellow at the National Endowment for Democracy and at the Human Rights Program at Harvard Law School, my project was to reform the Islamic school in the United States to conform to the human rights culture and American values. I decided one day while in Boston to take the chance and go to the mosque and pray. This mosque has two floors. When I went to a room in the upper floor, I was so scared when I started to read the newsletters in Arabic. It talked about taking America and taking Jews. It was like the same mosques in Egypt. I am not against the mosque, and I hope to find a mosque to pray that is not against peace.

I am famous and well-known among the fanatics, so I was scared. I prayed quickly and never went back to this mosque again. I opted to pray at my home with my wife and three sons, and moved to Virginia. Then I was informed about another fanatic mosque in Virginia that advocated violence in the name of Islam, and also about a plan to build the biggest mosque in the entire East Coast. I was told that some of the moderate Muslims felt unsafe, so they wanted a Muslim writer or scholar to work with them and to help them. Dr. Pipes gave them my name, so I began to work with them, have meetings, do media, and we made some progress. Together Charles Jacobs and Dennis Hale and I co-founded Americans for Peace and Tolerance.

I was the co-founder and board member of Citizens for Peace and Tolerance—Promoting a Hate-Free America since October 2004. As a famous Muslim scholar who graduated from Al-Azhar and the founder of the Koranic trend in the world, I more recently issued a public challenge to the leaders of the fanatic Islamic Society of Boston Mosque to invite me to give only one Islamic Koranic lecture in their mosque, but they ignored my challenge.

**CHRISTINE:** How do you place groups like CAIR, the Muslim Student Associations (MSA), the Islamic Society of North America (ISNA), etc., who claim to speak for the mainstream Muslim populations in the West?

**SHEIKH MANSOUR:** CAIR, the Islamic Society of North America (ISNA), the International Institute of Islamic Thought (IIIT), the Muslim Student Associations (MSA), and these groups are Wahhabis. If they are true Muslims, let them open the mosque for all people, the Shia, the Sufi, and to one like me, to preach. But they make it only for their own people.

Some students of IIIT asked their leaders to invite me to discuss my book, *The Penalty of Apostasy*, published on our website. I was invited and was so excited that I wrote another article for them to prove and confirm that there is no such penalty in Islam. It was a successful event, but yet the leaders of IIIT refused to invite me again when the students asked for more lessons.

Those people have their own Wahhabi agenda. They uphold the same Wahhabi culture of ISIS and al Qaeda. They are hijacking the name of Islam and abusing the American values of freedom of speech to create the American Talibans, or an American ISIS on American soil. According to their innermost Wahhabi faith, they are dividing the world into two camps: the camp of believers and the camp of war. It is needed for them to have the "fifth column" inside the enemy camp. This is the main cause of al Qaeda and its secret of establishing public organizations in and outside of the US.

Those fanatic leaders on American soil have a lot of money, influence, and contacts, while people like us reformist Muslims are struggling to defend America and to reform the American Muslims by our very limited access. The International Quranic Center, in spite of its role in reforming Muslims overseas, is just one room in my house in Virginia. Our powerful website was destroyed several times by the fanatics.

**CHRISTINE:** What are some of the ways that these fanatics are controlling American Muslims?

**SHEIKH MANSOUR:** They control Muslims without competition by utilizing the intellectual war against the US, by taking advantage of the Internet. But the most dangerous thing is the exploitation of the Sunni Wahhabi religion, which is widespread in America, and among the religious leaders, the imams. Followers of Sunnah are the ones who control the majority of American mosques. They exploit the American values of freedom of expression and freedom of religion to brainwash American Muslims to prevent their integration into the American society. They even try to turn them into enemies of their country and their fellow citizens, preparing them to become terrorists at the earliest chance. Consequently, they find fertile land to aid in their success.

**CHRISTINE:** So how are you trying to stop this?

**SHEIKH MANSOUR:** Koranist Muslims are experts in the intellectual war against the culture of ISIS and al Qaeda. We have 30 years of successful experience; however, what we lack is the means. If it became available to us, we would be able to spare thousands of American citizens' lives and save billions that are spent on wars. Ninety percent of the wars against terrorism are ideological wars, and when you face terrorism with violent war with only armed security operations, the result is failure.

But when Muslims who are devoted to their religion wage ideological war from within Islam against the culture of ISIS and its supporters, there will be success, because the war here is between well-versed Muslims who understand their religion and ignorant criminals who abuse Islam in order to access power and wealth.

We seek help in launching this intellectual war against the culture of ISIS and al Qaeda, not through money, but through the opportunity to meet the right figures in American agencies to explain to them how to win this war of ideas.

**CHRISTINE:** Does the Palestinian–Israeli territory issue have any merit in your view, or is it used by fanatics as a propaganda tool?

**SHEIKH MANSOUR:** This is a very sensitive dogma. Until Israel permitted the Palestinians to have authority in the Gaza Strip and West Bank, there was no Palestinian state. It is a historical fact, and no one can argue about it. From the time of the State of Solomon or the Jewish State, it was Judea, Samaria, and Israel at that time. Egypt occupied Palestine. Many Israeli leaders were born in Palestine before the Israeli state in 1948; now most of them are born in the same land under the flag of Israel, so they have the right according to any law to be there. I'm not talking as an Egyptian, but objectively as a researcher.

This needs to be confronted through the war of ideas that reaches the Palestinian masses, to convince them that their real enemy is not Israel, but Hamas and its group.

## UNDERSTANDING AND ENGAGING THE WAR OF IDEAS

**CHRISTINE:** Has radical Sunni theology become more aggressive across Europe and North America?

**SHEIKH MANSOUR:** Yes, because of what is going on in the Middle East. Let me explain this:

The Muslim Brotherhood Wahhabi culture has been rooted in Muslim Egyptians for forty years through Al-Azhar, the official Egyptian education system, Egyptian mosques, and Egyptian media. The current military regime of the President al-Sisi uses only the security and military troops in fighting this culture and its supporters. It is ridiculous to teach students Wahhabi teachings as Islam, and then when they act accordingly you arrest them and sentence them to execution while leaving the Wahhabi culture controlling the masses. That is the main mistake in the entire Middle East and North Africa, where the Sunni regimes uphold Wahhabism and don't use the war of ideas against it, yet they are killing the youth if they apply the war of ideas.

**CHRISTINE:** What country or regime is the biggest influencer of global fanaticism?

**SHEIKH MANSOUR:** The key problem is the Saudi crown family, its Wahhabism, and its oil influence in the so-called Muslim world and even here in the US. I recently published my large Arabic book about the Wahhabi opposition in the Saudi Kingdom during the twentieth century. The book proves that Wahhabism creates its enemy from within and they fight each other, and fight the outsiders as well. The founder of the current Saudi Kingdom, Abdel Aziz, also influenced the founding of the Muslim Brothers in Egypt, but then the Muslim Brothers became the real enemy to their founders, the Saudi family. The Muslim Brothers are in fact the founders of the recent last Wahhabi opposition that produced bin Laden and al Qaeda.

As long as there are the Saudis, then the Wahhabis, the Middle East and North Africa, Malay, and Nigeria will suffer chaos and civil war. Egypt could escape it if its military regime establishes real religious, political, and economic reform. It is the US involvement and the Saudi influence inside the US that may endanger American soil and bring ISIS here, unless the US handles the war of ideas to protect American lives.

**CHRISTINE: So the Muslim Brotherhood is a much worse entity to lead Syria than Al Assad in your opinion?**

**SHEIKH MANSOUR:** Yes, of course. Al Assad and his father are bad, but the Muslim Brothers are the worst. Mubarak put me in jail, but if these Muslim Brotherhood people had the chance, they would have killed me, according to their punishment for apostasy, plus they claim I'll go to hell. In the time of Mubarak, I used to write and explain the fact that Mubarak is bad, but the Muslim Brothers are the worst.

The Wahhabi religion of ISIS is the same religion of the Muslim Brothers, Al-Azhar, and Salafism. Had the Muslim Brothers controlled Egypt for some years, they would divide the Egyptian army, make massacres, and Egypt will be under the same chaos of ISIS in Syria and Iraq.

**CHRISTINE: Sheikh Mansour, given the global reach of the Muslim Brotherhood and Wahhabism, please provide more insight about the struggle for power between Wahhabists and the Muslim Brotherhood in Egypt.**

**SHEIKH MANSOUR:** Before the elections, the Wahhabists in Egypt were of two kinds, with the same fanaticism: the Muslim Brotherhood and the Salafists. The Muslim Brotherhood is very political, cunning, and preaches to Salafists. At the time of Mubarak, the Wahhabists wanted to enable the Salafists to control all the mosques. There was also some division, as the Wahhabists also wanted the Salafists to support Mubarak and to work against Copts and the church. After Mubarak, there were no controls.

The Muslim Brothers had plotted 80 years to take over Egypt, but they did not spend 80 minutes thinking how to rule Egypt. In many articles, I predicted that they would fail and lose and be put in jails, and if they still stayed in power, the only solution they would have had would be going to war against Israel to cover their failure. However, al-Sisi got rid of them quickly before they destroyed Egypt.

**CHRISTINE:** Any notable difference between Salafists and the Muslim Brotherhood?

**SHEIKH MANSOUR:** Salafists are like untamed animals, saying what's in their hearts, but the Muslim Brotherhood is very cunning, intelligent, and they know what to say and what to conceal, but they have the same ideas of the Salafis, but the latter is very primitive. They say publicly what is in their heart.

But Salafi ascension to power is connected to creating a state of chaos. For example, in Egypt they were in agreement with Mubarak's regime remnants and his state security organization, especially since the Salafi leadership was the product of Mubarak's security apparatus, and had the opportunity for thirty years to be trained and goaded by it. The biggest losers as a result of Salafi prominence are the Muslim Brotherhood and the Copts.

**CHRISTINE:** You advocate engaging the war of ideas, but is there not a fear in speaking out among Muslims?

**SHEIKH MANSOUR:** Some of us have suffered a lot, and there are those who feel scared. Koranists have suffered and experienced full waves of arrests in Egypt. One in 1987, the other in 2001 and 2002, and I escaped it to come here. Then again in 2007, and the fourth in 2009. Members of my family and my name were also put as "Wanted." On my website, I have this project to gather and rewrite all my published books in Egypt to be free for all people. Because of this article talking about my half-brother, they arrested him and others, and tortured him for three months. Most attacks come from the Salafists controlling the streets and the villages.

However, we still successfully wage the war of ideas against Wahhabism, using our very limited capacity.

**CHRISTINE:** What would you tell moderates and reformers who might be afraid to speak out because of radical groups and fanatics?

**SHEIKH MANSOUR:** I tell Muslims, you must be responsible to yourself first and ask yourself why Allah, God, created you and gives you the freedom of speech, belief, to be good, of choice and free will. So if you are a Muslim, you must be a good one in dealing with people and your environment. You have to respect the law and speak out against what is wrong. If you believe that Allah has revealed Islam as a good guidance, then look at other Muslims and ask yourself if they represent Islam well by being a good citizen, a good human being, and a good Muslim.

**CHRISTINE:** How do you explain controversy about Muhammad, such as his practice of violence and marriage to girls too young?

**SHEIKH MANSOUR:** In our belief, Muhammad is the final prophet and just a human being who was commanded to deliver the final Divine Message of the Koran and nothing but the Koran. Actually, there are two characters of Muhammad: one in the Koran and another in Muslim human-made religions and traditions. They are Muhammadans, because they idolize Muhammad.

You read about the true history of Muhammad in the Koran, as he was blamed and criticized because he was a human being. The many writings four generations and more after Muhammad were meant to justify the caliphate at that time of the Abbasid Dynasty in the eighth century. These writings were not true. It was written to please the Abbasid mighty caliphate who owned the wealth and the people as well. To justify its absolute rule, the history of Muhammad must be the same, so the caliphate became devoted to this cause of illustrating a certain character of Muhammad to be the same as the views in the Sunni traditions.

There is no difference in corruption between the Abbasid Caliphate and King Abdullah of Egypt and King Abdullah of Jordan. The Wahhabi regimes and ISIS are doing what the old caliphates used to do in the Middle Ages.

## ISLAMIC REFORM

**CHRISTINE:** Do you feel that there is a significant number in the Muslim population globally who are interested in your reformist views of Islam?

**SHEIKH MANSOUR:** Yes, because people get tired from listening to the same argument and discourse for decades every week in Friday service. They want something new. We bring something new. We are a trend, not a group. The Muslim Brotherhood is a group, for example. We operate through the Internet. Because of us, many people have become more educated, and I don't know how many more we continue to influence compared to the fanatics.

We have limited resources, but we reach out still in Egypt, in Muslim countries, in the world. No one wants to help us. There are few, like Dr. Daniel Pipes. I have hope. I told my sons that most of my articles predict what will happen. On January 23, 2011, I predicted the revolution in Egypt a week before. This regime must be resisted by blood, and I told my sons that.

**CHRISTINE:** Are there any majority Muslim countries you see in the world that will be willing to help reformists?

**SHEIKH MANSOUR:** I don't agree that it will be in any state anywhere, because this is politics. I want the freedom fighters to depend on themselves, because it is their own faith. They must work toward reform for themselves and by themselves.

**CHRISTINE:** What country is the most critical for the future of Islam?

**SHEIKH MANSOUR:** Egypt. It is the oldest country in the world, the oldest state in the world. We call it the Mother of the World. So when you look at Saudi Arabia, it was built in 1932, Israel in 1948, Jordon after the 1920s, Syria in the 1920s after World War I. Egypt is the oldest, with the most number of educated people. Egypt also has the greatest population in the Arab world and the greatest number of intellectuals. During its history, Egypt is the leader of Arabs and Muslims. If Egypt has its democratic state, it will be the end of the Saudi Kingdom and other dictatorships in the region. In the absence of the Egyptian leadership, you find that some tiny states like Qatar play a role. Without a strong democratic Egyptian state, you will find many Saddams, many Gaddafis, and many Gulf-corrupted states, along with lots of chaos, civil war, and bloodshed.

**CHRISTINE:** What keeps you fighting for reform?

**SHEIKH MANSOUR:** Someone has to do it. The Koran says you have to fight in the cause of God. For me, it is justice, free speech, human rights, and goodness. These people are against what I believe and I have to keep fighting. Koranists are against the Muslim Brothers.

I learn from human experience. There are people fighting intellectually within Islam. Once the people are awakened and know the difference between slavery and freedom and get rid of fear, and they come face to face with the soldiers of dictatorship, they will succeed.

## CHAPTER FOUR

# DR. TAWFIK HAMID

### Chair of Study of Islamic Radicalism, Potomac Institute for Policy Studies

Dr. Tawfik Hamid is a Senior Fellow and Chair for the Study of Islamic Radicalism at the Potomac Institute for Policy Studies and author of *Inside Jihad,* which analyzes radical Islam and describes Dr. Hamid's journey against Islamic radicalism. He was a former member of the Jamaat Islamiya terrorist group in Egypt alongside Ayman al-Zawahiri, the current leader of al Qaeda.[1] He is now a self-described "Islamic thinker and reformer" who promotes a "reformation based upon modern, peaceful interpretations of classical Islamic core texts." Dr. Hamid has testified before US Congress, lectured for the Pentagon and the US Special Operations Command, and was invited to speak at the Israeli Presidential Conference in 2009.[2]

In an interview with Ryan Mauro, Dr. Hamid described his work efforts as "trying to provide an educational system for young Muslims that encourages critical thinking, uses cognitive psychology, and uses religious texts in a way that promotes peaceful coexistence with others...providing education that fights radicalism through a thinking process, instead of just a theological one" and providing "a modern interpretation" of the Koran that will counter the effects of hatred and violence stemming from traditional interpretations. Dr. Hamid holds a medical degree in internal medicine and a master's degree in cognitive psychology.[3]

# INTERVIEW WITH DR. TAWFIK HAMID

**CHRISTINE:** What motivated your activism as a reformist?

**DR. HAMID:** Before I left Jamaat Islamiya, I was asked to kidnap a police officer with members of the group, burn him, and bury him alive. This was far beyond my human conscience to accept. I decided to leave them and had a time of thinking of what I should do. I founded a group called the Koranics who helped me think differently.

I was also affected by my upbringing. My father was an atheist and taught me a deep way of thinking. When I was very young, he showed me a picture of a father and two young children who were going to the ovens of the Nazis. I still remember that photo like it's in front of me now. My father explained to me what the Nazis did to the Jews, and I loved them since then. Despite my radicalism, I never hated them. The photos affected me.

I also remember reading about Jesus in the Gospel. I tried to criticize His words, but I loved Him and I loved His teaching. But then I became radicalized, until I left that life behind. When I see people killing and beheading human beings, I want to do something to stop this, and to stop the burning of churches. I am not a passive guy who will just sit on the chair and say, "Oh, radical Islam is bad." It does not change anything. You can say a car is not working for the rest of your life, and it still will not work unless you change the engine or battery or do some work.

I feel I am in the position to help. I have been given the knowledge to speak the theology and language to make things happen.

## ISLAM VERSUS ISLAMISM

**CHRISTINE:** How would you define an Islamist?

**DR. HAMID:** In my view, an Islamist is a person who wants to take Islam outside of his worship place in a mosque or a room, enforces his political views upon others, and changes the whole system to follow his understanding of Islam. He takes Islam from a way of worship to a way of controlling society.

**CHRISTINE:** What do Islamists aspire to?

**DR. HAMID:** Ultimately to control the world under Sharia rules. Islamists want to see the world controlled by the values of the Taliban and the Wahhabists of Saudi Arabia.

**CHRISTINE:** Is there a difference between "peaceful Islamists," in your view, and violent ones like the Taliban and al Qaeda?

**DR. HAMID:** They are the same when it comes to the mission and concept of domination in Islam, but they differ in tactics and in the understanding of certain elements within the religion. They also differ in the form that the domination should be. For example, Erdogan advances the economic aspect more than the Taliban would, but the concept of domination is what makes them both the same.

**CHRISTINE:** Explain the concept of deception among Islamists, especially among "peaceful" or stealth Islamists.

**DR. HAMID:** This is very important. When you approve of the deceptive Muslim Brotherhood, or others similar to them who portray themselves as moderates, and you believe them, then you are supporting them.

If their ultimate aim is to destroy you, then you are actually supporting their aim, and the very same group that will cause damage to you at the end. For example, the Muslim Brotherhood says, "we will respect the peace treaty with Israel," and people support them, but if you saw the reality before the election of Morsi in Egypt, he was sitting in an audience as a presidential candidate while there was a song about starting the "United States of the Arabs" and the capital will be Jerusalem. They went on about how Morsi will erase Israel from the map and they will all celebrate in Palestinian songs, not even Egyptian songs.

You should start to realize and ask the question of how this Muslim Brotherhood man can respect the peace treaty with Israel. You should also ask why the Muslim Brotherhood group does not even mention the name of Israel on its website. When you go to their website, you will see "the entity," not even the "Zionist entity," which they used to call them. They won't even say "Zionist" anymore, because they think it is too filthy to use on their website.

It is the normal Arab mentality to not mention the word "Israel" or the word "Zionist." This implies that they want to erase these people from the map. When you see strong celebrations against Israel and an intimate relationship with Hamas, you have to ask questions.

Morsi was depriving the Egyptians from gas to give to the people of Gaza. People were standing in queues seeing their gas going to Gaza. Morsi was calling Jews "apes" and "monkeys" and teaching hatred of the Jews. How can anyone expect a man like this to be true to Egypt's treaty? How can a man with such hatred bring stability to the area? This is where the deception among Islamists is, using Morsi as an example.

Islamists will use you as a step in their tactics by making promises. Their aim and strategic thinking need to be seen, and the West needs to understand when they are being used as a tactical step to achieve their aim. We cannot help them destroy us.

**CHRISTINE:** Can one recognize an Islamist through his view about Israel's right to exist?

**DR. HAMID:** This is not an accurate test, because Islamists can say things to deceive you. But if you ask them what they think of Palestinian terrorists exploding and killing indiscriminately innocent Israeli women and children in a bus, for example, or how they see Palestinian terrorist acts, and they immediately reply without hesitation that it is evil, then they are likely not an Islamist.

**CHRISTINE:** What if the person makes excuses about Israel being an "occupier" and suggests that Hamas is protecting its territory, then how should that answer be analyzed?

**DR. HAMID:** If someone is justifying the killing of innocent civilians because of some war between someone in history, this is not acceptable. The litmus test should not be the right of Israel to exist, but terrorist acts and killing innocent civilians.

If I go to Israel and say I am from Egypt, I am still welcomed, but try going to a Muslim country and say that you are from Israel, and see how they will treat you. This can tell you that the real problem is in the Arab world.

## ROOTS OF ANTI-WEST AND ANTI-ISRAEL SENTIMENTS AMONG ISLAMISTS

**CHRISTINE:** Islamists generally despise the West and Israel, if even secretly. What is the root of this?

**DR. HAMID:** The entire issue with the West and Israel in the Muslim world is one of supremacy. If you dig deeply into reality, China, for example, treats its Muslim minority much worse than in other parts of the world. In the West, Muslims have rights, and in Israel, they have full rights as Israeli citizens, even rights through Sharia courts.

Muslims also have mosques in Israel, and can freely worship. So logically, Islamists should go and attack China, not Israel and the West, but for them, the concept of superiority makes them go after America, because Muslims want to be number one like America. Throughout history, the religion was based on supremacy. In the case of Israel, it hits Islamists at the core when a small country like Israel defeats them. Even with all the money they have, with all the oil they have and with some 200 million Muslims, they still can't get rid of Israel. For them, it's an issue of challenging their supremacy, and their feeling of supremacy is vital to their religion.

Let me give you one example of a scholar I challenged in front of an audience, who is described as a "moderate" imam in Dearborn, Michigan. I asked him if he would mind inviting me and some Jewish friends to his mosque at Friday prayer, and whether he will say out loud in front of the audience that Jews are not pigs and monkeys, but he did not say one word. This man was pretending to be a moderate, but he will not answer me in public.

I challenge such leaders to put words on their websites and say publicly that they do not approve of calling Jews apes and pigs if they are moderates, since a real moderate will say it publicly. An Islamist will not.

Going back to Muslim supremacy: For Muslims, the ability to show power gives them the psychological satisfaction that the religion is correct and is coming from God. When Muslims start to question the reality of their religion and whether it is truly from God or not, this creates psychological frustration. It is a deep psychological phenomenon and it is all about supremacy.

**CHRISTINE: As a one-time radical yourself, please explain some other factors for that antipathy toward the West and the extent of it.**

**DR. HAMID:** The reason simply was the complete contradiction between Western values and our values of suppressing women, making women wear the hijab, the separation of sexes, the style of life that Sharia implemented, of beheadings, stoning, and putting people on a cross or amputating hands and feet. This is what we wanted to implement, and Western values were completely against this. We want to suppress women; they want to give them freedom. We want to kill the apostates; the West wants freedom of religion. We want to implement corporal punishment; the West is against corporal punishment. We want to see slavery. In fact there were many books saying slavery is part of Islam and encouraging this. The West stopped the slavery.

I and others wanted to remove the West from existence. If we could do it with nuclear bombs, we would do it. If we could do it with viral terrorism, we would do it. We felt we were at war. In fact, I always give the example of a soccer player: When he doesn't know how to play well, he starts to use violence. It seems that we were unable to be convincing enough to others with our ideology, so we resorted to thinking about ways to use violence. We quoted the Koran and we quoted the Sunnah to justify the violence, but the hatred was predominantly because of this serious contradiction in values of existence, which were a main threat to our values.

## ISLAM VS. ISLAMISM

**CHRISTINE: How can one tell an Islamist from a moderate Muslim?**

**DR. HAMID:** I call it the ABC test for Radical Islam. It is about ideology, and the test is simply A B C D E F G.

A   is for apostate killing.

B   is for barbaric treatment of women like stoning, beating, and polygamy.

C   is for calling Jews pigs and monkeys.

D   is declaring war on non–Muslims to spread the religion.

E   is the enslavement of human beings.

F   is fighting Jews before end days and killing all of them.

G   is gay killing.

**CHRISTINE:  The average Westerner may look at an Islamist and say that person looks kind, friendly, a pleasant co-worker, easygoing, accepting. In that scenario, how can the average Westerner tell?**

**DR. HAMID:** You can ask about the same ABC test, and some other questions can be what he thinks about someone converting to Christianity. Should there be punishment or not? Ask him about dealing with minority riots, building Baha'i temples in Egypt or in the Muslim world, or churches in Saudi Arabia. And if he says that it should be OK, then you say, "How about putting it on your website on my expenses, I'll pay for it?" When you talk about these issues of Muslims against other faiths, a true moderate person would be able to tell you this is unacceptable.

**CHRISTINE:  What is your analysis of the Muslim Brotherhood plan for the West?**

**DR. HAMID:** At the high levels of the Muslim Brotherhood, the desire is to dominate the world, and when you are close with them as I was, you will feel it in their words. They will not come and say it in your face in the West, but they certainly do it in their private talks. They say that they see decay in the Western civilization and an ultimate collapse, that failure is going to happen, and they see themselves as the ones who will provide the replacement for it.

So their project and their mission is this: They started to learn how other minorities work in the American system; for example, how to use lobbying effectively and other resources. They try to convince some journalists by giving them wrong information, so they can use them in promoting their views or ideas. They are very tricky, so they can talk to you about how Islam, for example, respects the freedom of religion, but they would never tell journalists openly that killing apostates is unacceptable. They have a lot of money—billions and billions—and they are dedicated to their cause.

**CHRISTINE:** When one looks at the power of Saudi Arabia, driven by petrodollars, how can we challenge Islamism in the face of the far-reaching power of all that money?

**DR. HAMID:** We already did. We already challenged it, and the Islamists are on the defense. We see the highest level of atheism in the history of Egypt. There are two-and-a-half million atheists now in Egypt. The highest rate of atheism in the Arab countries is in Saudi Arabia, so we already challenged Saudi Arabia through the Internet, social media, and through the power that they cannot stop reality. You can pay a lot of money to stop reality, but you can't forever succeed in this. At the end, reality will confront you, and this is what is happening.

## ISLAMIC REFORMISTS

**CHRISTINE:** What is the difference between a reformist and a moderate?

**DR. HAMID:** A reformist sees a problem in the religion and tries to find solutions by changing interpretations. I distinguish between the vocal moderates that speak out in the media, but they really don't go to the theology to change it. A vocal moderate is great to demand secularism and separation of mosque and state, but a reformist is the one who will try to give a theological foundation to the concept of secularism.

**CHRISTINE:** Can a pious Muslim be a reformer today?

**DR. HAMID:** Yes, a reformer can be pious, but not in the Muslim traditional ways of the word pious, as Islam never got any real reformation since it started.

There were those reformers in history whose main point of view was that thinking is more important than what is written. They contradicted views where the written text was deemed more important than thinking. So the reformist view was based on the fact that you reach the concept of God by thinking. Thinking is the beginning of everything, including the belief of religion itself. Thinking has to be above and superior to the text to a reformer. But the reformists were killed throughout history, including those who rejected the Sunnah. But if you talk about the word pious, meaning worship, praying, and reading the Koran, then certainly it is possible to be a pious Muslim and a reformer.

**CHRISTINE: You created a reformist Koran based upon modern peaceful interpretations of classical Islamic core texts. Can you give some examples of the methodology you used to provide certain interpretations? For example, stoning.**

**DR. HAMID:** My interpretation is that stoning is not in the Koran. It is in the Sunnah, and I reject these books. Also, for example, if it says at the end of a verse that someone repented and God forgave him, I conclude that you cannot punish that person by stoning, since God forgave him. So now you have a Koranic justification to follow commonly acceptable things in humanity, like repentance and human rights.

**CHRISTINE: What's the ultimate goal of reformers?**

**DR. HAMID:** To bring more peace to the world and to see more stability, less violence, less hatred, less discrimination against people for their views, religion, or opinion, and stopping sex slavery. You are dealing with an evil phenomenon in Islamism.

**CHRISTINE: What is your view of ijtihad and its significance in reform?**

**DR. HAMID:** Ijtihad is not a word in the Koran. It is a Sharia word that developed later, and is seen as the spirit of the religion, so that whoever follows it will build the religion, and whoever wouldn't follow it will destroy the religion.

Ijtihad is a new understanding of the religious concept of renewal, and adds completely new religious concepts to Islam. For example, someone like Umar ibn al-Khattab, who was the second Caliph, said that he will not implement the concept of amputation of hands of thieves, because there is something called justice in the Koran, and this would be unjust because some people are poor, so in justice I can't punish someone if he stole because he was poor; it's against Koranic understanding. The mujtahid, or the person who uses ijtihad, should be able to see different verses in the Koran and reach different conclusions, non-literal usually. Those conclusions introduce and justify something. You need someone to think differently to bring a Koranic or religious justification for new concepts that are significant and serious.

**CHRISTINE:** Do you believe that moderates are important players to the reformist movement?

**DR. HAMID:** I love this question. It's a very accurate and great question. They are extremely important because the reformers provide the theory, but the moderates are the ones who show others that the theory could be practiced and can be followed also. They are the role models for others. It's like a crystallization phenomenon. You have the reformers at the theoretical level, then you have the moderates, who join the rest of the people to follow the movement. Without the moderates to follow, there will be a big gap. It's a symbiotic relationship.

**CHRISTINE:** There are some that say that a reform movement flourished between 1850 and 1950. Was there a reform movement thriving during that period?

**DR. HAMID:** Yes, there was, and it was led by Muhammad Abduh, the head of Al-Azhar University, who struggled for change and reform in Al-Azhar and in Egypt. I read his books of interpretation. He was a reformer who accepted rational thought, modernity, and evolution theory. But this wave of reform was aborted, because Wahhabis came and aborted it. Muslim women in this time were starting to take the veils off, burn them and starting to be free by the '60s, but when the Wahhabis came in the '70s, and the Muslim Brotherhood came, they made the women wear the hijab again.

**CHRISTINE:** Do you see such a period of reform rising again?

**DR. HAMID:** Yes, especially after the Arab Spring and following the failure of the Muslim Brotherhood in Egypt, which was significant. Many of the Salafists will speak about morals, and they were discovered doing terrible things, so they really collapsed on civil dimensions and economic promises. They make promises and then break their promises, so I think the failure of the Islamists when they came to power is the main factor behind this beginning of change.

I have gotten a lot of attention on Facebook for my work on the reformist Koran. A few years ago, I would have gotten only about 500 people interested in my work, not the 500 thousand people, which I got in a few months and with limited resources. I think the difference now is that many people are criticizing the Muslim Brotherhood and the Islamists in a way that never happened before.

**CHRISTINE: Despite this interest in Islamic reform as you suggest, can you identify a stumbling block?**

**DR. HAMID:** The stumbling block is that Muslims have a problem when you ask them if they want Sharia. They have a phobia about saying no to Sharia. They feel they would go to hell. If you ask them if they want to be like the Taliban, they will say "No, of course not." It's like they want Sharia as a title for principles. They want to have a touch of religion, but don't want to make Egypt like the Taliban, and Egypt is central to Islam, because Al-Azhar is in Egypt. Whatever happens in Egypt happens in other countries as well.

**CHRISTINE: How do you see reform happening, given this phobia in rejecting Sharia?**

**DR. HAMID:** The problem for many Muslims is that they don't have an alternative. That's why I rushed to create my translation of the Koran, because without having an alternative, the radicals will always win this war. In Islamic states, people can say we want Sharia, but what interpretation for Sharia do they mean? What understanding? It should be one that provides and promotes freedom of religion and no compulsion of religion. The Koran clearly states whoever wants to believe or not believe, it is up to the person, not forcing anyone to religion.

You may have people afraid to criticize Sharia as a name, because for them it is an Islamic law and contains principles of Islam, which are so holy to them, but now the real war is about how to interpret Sharia. This debate is now happening on TV in the Muslim world. People are discussing what interpretations of Sharia they should follow. This has not happened before, or seldom has. They have not reached the level of saying they don't want Sharia yet. In the end, it may turn out that they will use the same word but have a different context or understanding for the word.

**CHRISTINE:** When do you see this new reform taking root and gaining enough strength to be called a full-blown reform movement?

**DR. HAMID:** I think that we may see a full-blown reform movement within this decade because of the failure of Islamists and exposure of their crimes, and criticism of Islam on the Internet, Facebook, and social media. So I think with technology, what we used to see in thousands of years can happen now in a decade. I see the rate of change.

## PROBLEMATIC TEXTS IN THE KORAN

**CHRISTINE:** Many moderates say they don't believe that Muhammad consummated his marriage with Aisha when she was nine. What is your view?

**DR. HAMID:** There are many analyses here. Many Muslims, when they are exposed to this question about Muhammad, feel embarrassed, so they try to say, "Oh, he consummated the marriage after that," but when you go to the Hadith, "after that" means nine years old. It is still disgusting; seven years old when they married in paper and then nine years old when consummated, so do you accept this? Was this information wrong? This story is not in the Koran; it is in the Hadith.

Some Muslims also try to betray interviewers. For example, a Sunni Muslim leader was talking to me about it on the BBC. He was a Muslim leader in London, and said, "That doesn't exist in the books. It's 18 years old and I have a book in front of me saying 18 years old." I said to him, "You are not telling the truth." This guy was a Sunni and was intelligent. He went and brought the book for Shia, which says the age of marriage was 18. So as a Sunni, he swears in the name of God on this book to embarrass me on the radio and make me look as if I am the one who is lying, but yet he doesn't believe in this book himself because it is a Shia book, not Sunni book. So there are a lot of tricks here.

There is an important question for many Muslim groups: Who is Muhammad? For the Sufis, Muhammad is an imaginary guy full of spiritual things. Sufis don't think much about issues of his personal life. For the Salafi, Muhammad is the guy who married this young girl. For a reformist, Muhammad has nothing to do with this story, because it is not mentioned in the Koran. Each one has a different Muhammad. Which Muhammad do they follow? This story is certainly disgusting about Aisha, and many try to trick and lie about it, saying his marriage was consummated later on.

**CHRISTINE:** Does this specific issue about Muhammad and the young Aisha shake the faith of a Muslim?

**DR. HAMID:** Absolutely. When your role model is doing this, it's not like one of the differences between the Old Testament, for example, and Islam. In Judaism and even for Christians, you see someone like Joshua, who is known as a warrior. He entered Jerusalem and made war, but Joshua is not a role model for every Jew. But Muhammad is the role model for all Muslims, so when the role model is a pedophile according to the Hadiths, then you have a problem. Those who believe in the Koran, not the Sunnah, do not believe in this story at all, because it's not in the Koran. We don't believe in these books of the Sunnah and Hadiths.

**CHRISTINE:** Do you reject that Muhammad took a nine-year-old, as reported in the Hadiths?

**DR. HAMID:** If I believed it, I would have never followed this faith. You can't follow someone who is described in this way of having sex with a nine-year-old child and asking the world to become followers, and see him as a role model. That's a big problem.

**CHRISTINE:** The range of subjugation to degradation of women seems to be wired into Islamists, from the niqab to sex slavery. Can you explain the root of this?

**DR. HAMID:** Let me tell you something about those people and their level of hypocrisy, who claim they are promoting Sharia and they want women to cover. I asked a guy one day in Saudi Arabia, which was very risky to do in Saudi Arabia, if a woman has a friend and they have sex together, that is a big sin that you punish by death or lashes; but if the same woman was owned by a man and he sold her against her will to another man to rape her literally, that's okay for you. Can you explain this to me?

The way women are taught to be modest is not a modesty issue, as many people think. It's about controlling women. For example, according to Islamic Sharia, slave girls are not permitted to cover completely. They are only permitted to cover from knees to umbilicus, so they are topless. So they criticize someone exposing her hair. In the Islamic slave market of Sharia throughout history, slave women were semi-naked, so how can you talk about modesty and morals? It's hypocrisy to control women. When they control the women it is OK, but if the women did the same thing on her free will, then that is a problem.

The issue is the freedom of women, and this was the central cause of why we hated the West, if you asked me about the freedom issue back then. In our personal talks, we had nothing to talk about but how the evil West allowed freedom for women. This was the number one issue for us.

**CHRISTINE:** Why the targeting against women and the need to control women?

**DR. HAMID:** The woman issue is an obsession throughout the religion. They go to wars to take women as their sex slaves. We used to dream about paradise, just to have sex in paradise. It was a repetition, and also the sexual descriptions of Muhammad who used to have sex with all his wives in one night. He used to have the power of 36 men in having sex, so there is a lot of sexual emphasis in the tradition of Islamic thought and interpretations.

Wars are a way to get women, or dying for Allah is the way to go and get women in paradise. The role model according to the Sunnah is a man who could be ready to take women in war and have sex with them, and there are a lot of descriptions of the sexual elements of women in paradise, so there is an obsession, and the more they cover women, the more they think sexually. You see the highest level of sexual harassment in the Islamic countries.

There is a psychological factor that comes historically from the Arab culture, that Arabs are in the desert of Saudi Arabia, and they didn't own anything. There is no river, no assets, no agriculture, no buildings compared to Europe or other parts of the world, so in the desert they had nothing to own. The only thing a man could feel he could own is the woman, because she is physically weaker than the man and this is what he can control.

They have no control over anything else, so it became a central core of the Arabian mind of fighting to get the women and show that they are now controlling what they own. It became a central core of war and battles. This became transmitted throughout the religion, and here we have this problem today, a big problem.

**CHRISTINE: Can Muslims just pick and choose what they want to take and leave from the Koran?**

**DR. HAMID:** The Koran states to follow the better of what God has revealed to you. So there is better and "less better." So choosing from the Koran has a Koranic justification in itself. An example from Islamic history is on the concept of amputation, where Umar ibn al-Khattab, the second Caliph, stopped amputation completely, and he was a Muslim leader, so stopping such values or corporal punishments is not against Islam, as many think.

**CHRISTINE: What is your view on defamation of religion laws in Pakistan, and subsequently a post 9/11 UN defamation of religion resolution 16-18, an initiative of the Organization of Islamic Cooperation (OIC) to end criticism of Islam?**

**DR. HAMID:** I talked about this one day in the Heritage Foundation, and my view was that I welcome this as long as Muslims are also not permitted to criticize other religions, so you don't expect it to be one-sided. In other words, if you want to stop criticism of Islam, you also stop any criticism in Islamic books about Christianity and Judaism. You would stop calling Jews pigs and monkeys, and you would stop calling Christians infidels or any word that is insulting to them. When you pass resolutions like this, then you have the full right to ask for reciprocation.

When the Muslim world was criticizing Jews and Christians publically in their many mosques, calling for a curse on them, using evil words in their prayers loudly at every Friday prayer, no one was talking about defamation of religion, but when in turn there is criticism of Islam, everyone talks about defamation of religion. I like justice and I like to have one single standard; don't judge things with double standards. So the concept could be great, but only if it is reciprocated.

A second point is that you have to distinguish between scientific analysis and scientific criticism. This must be allowed, and can even be insulting. For example, there is a difference when I say Muhammad is a devil and an idiot from when I say, that according to al-Bukhari, the prophet Muhammad in the Hadith married a 7-year-old child and consummated the marriage at 9 and this is a form of pedophilia. The latter is fact that you cannot stop. When someone puts on his website that Prophet Muhammad married a girl of seven years old, you consider it criticism for Islam. But it is in al-Bukhari. Does this mean al-Bukhari criticizes Islam? If we opened it for discussion, al-Bukhari describes Muhammad as a pedophile, while the Koran did not describe him as a pedophile, so then al-Bukhari is insulting to Muhammad.

The real cause of insult to Islam is when someone says Muhammad used to bring women in the war and rape them, or someone beheaded her because she criticized Muhammad, and they portrayed Muhammad in al-Bukhari as a war criminal. So then who is to blame for criticizing Muhammad? Blame the ones who quoted al-Bukhari or blame al-Bukhari.

This is a very sensitive issue, because if it is really opened up, we will have to stop publishing and printing al-Bukhari, because it is insulting to Islam.

## RECENT PAST AND FUTURE OF ISLAM

**CHRISTINE: Some main thought leaders in Islam were not even scholars, as often deemed necessary among proponents of the religion. Tell us about these influential thought leaders.**

**DR. HAMID:** They were ordinary people. Some of them were teachers, like Hassan al-Banna for example, the founder of the Muslim Brotherhood. He was a teacher for gymnastics and sports, and Sayyid Qutb was another. He was one of the main leaders of the Muslim Brotherhood who influenced al-Zawahiri. Qutb wrote a book that is an interpretation of the Koran called *In the Shade of the Qur'an*, and he set the foundation for the Islamist way of thinking.

You also have Mustafa Mahmoud, a Sufi scientist and doctor who was famous and influential. Amru Halat is a modern scholar who affected many young women in making them wear the hijab in the last few decades. He is younger than many other scholars, and he is just an accountant.

In the Sunni world, the system is different than Shia. In Shia, you have a top leader and cannot go outside the system, but in the Sunni world each group has its own views. There is no top-level authority. You can have many views. That's why it's difficult to work with Sunnis, because each group works independently. You can have many scholars and many reformers.

**CHRISTINE: Which countries do you deem to be the most critical to the future of Islam?**

**DR. HAMID:** Saudi Arabia, but I give Egypt the priority because it controls the media of the Arab world, including the movies. Egypt is also seen as a mother of the Arab nations. Among al Qaeda's top leaders, 70 percent are Egyptians.

**CHRISTINE: How influential do you see Pakistan, given that al Qaeda operatives are being trained along the borders with Afghanistan?**

**DR. HAMID:** The Arabs went there after the Mujahideen, so the Arabs have influenced Pakistan. The Arabs are the owners of the religion and its understanding. The Arabs are authentic, not the imitations, so if the Arabs changed the interpretation or understanding, then Pakistan will be influenced and follow. All attempts are weak until Arabs come into the picture and suggest different meanings. Pakistanis don't know and feel the message. The role of the language is that deep and integral to the religion. The Koran emphasizes that we have revealed it in the Arabic language.

**CHRISTINE:** What is your opinion about other countries such as Turkey, Pakistan, and Indonesia?

**DR. HAMID:** Not influential theologically, because if you are not an Arab speaker, you will be deemed not being able to understand the Koran. You need to know and feel the Arabic language. An Arab would never follow the interpretation of an Indonesian or Pakistani who does not know Arabic. Arabs brought Islam to the world.

## CHAPTER FIVE

# DR. SALIM MANSUR

### Historian and Political Scientist

D R. SALIM MANSUR IS AN ASSOCIATE PROFESSOR at the University of Western Ontario in Political Science. He is a former columnist for the *Toronto Sun* and the *London Free Press* and author of *Islam's Predicament: Perspectives of a Dissident Muslim* and *Delectable Lie: A Liberal Repudiation of Multiculturalism*. Dr. Mansur has contributed to many publications including *National Review* and the Middle East Forum, serving as an analyst on Muslim issues.[1]

He is also a member of the Board of Directors for the Center for Islamic Pluralism, based in Washington, D.C., a consultant with the Center for Security Policy, and a Senior Fellow with the Canadian Coalition for Democracies.[2]

In 1971, during the creation of Bangladesh, Dr. Mansur was both a victim and a witness when the military government of Pakistan made war on its own population, leaving half a million dead.

In an article "Canada's Angriest Moderate," Dr. Mansur is described as "angry [and] violent [at] evil men who have done their best to ruin the reputation of his religion" and "furious at their many apologists in the West who explain away Islamist atrocities in the name of social justice."[3]

In an example of the distinction to be made between moderates and crypto-moderates, after the brutal riots following the release of the Danish cartoons insulting to Muhammad in 2006, Tariq Ramadan, the Swiss-born theologian and grandson of the founder of the Muslim Ramadan, explained that the reaction of his co-religionists was "a principle of faith ... that God and the prophets never be represented."

Mansur warns, "Non-Muslims went to the wrong Muslim for an understanding of the faith."[4]

# INTERVIEW WITH DR. SALIM MANSUR

**CHRISTINE:** Who inspired your work, Dr. Salim?

**DR. SALIM:** I was lucky growing up in a family with my parents and extended family, even though my father died when I was 10. My family was one of learning and scholarship. My father's library was a marvelous place to be, with books passed down from his father. I abided in this library and learned from it.

The largest English-speaking country is India. People forget that because Britain ruled us for 200 years. My favorite and most influential person was Shakespeare. I loved Shakespeare and I enjoyed that literature and also the great Persian poet Rumi, identified as Sufi in Islam. It is a synthesis of various trends that are part of my life. My culture in India is a genetic code but I am a Canadian and this is the other part of me I embrace. It is part of the Western civilization. Canadians need to be reminded of this with their emphasis of multiculturalism. Wilfrid Laurier, Sir John A. Macdonald, and John Stuart Mill built the tradition of enlightenment that in turn built what the West is today. John Keats's line was: "A thing of beauty is a joy forever."

## ISLAMISM

**CHRISTINE:** Why is it necessary to differentiate a moderate Muslim from an Islamist?

**DR. SALIM:** Because an Islamist is a person who takes Islam and makes it into an ideology in contrast to Islam as a personal faith. In our time it is a movement seeking to reconstruct a Muslim society in keeping with a Sharia value. By definition Sharia is a closed system that was constructed way back a millennium ago in the tenth to twelfth centuries and within a legalistic tradition. There is no room for independent thinking that we call "ijtihad." Groups like the Muslim Brotherhood, ISNA, and CAIR are Islamist organizations as their goal is to promote Sharia.

**CHRISTINE:** How can we tell the difference between a moderate and a crypto-moderate?

**DR. SALIM:** I believe that over time you can tell the difference. I don't think there is a litmus test to spot a moderate Muslim from a non-moderate. Over time you see the distinction. Litmus is a quick pressurizing question and an Islamist activist will be trained on how to deal with such litmus questions to tailor his answer to the needs of the questioner. In my view, it is the behavior of any human over time that provides the indication, not the claim or answer.

In the Koran, there is a verse that says that in the eyes of God it is the conduct of a person that matters. Another verse says that God does not change the condition of the people unless they change what is in their heart. What is in the heart of a person can only be disclosed over time.

**CHRISTINE:** What about Israel, could it be an indicator to find out what is in a person's heart?

**DR. SALIM:** Yes, I think so. On a political level, yes, but if made into a test question, the problem is that a person who says no will draw their confidence by saying that the same stance is also among non-Muslims. It is not only a Muslim issue. Those who oppose Israel could be a cover for a non-moderate Muslim to say they don't recognize Israel's right to exist. Even among the New Democratic Party in Canada there are members who are militant and, proudly so, in opposing Israel.

From my personal point of view, Israel has a right to exist. It is a wider issue than a Muslim one. The Jews have a moral, historical, and legal right to constitute a state just like any other people. Take for example the Hindus of India. Nepal is a Hindu state, Thailand is a Buddhist and Hindu state, and the OIC is comprised of states that are defined as Islamic countries. The Jews deserve a state and have a right. I would go even further, speaking as a Muslim who takes my faith and tradition seriously, that in the case of the Jews having a place in the Holy Land, it is mandated by my faith and defended by the Koran. So there are Muslims who deliberately pervert those verses of the Koran or say they have been abrogated.

**CHRISTINE:** What are some of the signs to determine if a person is an Islamist over time?

**DR. SALIM:** Most would appear like everybody else but a fraction take on a certain attitude to demonstrate their faith, but it is strident in some ways, along with their attitudes about women and other faith traditions. This should ring bells. In looking at the long term, further exploration may lead to disclosure that they hold on to the value of the Muslim Brotherhood. They would support Sharia, would say that women should hold a certain place in society; the problems about Israel would come up and they would have an attitude. Upon further discussion, 9/11 would come up and they would expose their attitudes about suicide bombings and violence by taking an apologetic stance and make excuses about it. This is a clear marker. It shows that they are seeking a way out to explain this kind of behavior as part of a larger political agenda, other than saying that this is unacceptable under any condition.

**CHRISTINE:** Do you see a difference between violent Islamists and "peaceful" Islamists?

**DR. SALIM:** These are the classical problems for any culture; it is a question of means versus ends. They all share the same end, but the means are different. So for a group like al Qaeda, the instrument of violent Jihad is a public policy. They take their Jihad struggle, or war, from the personal domain—that every individual engages in to become a better human being—to a public domain, which is the pursuit of power. The end result is to obtain a Sharia-based society.

**CHRISTINE:** Is there dissension among Islamists themselves on methods they choose to achieve their end?

**DR. SALIM:** Osama bin Laden shifted away from the Muslim Brotherhood. Historically the Muslim Brotherhood emerged into splinter groups, where al Qaeda was one of them and bin Laden became in command. Muhammad al-Zawahri, who is Egyptian, also came from the ranks of the Muslim Brotherhood.

**CHRISTINE:** Islamism has been likened to communism and fascism, so do any parallels come to mind for you given this evolutionary shift between al Qaeda and the Muslim Brotherhood?

**DR. SALIM:** The great movement associated with Marx and Engels splintered into the Bolsheviks during World War I and the Stalinists/Leninists, but then they splintered into the Maoists, Che Guevara and Castro. So these splinters become the disagreement on how to reach the same end. So the question of means becomes a problem in the ranks. The Muslim Brotherhood in Egypt disowned al Qaeda for violence. But the greatest relevance is that the end is the same: to create a Sharia state.

**CHRISTINE:** From your explanation, are you indicating that the Muslim Brotherhood is the umbrella organization to both violent and stealth Islamism?

**DR. SALIM:** It is the Muslim Brotherhood and its view that set everything in motion. Tariq Ramadan, the grandson of Hassan al-Banna who founded the Muslim Brotherhood in 1928 in Egypt, will stand up in a public platform and say that the Muslim Brotherhood has nothing to do with violence, that his own grandfather that was killed was reactive and that he was reacting to oppression.

**CHRISTINE:** How much has the Muslim Brotherhood affected mosques?

**DR. SALIM:** Most mosques in North America, in Europe, and around the world are basically reflecting the argument of the Muslim Brotherhood and Jamaat Islam. This has been facilitated by petrodollars. It exerts an influence on the world stage since 1972–73 when oil prices went up. The influence of the vast majority of mosques is that they are as bad in the West as they are in the Middle East and everywhere else.

**CHRISTINE:** What about the practical role of the Organization of Islamic Cooperation (OIC)?

**DR. SALIM:** The intent of the OIC, its charter and program, is to create the Sharia state. Their program outside the OIC is to make all countries compliant to Sharia and make Western governments tailor their policy—domestic and foreign—to what the OIC wants.

**CHRISTINE:** How has the Muslim Brotherhood been allowed to infiltrate Western society?

**DR. SALIM:** They have infiltrated Western society because of the nature of Western society and its commitments to the values of individual rights and liberalism, which is an old problem since democracy is very vulnerable to the very principles it espouses. The Islamists have taken full advantage of that and reformists seek to oppose them and to warn the people that it is our citizens that must to be alerted to this problem [in order] to fend off and oppose the Islamist agenda.

The Islamist agenda is secured by petrodollars and they use votes to advance their agenda in a democratic society, whereas those who oppose Islamists don't have that kind of funding and organization.

## ISLAMISM'S EXPLOITATION OF MULTICULTURALISM

**CHRISTINE:** How have immigrants arriving from closed societies contributed to the problem of the spread of Islamism?

**DR. SALIM:** Immigrants arriving from societies that are pre-democratic and closed bring the baggage of their own culture, so there is a profound psychological disorientation given where they come from and where they arrive at. Muslims from countries like Egypt, Pakistan, Africa, and the Middle East who want to protect Islamism are comfortable in their closed societies. Many of them come here because they are refugees, because of war, starvation, etc. So they find themselves in a situation of being comfortable and the West says, "Yes, be comfortable, we celebrate you as a multicultural society. We say be who you are."

Such closed societies with gender inequities, judgments about heresies, etc., are told by Westerners that you don't have to change. The patriarchs then celebrate that they are in a society that permits them to be comfortable with what they are. Now the West is caught in a conundrum of being a liberal democracy and its sensitivity not to question the values of another society in order to avoid being accused of bigotry or being accused of falling back into old attitudes of imperialism and colonialism. The West does not want to be labeled so instead it gives these patriarchs of closed societies reinforcements not to be questioned and not to be challenged.

**CHRISTINE:** So what advice can you provide for the West to break this pattern?

**DR. SALIM:** Every equation has two sides so in first looking at the West, post-9/11: The West must become far more assertive about its values historically. It should not be nonchalant about these values and see them as natural and God-given. People have fought and died for values like gender and race equity, free speech, and the fragile notion of freedom. Such a notion does not exist around the world but has emerged in Western civilization. Therefore we must become serious and assertive about protecting what we have.

**CHRISTINE:** Some ideas on how to do this, Dr. Salim?

**DR. SALIM:** Fight for free speech where the individual has the right to espouse and express whatever he thinks on any subject no matter how offensive. According to the old English saying, if a cat may look at a king, then a king or queen can be open to a critical discussion, an offensive cartoon, etc. Then there is nothing sacred. The only sacred thing is the individual in which his or her free speech can be violated. That is something upon which civilization and our culture is built. It must be defended with difficult consequences against those who impose parameters. We have to tell Islamists that the value of free speech transcends and trumps whatever faith tradition they bring into Canada and the US. We have lost that perspective and have to bring it back.

On the Muslim side, there is a historical problem but they must be challenged to accept this country, to embrace it, and also to be true to their faith. This is a tremendous challenge for Muslims talking to other Muslims from closed societies because the whole paradigm of the latter must shift—a paradigm that advocates that everything must be sanctified by Muslims in the name of Islam. But the Koran itself is not a static book. This is the great debate inside Islam. To a Muslim the

Koran is the word of God and I say to the Muslim, the word of God is eternal and God is speaking to me in the twenty-first century, not the seventh, and I read the Koran from the eyes of a twenty-first-century man, not a seventh-century man. The Koran is no more static than any other culture or society. I see women as equal partners with men. I see a woman living her life and achieving her goals as fully sanctified by the word of God.

**CHRISTINE:** Given the resulting clash of civilizations between seventh-century Islam and modernity, how could Western authorities take more action in asserting Western values?

**DR. SALIM:** The time for that is long past. The West is entangled in the problems of the Muslim world and is an integral player in the life and politics of the Muslim world. So to the extent that the Muslim world tries to come to terms with the modern world, the West has to ask itself to what extent is it involved with the Saudi family and the Saudi state. They need to also ask if this is more important than the nature of change needed in the Muslim world.

## PROBLEMATIC TEXTS

**CHRISTINE:** There are texts in the Koran that I refer to as "problematic texts" because they advocate what we deem as atrocities as measured according to the Universal Declaration of Human Rights. How do you reconcile your faith with such texts?

**DR. SALIM:** In my view it is about how the Koran is interpreted and understood. To another group it is timeless as a word of God. To others, it is a frozen book, the word of God, and speaks from the seventh century. The Muslim faith is frozen in those centuries. Such texts are also in the Bible. I read the Koranic texts in the context of the twenty-first century. For example, violence is part of human nature. There was no Jew, Buddhist, Christian, Hindu, or Muslim at the time of the murder of Abel by Cain, so I view it as a metaphor of human nature. All of God's word refers to human nature and how you will constrain and deal with that violence. So in the Koran, violence is the acknowledgement of human nature. As with a physician, you must recognize and acknowledge the existence of a disease to find a cure.

The cure is also there. One cannot take out texts in isolation. Violence is a [part of] human nature. God cannot change the condition of the people unless they change their heart. It is us who have to change. The Islamists have fused their texts to legitimize their politics. It is easy to do that in certain societies. For example, in Afghanistan up to 90 percent of the population is illiterate and the imam too is uneducated. It is a sociological reality, but is seen as only within the Koran and Islam. In all religions there is a sociological reality and to the believer it is a sacred reality.

The world has more than 6.5 billion people and not one of us is the same. Our fingerprints are different and yet my heart will beat inside you and yours will beat inside me. We are simultaneously unique and at the same time we are in common. Coming back to the text, it's how you read and understand. That is the great debate within Islam today. On the one side are those who malign Islam—and the Islamist's conduct deserves to be maligned—and on the other side there are the voices that people don't hear about who have not abandoned the text because they see the text with completely different eyes.

**CHRISTINE: Do you view Muhammad as a model for today?**

**DR. SALIM:** No. A man from the seventh century will not be at home in the twenty-first century, but a man from that time like Muhammad was an iconic figure in the context of that time. The Koran talks about Moses as the greatest prophet, but Thomas Carlyle, the nineteenth-century Scottish philosopher and Presbyterian, chose Muhammad as a "hero as a prophet" in his book called *Heroes and Hero Worship*. At that time, Britain was coming into deep conflict with the Muslim world. Carlyle felt that Muhammad was sincere and true to himself and fought for what he believed. He fought because he was attacked. War philosophy is not negative because the issue becomes, what are you fighting for? Abraham Lincoln fought to emancipate the slaves while Jefferson Davis fought to keep the slaves. One has to bring perspective. Abraham Lincoln is not Jefferson Davis. [There is] no question that Muhammad fought because he was attacked. If he had been killed, there would be no Islam. If Moses was overthrown and killed and miracles did not save him, Jews would not have their freedom from Egypt—so again, context. Muhammad in the twenty-first century would not be the Muhammad as we know him from the seventh century. The problem with Islamists is that they have frozen their own understanding and use that understanding to pursue an agenda, which is completely contrary to the values of the modern world.

## ISLAMIC REFORM

**CHRISTINE:** Do you see the goal of Islamic reform coming from the West?

**DR. SALIM:** No, the West will not achieve the goal. In the long term it will happen despite the West and despite Islamists, because women will drive the progress in Saudi Arabia. Once this happens, the thinking in Saudi Arabia will collapse with it. I believe women are the most important instruments of change, and not just today but historically.

**CHRISTINE:** How do you reconcile your views of gender equality with that of your faith?

**DR. SALIM:** I cannot even go to mosque. The leaders of the mosques in my own city have publicly declared me an apostate, so they don't listen to me and wouldn't invite me to speak. But the Muslims themselves don't know their own history. There would be no Islam in the sense that there would be no Muhammad if it were not for his wife, Khadijah. She is the very person who embraced the word of Muhammad, the word that there is only one god which is of the Abrahamic faith. Without her there would be no Islam because he would not have the protection that she provided. She was 15 years older than him. It was [due to] her wealth and her status in society, because when she died, he no longer had the protection and Muhammad had to leave the city of Mecca. That is the flight, marked as the hijrah. It is so significant an event. People asked why it happened. It was because the protection of his wife was gone. In the Muslim world, ironically, women—half of creation—get excluded, but change in the Muslim world is happening. There is a great void in the Muslim world. It is underdeveloped and per capita income is a couple dollars a day. The focus on Islam came after 9/11 because people wanted answers, so in looking at the history, there is a void but there is also a historic reality.

My wife is a physician. She is from North Africa. She is everything to me. I also adored my mother. My daughter is the jewel of my eyes. My wife had to escape Algeria in 1990 when Algerian society became consumed with the violence between the government and Islamists and for a whole decade the government of Algeria was devastated by terrorism. Two hundred thousand people were killed. Women were targeted by the Islamists in their pursuit of creating an Islamist society. My wife had just graduated from medical school and was working in the main hospital in the capital of Algiers along with her friends. But they were targeted and killed or beaten up if they didn't live according to the values of the Islamists. They were forced to wear the burka and the niqab. My wife belonged to the first generation after the independence of Algeria from France in the early 1960s. That was the first generation of women that went to graduate studies. The greatest stories you want to talk about in societies are the stories of individuals such as Rosa Parks when she did not get up off her seat on the bus during the Civil Rights Movement. My wife's story is important and there are others.

**CHRISTINE:** Your story provides a historic plane of Islamism, operating in another society, in another time. We in the West are new at contending with such violence as your wife witnessed and responded to. Given what the average Westerner is now hearing in the news, many are skeptical about any notion of Islamic reform. How would you respond to this skepticism?

**DR. SALIM:** The Islamists would like to create a monolithic Islam and impose a view that has emerged in the twentieth century, a view that is generated by the Muslim Brotherhood and which is now tied with petrodollars. Islam is not any more monolithic than Christianity is. The Muslim world is vast and diverse with its 1.6 billion people. Look at Indonesia, Morocco, Nigeria, Uzbekistan, which ranges in ethnicity, in language, in culture and customs. As a religion it differs with the region. It is not monolithic, just as the Philippines, Iceland, Norway, are different in their Christianity. In our time in North America, a reformer can be identified as one that is completely at home in the West—culturally, intellectually, philosophically, and politically—because Islam to them is a personal faith.

The West took five centuries to struggle and establish these values of secularism. There are other cultures and civilizations that have not achieved that. The West has. There is a tragic pattern of a trajectory that Muslim countries are now facing, as are Muslim societies in the West. In India, there are Hindus and Muslims. In Hinduism it is divided in terms of the caste system; even so, India has a democratic constitution. Since its inheritance of the British system of government, India has been trying to work out its problems and be a modern country where religion and politics are separated. We have a Sikh Prime Minister where Sikhs represent less than 2 percent of India's population, and a woman who is not even Indian-born nor Sikh and is the wife of the former Prime Minister Rajiv Gandhi, Sonia Gandhi, who is also the head of the largest Indian political party, the Indian National Congress. This represents the historical movement and efforts going on. The Muslim societies have to struggle with what it means to be at home in the modern world of globalization and of individual and human rights.

I see the convulsions going on in the Muslim world as the convulsions of a civilization that is going through the process of implosion as a way of coming to terms with the reality around them.

There is denial and a fight back but there is also acceptance and coming to terms with it. For instance, I see Muslim women as an instrument of change as more women enter the economic life of the society. Half the population of the Muslim world ignores the presence of women. As women become more engaged, it will be fundamental. The process is happening even though it may not be as fast as we want.

If a Saudi woman says she is going to drive a car because a woman in Toronto drives a car, it is that little change like the drip of water that cracks a stone. This is what is happening.

**CHRISTINE: Do you have an expectation of a time frame for Muslim reform?**

**DR. SALIM:** It will not happen in the immediacy of our time because of the polarization in the Muslim world post-9/11. This polarization must work its way out and Muslims have to do it. Every society is in a state of movement, not inertia, so the Muslim societies will move, and

I already see it taking place. Another issue altogether is whether our media covers it. For example, 3 out of 4 Muslim countries are not Arab. Only 20 percent of Muslim countries are Arab and from the Middle East. There are others like Indonesia, Pakistan, Bangladesh, and India. Bangladesh is very large and a woman was elected, which is indicative of something. In Saudi Arabia women cannot drive a car, whereas we see women as leaders in Bangladesh and Pakistan. Pakistan is in the middle of a convulsion. Benazir Bhutto was assassinated; otherwise she would be the Prime Minister. The most significant change in a society is the status of women. Where women are free and educated, that society is marching forward toward a new culture. Women are indicators of whether Muslim reform is moving. Those Muslims who are uncomfortable with women in public life and women who are economically independent and want to constrain them are using Islam as a tool, so it becomes an instrument or tool in the hands of a patriarchal version of Islam: militant, aggressive, and misogynistic.

This is an internal struggle going on even in Canada in the face of honor killings, where women try to assert their identity but get punished or killed by a member of the family, [such as] the father or brother. These are huge issues and must be discussed. They force Muslims to take a stand and force the genie out of the bottle. Islam is being reformed. Who is making the reformation? No single individual. It is a cyclical process, a historical process. There will be casualties. America was founded upon the republican principle that men were created equal and they had to fight a civil war and a civil rights movement in our lifetime. Nothing is static because the process of reaching one's fullness is a struggle that goes on. That's why Jihad in the classical sense is an internal struggle. The Islamists have made it into a weapon for their own political agenda.

**CHRISTINE: Is it too late for reformists to rewind the infiltration into the West and modern society of Islamists?**

**DR. SALIM:** No, it is not too late. You and I are sitting here engaging in that. If we came to a conclusion that all that matters is me and myself, then why am I making this effort? It is part of a continuum. Generations have lived and died. Islamists will be defeated. I oppose Obama on political grounds, but a black man was elected and that was a historical thing to celebrate. I oppose his policies, but that was part of the continuum. India was liberated in the war of independence. Mahatma Gandhi prevailed. This man that Winston Churchill called a half-naked "fakir" shook up the British Empire, an empire in which the sun never set. You and I are both from the British Empire and Gandhi shook it up. Nelson Mandela shook up South Africa.

These things happen because God is in us despite the human nature of Cain murdering Abel. He has also provided in us that other dimension. In the Islamic term, that dimension is "God breatheth into us the human soul." In the Koran Jesus is referred to as the spirit of God, the soul of God. As humans we are fashioned out of mud, the lowest of the lowest, but into that God breathes His spirit, the highest of the high, so we are the composition of the lowest and the highest. A beast of the jungle has no ethics but we human beings are both angel and devil and beast at the same time. The question is, which one will prevail in us? There will be no value if all were angels. The Islamists will fade away.

# CHAPTER SIX

## DR. QANTA AHMED

### Physician, Author, Columnist

Dr. Qanta Ahmed is author of *In the Land of Invisible Women*, a chronicle of her experience of living and working in Saudi Arabia. This book has been translated and published in 13 countries.[1] She is also a regular contributor to numerous publications including the *Huffington Post*, *Jerusalem Post*, Israel's *Ha'aretz*, *The Times of Israel*, *The Guardian*, the *Wall Street Journal*, *New York Post*, *The Telegraph*, CNN, The Investigative Project on Terrorism, and the *World Policy Journal*. She has provided radio and television commentary, including to the BBC, CNN, Fox, C-SPAN, and Al Arabiya.[2]

Dr. Ahmed is the first physician and first Muslim woman to be selected as a 2010 Templeton Cambridge Fellow in Journalism at the University of Cambridge, England. During this time she completed her treatise on the psychological manipulation of Islam in the service of terror.[3] Dr. Ahmed's focus was on the cultural phenomenon of suicide bombings. Her expertise led her to testify before the US Congress in June 2012, at the request of the Homeland Security Committee, as a witness in the 5th Investigative Hearings on Radical Islam in the United States.[4]

Dr. Ahmed is also a practicing sleep disorders specialist and faculty attending physician at Winthrop University Hospital in Mineola, New York, an Associate Professor of Medicine at the State University of New York, and a recognized expert in health issues pertaining to the Hajj, the annual pilgrimage to Mecca that Muslims make each year.[5]

# INTERVIEW WITH DR. QANTA AHMED

**CHRISTINE:** Who or what has motivated your work and convictions as a moderate the most?

**DR. AHMED:** I have always been a voracious reader and wanted to do journalism but my parents steered me into medicine. *From Beirut to Jerusalem* by Thomas Friedman was a book so vivid that I was compelled to write to the author and we eventually met. I described some of my experiences and he motivated me to tell my story. Much more profound has been my relationship with my psychotherapist who is a Jewish woman and a New Yorker.

We were working over 12 years and I tell her what troubles me. This space we created is of me—a British Muslim—and her, an American Jew. Her insights on Judaism have very much unlocked my curiosity. Along the way I have read incredible works by Stephen Schwartz, the first person to capture the big picture for me as I lived in both worlds. Another inspiration is the country itself, the US, since 1992. It has been astonishing, the amount of opportunity here and grace the American people have shown me.

I came with a medical degree and then enrolled in a residency and fellowship. They asked for no money but paid. I took the credentials and along with it the freedom to work where I wanted to and I chose to go to Britain, then back to the US after obtaining a green card; however I did not need a visa but a special immigration status on contribution to the field to get a green card. I don't know anywhere else that would have given me that kind of endless opportunity, even Britain. I find that perpetually inspiring.

Any accusation about being alienated or excluded is such anathema, because my experience has been anything but. The only requirement America had of me was to just show up. The opportunity has been most inspiring.

I am also continuously amazed by my parents. They are supportive, understanding, and a constant source of validation even when it is difficult for them when I am transitioning and changing my mind.

My parents have always taught me that Islam is about justice and taught me a very simple message of keeping your beliefs so that they don't impinge on others, but to expose injustice and deceits if that falls upon you as your responsibility, so I feel that has been a good map for my life.

**CHRISTINE: Do you consider yourself to be a reformer?**

**DR. AHMED:** I don't consider myself a reformer as I don't see what there needs to be reformed in Islam. But I am a moderate. The distinction should be made between an Islamist and a Muslim. An Islamist to me is someone who has an aggressive political agenda or nihilism, that is, the extinction of all other elements in favor of the Islamist ideology. An Islamist is one who seeks supremacy of a political ideology for an orthodox or neo-orthodox version of an intolerant expression that they deem Islam.

The ideology of Islamists is to dismantle constructs that are integral to our society, like the expression of Western democracy and the freedom to choose a particular path or existence. Their expression of the rigid Sharia involves very harsh and punitive laws that are particularly harmful to people who are not deemed Muslim enough.

This question about Islamists needs to be asked frequently until the difference becomes apparent in the mainstream. This question is difficult to explain. For example I have many friends that are Saudi Arabian who dress according to the laws of Saudi Arabia but are not Islamist. When I meet them in London or New York, they lose their external religious wear, yet their views never change wherever they are. But Islamists claim they are being persecuted and they claim they are being silenced when, underneath, they are stealthily advancing their own mission.

## THE ISLAMIST AGENDA

**CHRISTINE: How do you recognize an Islamist?**

**DR. AHMED:** By his or her actions and how he or she is contributing to society. A Muslim is someone who engages with his or her surroundings and serves others and is very inclusive, but with an Islamist, the salient feature would be supremacy, a sense of exclusivity, and a sense of disconnection.

I would go another step and say if I come across individuals who say Israel does not have the right to exist, that would be quite possible they have Islamist sympathies. I don't see why a Jew does not have the same right to worship and nationhood as the 1.6 billion Muslims in 50-plus nations. Even those Muslims who are among the most educated can be Islamists who have astonishingly anti-Semitic views and who deny the Holocaust.

We fall into the trap of trying to identify Islamists by head coverings or adoption of Arab region clothing, but we have to become more penetrating in our questions, more informed about background, like who are their friends? Do they attend gatherings where people of other faiths like Christians and Jews attend? Muslims are a minority in the US so the onus is on us to engage in our surrounding society. That scent of supremacy is the most telling identifier of an Islamist. It is not a relationship between intellect and education, or even access to privileged opportunities. It is an ideology stemming from Muslims who feel alone, feel apart and in order to feel secure need to feel superior.

Islamists act on their ideologies, sometimes with dire consequences, and I don't mean detonating an explosive or harboring a prospective terrorist. Much more dangerous I think is the puppeteering of the masses and the influencing of the masses.

When Muhammad came and gave the message of Islam, he taught us to also submit our will to God, so everyone who submits to the will of God is regarded as Muslim. There is no room in there to be better than, or in contempt of any, of God's followers.

**CHRISTINE: Should Westerners be trusting mainstream Muslim advocacy groups?**

**DR. AHMED:** The problem with Islamists is that they become self-appointed advocates for the Muslim communities that never elected them to. I have rightful access to all my elected officials. I do not need organizational bodies to represent what they think my interests are without me having any influence. This is what is happening in the US through organizations like ISNA and CAIR. They claim to speak for and represent all Muslims in America including me. I did not accord them that authority.

In our culture we have lobbies and that is a tradition, not under-handed organizations that drive an underhanded agenda when most people are not even sure of the intent. The intent is portrayed to represent and protect Muslims. Yet Muslims like me will say we don't need their protection.

**CHRISTINE:** As an educator yourself, do you think that Islamists have made inroads in our school system?

**DR. AHMED:** We can see changes happening in the West. When I was growing up in England, there was no such thing as the concept of Islamic schools. In my school you were just a schoolgirl who went to a Church of England school and we learned with all the other children. Every day we started with a Christian assembly and I sang from my hymnbook. My parents never prevented me or pulled me out of any service. I did Bible reading like all the other schoolgirls. All of my education about Islam came from my parents. There was no concept that you would give your child over to some system who will instruct them in unknown values.

I saw my parents as caring enough to want to educate their children about religion and not take chances. Now fast forward 30 years, we have parallel Islamic schools with very aggressive views about pursuing their own religion, their own schools, their own agenda, and curriculum.

**CHRISTINE:** A frequently heard outcry is, where are all the Muslim voices like yours that are friendly to the West? Can you provide an answer?

**DR. AHMED:** I think there may be a silent majority like me, which we cannot quantify. Yet there are also people who are extreme, who buy the Islamist groupthink because they want to be part of something and they don't give countries like America and Britain a chance to see how completely accepting these countries can be and how they can acquire many Western values without conflicting with beliefs and morals. There are also those moderates who do not wish to identify themselves publicly. I would think there are many who will hear my message and agree but will not put it in print or on tape.

Another category is those who are undecided. I think we are now in a battle to win over the undecided, who can go either way, but because the Islamist activities are more vociferous and more animated, the people are more drawn into that. If you happen to be disaffected—whether young or old, a new immigrant or not—it might be appealing if you don't see an alternative.

In Islam, we have three duties: to God, to ourselves, and to society. Our duty is to enhance society, not to separate and dismantle society. We have to take a leap out of the Islamist book and anti-Islamists like me have not consolidated ourselves very effectively. As a society we have not done enough to protect the people who try to dismantle Islamist activities and the media is cowardly.

**CHRISTINE:  Please elaborate about the media.**

**DR. AHMED:** The mainstream media condemns scrutiny into Islamist activities, even discourse on the identity of Muslims and they cast anyone who says anything negative against Muslims as an Islamophobe. What has happened to our freedom of speech? Discussions are being shut down and Islamists use the word "apostasy" to intimidate us.

I found the movie *The Third Jihad: Radical Islam's Vision for the Future* to be fascinating even though the New York City Police Department was criticized for it. For those trying to investigate this, they get intimidated, vilified, and this kills further inquiry.

**CHRISTINE:  What do you anticipate will be the consequence of a reluctant mainstream media, and also of fearful politicians in addressing Islamism on American soil?**

**DR. AHMED:** The undecided group of Muslims of whom I hope are a majority are the ones who stand to lose the most. If we allow the Islamists to lead the fray or to lead discussions and debates, our rights, access to free expression, to worship how we want, to marry or divorce, and raise our children how we want will be contained. We risk losing our freedom.

I have lived under Sharia in Saudi Arabia and democracy in England and America and I know which I prefer. Although we want to protect individual rights, anyone who criticizes these kinds of investigations doesn't realize that protecting individual rights over the rights of the group can end up costing us all our individual rights in the future. And at this rate, it will be probably sooner rather than later. Those people that criticize these investigations, let's send them to a climate of Sharia law for a few years and let them tell us how they feel. Let them tell us how they feel when you are not allowed freedoms, not allowed to leave the country without many documents, to hold your passport, to worship publicly as a Christian and afraid to worship privately. You are not allowed to identify that you are Jewish publicly or privately, you are afraid to tell people what your religious beliefs are, you are not allowed to open a business as an individual, you cannot sit with a man to whom you are unrelated and to do so will be a risk. I have lived there, and it's not something you want here.

## VIEWS ABOUT PROBLEMATIC TEXTS IN THE KORAN

**CHRISTINE:** A common criticism of Islam is toward the violent texts and other "problematic texts" which includes Muhammad having 9-year-old Aisha as a wife. How do you explain these texts?

**DR. AHMED:** What I understand about polygamy and the Koran is that it allows a man to take up to four wives simultaneously. The Koran also says it is only legitimate if the husband can afford to keep them in equal status and emotionally treat them exactly the same. The next line in the Koran acknowledges that men are human so this will be difficult; therefore it is inherent that it is not recommended. We think polygamy became sanctioned in the life of Muhammad because in early Islam there were lots of battles, which created lots of widows, and in the pre-Islamic and early Islamic Arabia, women had very limited rights. That's why Islam was very revolutionary at the time as it gave women something they had never had in order to accommodate all these widows who had no livelihood, no fathers, no sons, no husband, no brothers, so polygamy became permissible.

But now, there is no basis for it. It is heinous according to Muslim values for a man to have wives recreationally and to have a preference. There may be an instance where the first wife cannot have children and a second wife is permitted by the first wife. This is legitimate under Islamic law if the man can equally divide his affections between the two, but humanly that is not possible. Even parents say it is hard not to have a preference for a child. However that nuance has gone by the wayside. We see terrible outcomes in children from a polygamous relationship and terrible hardships to women who in Saudi Arabia are not accorded the rights that Islam would give them.

**CHRISTINE:** Returning to Muhammad's young wife Aisha, can you tell us more about your thoughts about her?

**DR. AHMED:** Aisha was a very special wife to Muhammad and she never had children. She outlived him by over 50 years. She was 9 when betrothed according to accounts and cohabited with him at about 13. We need to remember that the lifespan of individuals in pre-Islamic and Islamic Arabia was very short so it was reasonable to assume a person will die in their third and fourth decade and that's why marriage was customary when a female became biologically able to support children. Now we have the technology to delay biological motherhood and control reproductivity, so it's conceivable that marrying Aisha was appropriate for that era.

In the philosophy of polygamy, the prophet exceeded four wives and we believe the marriage was for tribal and political reasons as a means to unite various tribes in Arabia. Aisha was often called one of the most favored of Muhammad's wives. His first wife was Khadijah and she chose him in marriage. She was a divorcee, previously married to two others. She was a woman of wealth and autonomy and while they were married, it became revealed that he was a messenger.

He was monogamous to Khadijah. After her he had a number of wives. Aisha became more important because she was the youngest, the final, the beloved and therefore her memory lives on. So to call the prophet a pedophile, I can understand why people would look at the age of her as a bridal partner and decide he was a pedophile, but one must look at the historical context. I would say no thinking Muslim today would advocate either polygamy as the Koran says because all of us know that men cannot divide their affections equally and nobody would agree that a child is intellectually ready to marry at 12 or 13 in today's world.

Unfortunately there are those Muslims who don't feel like that and they take this historical account and perpetuate practices tantamount to pedophilia. We see that in Afghanistan through forced marriages and in Pakistan where girls have the least number of years of education in the world. While they want to emulate a practice they think is coming from the root of Islam in terms of polygamy and very young wives, they're not willing to emulate all of the other things like autonomy for the woman, power and wealth, as well as her right to choose a marriage partner and to terminate a marriage. They can't have it all.

I have studied further accounts on Aisha whom we think her mission was to become the centerpiece of the "Ummul Mu'minin," or mother of the faithful. She outlived Muhammad and went on to become a very important scholar. She trained future Muslims for the rest of her life. If you think of the idea of a pedophile, from a medical point of view a pedophile is someone who indulges in a child for sexual gratification at the expense of all other status, health, or mental integrity of the individual. And this is not how the prophet treated Aisha. Other than Khadijah, Aisha became more acclaimed than any other Muslim woman as a scholar. There is a very famous Hadith that tells of Muhammad being asked a question and instead of explaining this nuance of Islam, he said, "Ask the one with red hair." It was Aisha who was a redhead and he was identifying her to another follower. So her hair was visible, not covered, and he was indicating her authority was as good as his. This is not the characteristic of a pedophile.

**CHRISTINE: Khadijah is an important figure that many of your fellow moderates refer to as an example of the place of women in the religion. Explain your view.**

**DR. AHMED:** The first Muslim was Khadijah, the wife of the prophet. He was married to her for a number of years and would go to a cave outside Mecca to meditate. One day he came back very disturbed, cold and trembling. He had seen a vision of the angel Gabriel and the angel Gabriel instructed him to recite. Muhammad was illiterate. He said he didn't read, yet the angel said to recite. Then words emerged from the prophet and these became the first words of the Koran. This brings us to the Jihad of the pen. Muhammad went back to Khadijah who reassured him and said not to worry, that they will go and seek advice from her wise uncle who was a Christian priest, but some scholars say he was a rabbi, so this is the woman that chose Muhammad as her husband. She chose Muhammad, was the first to believe him and therefore the first Muslim so if this is our first prototype of a Muslim, any Muslim that puts women as inferior is not coming from Islam. It is coming from Muslim men and it is profoundly un-Islamic.

**CHRISTINE:** The issue of supremacy within Islam, which includes supremacy over women and blacks, how do you respond?

**DR. AHMED:** I get very upset about this. In the center of Mecca is the house that Abraham built 4,000 years ago, called the Kaaba or the House of God. The first Muslim to give the call to prayer was Bilal. Bilal was a black African, and Muhammad gave him the rare honor to show that Islam does not distinguish between races. Islam was meant to be gender blind and color blind to Muhammad. He could have chosen anyone, but instead he chose an African. Many Africans that were with Muhammad at the time had been enslaved and he would free them. Islam is very detailed on the rights of all orphans and slaves, on what happens to their inheritance, and your responsibility when you free slaves, so the idea that Islam is racially discriminating is anathema to what we see in Islam in the life of Muhammad. I agree there is terrible racism in lots of Muslim communities but they did not come from inside Islam. About women's inferiority, I will accept that almost every Muslim-majority community you look at has examples where women are badly inferior to men. They are actively disempowered or effectively enslaved by men legally if not literally. I lived in Saudi Arabia where male supremacy is legislated. I was deemed inferior living in Saudi Arabia even though I was a physician with American and British links. I do not believe these practices come from Islam because Islam says very clearly that this is not so according to its requirements.

One requirement when you go to Mecca is to have a male accompaniment. I didn't have one when I went and my advice to women is to go with a male because you feel safer in those crowded places. So there certainly is a role for men to protect women but protection of women does not mean suffocation and subjugation. Protection of women means making them as powerful as your sons.

**CHRISTINE:** Please explain your notion of the word "Jihad," which is another problematic notion that is incited by Islamists.

**DR. AHMED:** In our moderate belief one has the right to bear arms and defend oneself. So hypothetically by those same means if a Christian living in Saudi Arabia is not allowed to practice his faith, show his faith, and is punished or attacked for it then under Islam he would have a right to defend himself. If one is prevented from worshipping in their faith, they can engage in violent Jihad.

This is how Islamist puppeteers mastermind and use the word Jihad to falsely wage unholy, unauthorized wars that are unjustifiable by the Koran. Yes Jihad is in the Koran but we live in an era that has moved beyond violence.

Islam is very clear about who wages these wars and they are just wars only to be waged by men who carry arms. Listed under Islamic law in war are non-combatants, which include women, children, the elderly, and the disabled, so the political Jihads in the Palestinian territories are completely anathema to Islam because they are engaging women and children and targeting civilians. They get around this by saying that every Israeli serves in the military so is not a civilian, but this is rubbish.

Palestinians sending their children to become suicide bombers and calling it Jihad is an absolutely false justification. They are allowed to practice their faith. Their situation may be very difficult but Israel even allows them Sharia court in Israel to settle disputes, and you also have the choice of Israeli secular court. Israel allows them to build mosques. The Palestinians have mosques in the "disputed territories." If you want a war of a territory, then call it a war of a territory. It is not a Jihad. Same thing with bin Laden. He used this very seductive language for his political motives. Such language to an illiterate and uneducated group has powerful appeal. Also, if you do not exercise a mind of your own and are not secure, or don't feel as privileged, this becomes alluring.

I admit that there are ways in Islam that you can bear arms, but the best retaliation will be in the written and spoken word, grossly underutilized in the post-9/11 era in the face of a noisy, hysterical, and far too uninformed media. The media also collaborates with a possibly equally uninformed government leadership. It's been quite a spectacle to watch.

There are many ways to defend a right to practice the faith and we believe in Jihad of the pen. I cannot go out and face real bullets as a soldier. I don't have that kind of bravery, but I can take ideological bullets, the Jihad of the pen, where you dismantle monstrously destructive ideological elements with words and articles to expose the monster, which will crumble. It is very protected when you don't expose it.

If there is an idea I don't like or I think is false, I pick up a pen and there is no weapon more powerful than the pen, because words are timeless and words can be very damaging if you use your words wisely. Hopefully this is how we will damage Islamist ideology: with words.

Jihad has two other meanings: the lesser Jihad and the greater Jihad, the latter being your own internal struggle. This involves the struggle to do good, to stay on the good path and be moral. There is always a chance to do things that are not moral, a struggle to fight your baser inner instincts, which we all have as human beings.

## CHAPTER SEVEN

# DR. JALAL ZUBERI

### Medical Specialist and East Director of the Center for Islamic Pluralism

Dr. Jalal Zuberi is a pediatric infectious disease specialist in Atlanta, Georgia. He is US Southeast Director of the Center for Islamic Pluralism (CIP).

In an article, Dr. Zuberi once took Bollywood to task for perpetuating myths of Muslims being victimized in the West. He states that while it is fair to note that "isolated cases of the harassment of individuals with Muslim names and Middle Eastern backgrounds are an undeniable part of recent history," he stood against the message projected that in America, Muslims are victims of discrimination solely because of their religious affiliation or identity without proper context. He states that transport security officers must detect and stop potential terrorists who are mainly coming from "Muslim backgrounds and brainwashed with the radical Wahhabi, anti-Western ideology of al Qaeda." Yet true to his conciliatory nature, Zuberi also poses the question: "How do we save lives and property without appearing insensitive and racially discriminatory?"[1]

When I visited Dr. Zuberi's home, I was introduced to a Muslim English professor and two supporters of CAIR who were adamantly against the notion of reform. Dr. Zuberi encouraged dialogue that took place between his three visitors and myself. We ended up in a heated debate about the notion of reform, their reference to colonialist "sins," racism, the politics of Israel, and free speech in the West. One of the guests started to walk out during an impassioned moment of disagreement with me. Dr. Zuberi discouraged this move, asked his guest to sit down and approximately three hours later, the outcome was that peacefulness resumed, with a willingness for Dr. Zuberi's guests to further engage in such dialogue and debate. Dr. Zuberi believes that Muslims of all stripes must be pluralistic and hash out issues of ideology amongst themselves and also be willing to engage with non-Muslims in public forums.

# INTERVIEW WITH DR. JALAL ZUBERI

**CHRISTINE:** What and who motivated your ideas toward moderation and reform?

**DR. ZUBERI:** My own father Wahiduddin who passed away some years ago. He would sit down with me and made me read the newspaper as a very small child. From him I have a passion for reading the newspaper every day. He was an avid reader who would read material and write about it. He taught us about Islamic history, British history, Greek history and politics, which opened my mind. The other thing is my heritage from the university I went to, Aligarh Muslim University in India. The founder, Syed Ahmad Khan, was the greatest reformist of all time. These factors compelled me to search for balance in life and I take this heritage and hope that I can advance the cause.

## ISLAMISM

**CHRISTINE:** Define an Islamist.

**DR. ZUBERI:** The word is not without controversy and I question how effective it is to identify extremism. In the eyes of other Muslims, they don't see this as helpful in the debate but the word is used to define extremism ideology now for the lack of a better term. With that said, Islamists are those that hold Islam as all-embracing. Everything they do has to conform to their religious being so it is difficult for them to separate their religion from social aspects of life.

**CHRISTINE:** Do you differentiate between violent and stealth Islamists?

**DR. ZUBERI:** There is a difference. Erdogan of Turkey and the Muslim

Brotherhood have an ideology, which has legitimacy with the public. They work with the local population, taking away the governance of secular fascist governments that don't allow religious expression and the hijab. So a reaction to such governments is the takeover by the Muslim Brotherhood.

**CHRISTINE:** So how can one differentiate between representatives of the Muslim Brotherhood who have legitimacy among the populace from a genuine moderate?

**DR. ZUBERI:** The devil is in the details. The ability to live at peace with a critical view of Muslims and Islam and not become very defensive of other viewpoints and unaccepting of a difference of opinion is important. For example, I may not believe in certain sayings of the prophet, which may not be applicable in the present environment or time, but there is rigidity about the beliefs in someone who cannot accept this. That will cause me to question whether they are a moderate or not.

**CHRISTINE:** What about groups like CAIR, ISNA, and ICNA—are they Islamists in your view?

**DR. ZUBERI:** They are more so than moderate, yes, because they do not create the space for dissent, which in my opinion is the biggest litmus test. I have attended their conventions so I have first hand experience. They are very established and any criticism of their groups is deemed to be anti-Islamic. I don't attend when they come out to Atlanta anymore. Neo-Muslims are drawn to them because it jibes with the religious vigor, it renews their faith and that is where they are in their own journey. I do not see them as healthy at this time in furthering the cause of moderacy and diversity. All of these groups have the same basic ideologies and they are part of the same establishment.

Criticism is the opening of that watershed that will lead to the real change to take place in the Muslim mind. This opens the mind and creates free thinkers, but they want to keep the collectivist thinking and influence. They want to perfect how Muslims behave as back home, so anyone who challenges them is seen as a challenge to their own authority.

I am part of a mosque myself and these people's biggest interest is to expand the ideology of the ritual faith system. That includes groups like CAIR. For them, it is a cultural medium and may not in itself be growing anything like terrorism or aiming toward an Islamic Caliphate, but it enriches a particular strain where an individual with those kinds of dangerous extreme ideologies will be more comfortable in that environment. But not everyone is of that same strain.

**CHRISTINE:** How are mosques impacting the cause of reform in your opinion?

**DR. ZUBERI:** I won't call mosques a detriment but they are not helpful either. They provide an opportunity for Muslims to fulfill their ritualistic observations. In debating contentious issues, these are not able to be discussed at the mosque because of the universality of the views of the administration. This leaves me with a void, as I would like to see different points of views expressed.

## PROBLEMATIC TEXTS

**CHRISTINE:** In looking at the Koran, how do you reckon with problematic texts in a modern world and in living in America?

**DR. ZUBERI:** The biggest problems are the verses of the war in view of looking at them in a modern context. We need to see them as contextual to the historic times of the prophet. Those verses are there and we don't need to take them out or hide them as they are part of a context. Similarly we see verses in the Torah and Christian Bible where the Divine was asking his followers to kill. The faithful followers have evolved from that thinking while still maintaining those verses in the texts. Muslims can also do the same. They do not face an existential threat as in Muhammad's time, so context is important as such conditions no longer exist.

In the US we are growing. My plea to fellow Muslims is that those war verses do not apply to the current world environment, especially in the West. With specific references to Jihad, there is no Jihad, except the challenge of internal Jihad to become a productive citizen and pledge allegiance to the state of which they live. It is not contradictory to my beliefs and it does not make me any less of a Muslim to pledge my allegiance to the flag of the United States of America while I still maintain my identity as a Muslim.

**CHRISTINE: Is Muhammad a worthy paradigm in a modern world?**

**DR. ZUBERI:** Yes, certainly. He had a complex personality. He had to be too many things at the same time: a prophet, a strategist, a statesman, a military man, a husband, and a father, so he had to fulfill these roles and I think sometimes they conflicted with one another. He is still a revered figure for us.

For example, he never took any personal insult to those people who opposed him. He respected them and although the verses of the Koran contain the punishing of women, Muhammad himself never raised his hand, so we know that even though Muslims have that permission, Muhammad never indulged. He was an example of supporting gender equality. He was the father of four girls and would stand up when his daughters came in to greet them with respect. I do the same with my daughters and I tell them this is our legacy of respect to our daughters in giving them regard. He also famously said that paradise lies at the feet of the mother, so that, I think, is a great testament to how he felt toward women and wanted his follows to do the same. I can also cite numerous examples where he said the pen is mightier than the sword. People in the West want to portray him as a warmonger, but he said that, and also that the ink of a pen is much more valuable than the blood of the martyr. These are the ideas Muslims need to espouse and make people aware of. This is why I think Muhammad is a human being that we can be educated from in our time.

## ISLAMIC REFORM

**CHRISTINE: Do you consider yourself a Muslim reformer?**

**DR. ZUBERI:** I would rather call myself a thinker and one who aspires for reform to take place. I see reform as more of a responsibility than being a leader.

**CHRISTINE:** What do you personally believe to be the most identifying character-istic of Muslims who would support the notion of reform?

**DR. ZUBERI:** I like to make sure I am walking the right path myself and asking others to come with me. Coming to the West gave me the opportunity to think and created a state in my mind to digest criti-cisms without becoming so upset. That is the first gift I have received, which is the idea of separation of church and state. From there is a fundamental shift in mind. People need to learn history and what made the ideologies of America and such societies advance.

After accepting criticism then the journey becomes easier. Most Muslims have not crossed that threshold but feel victimized by forces that they see as demonizing Islam and Muslims. They cannot cut through that and see that some of these criticisms have some valid-ity. Muslims have not gone through this phase of evolution as other religious faiths and races have. This will make a very big difference in my view.

In addition to not being open to criticism, Muslims think collec-tively as opposed to individually. They have a problem with the West. The problem is the collective identity as a Muslim and that is because of the forum created for them. They have seen it in the Arab and Muslim world of establishment. They come here like business as usual. They discover this new reality without anyone or enough to lead them.

**CHRISTINE:** What about the Israel–Palestinian issue. Do you consider Muslim at-titudes toward Israel a litmus test to determine a moderate and reformist?

**DR. ZUBERI:** Israel has a very distinguished role by default because of the issue of Palestine and the suffering among Palestinians. Denying that will be a fool's errand so therefore I do accept that as very important and critical.

I think the presence of Israel is a good thing for Muslims. Jews have not been historically favorable to Muslims and to Muhammad and we have to separate historical incidents from what we are facing right now. Supporting Israel is a difficult thing for Muslims to do and we have to come out of that and be able to at least call a spade a spade.

You have to accept Israel as a state. So this is a litmus test but not the starting point. This issue of being a moderate goes beyond the question of Israel and the Jews. It is more about acceptance of what is decent. That is the key and we need to review our own history and how Islam has involved itself in violence and internal struggles. We are only dealing with the twentieth century of Israel's creation. It is not the only issue.

A litmus test for being a moderate is acceptance of another opinion without labeling them an apostate, a kafir, and such terms. These terms have very serious connotations to Muslims and Muslims need to reject such terms.

## INSTITUTING REFORM AND THE CHALLENGES

**CHRISTINE:  What is your vision for reform, Dr. Zuberi?**

**DR. ZUBERI:** I am admiring the idea of reformist mosques. It asks the question: Do we have the means or the resources to set up this up? So rather than go this route, it might take an evolution to get there; otherwise it would create discord in the community. I think we need Muslim secular forums first before reform mosques so we can develop a pluralistic mindset or at least the notion of a dialogue.

Once the communities are organized those Muslims can decide whether we are organized enough and our numbers big enough to afford our own centers that promote different views where we do not all agree. In the midst of the congregation at mosques, 50 percent may not agree with what the imam is telling them. But because they have no other way of doing it, they sit there to fulfill their obligations without the same organizational capacity as the fundamental Muslims or orthodox Muslim groups, who are organized and building mosques rapidly with the help of petrodollars.

The number of mosques in the US has doubled since 9/11. Muslims feel very proud of that, but I don't have to feel proud of that. What affects me is that this country has allowed us to build the mosques, despite the accusations about victimization of Muslims. But in America, Muslims are actually free to express their religion in a way they have not been able to establish in their own countries. Muslims should be proud of the victory they have to be free to express themselves and their religion in America instead of presenting themselves as victims.

**CHRISTINE:** What stage would you say that the evolution of Muslim reform is in today?

**DR. ZUBERI:** It is in an infancy stage. The biggest challenge is crossing over the threshold into the next phase of progress. Most Muslims don't even agree that there is a need for reform, let alone what reform should be. So our goal needs to be to make clear what we are trying to reform. There is a lot of resistance to the concept of reforming the religion itself. There is more general agreement to the idea of how we think about religion and how we integrate our religion with our society and our fundamental human rights.

**CHRISTINE:** Do you believe that such a small group of Muslim reformists can challenge the larger institutions?

**DR. ZUBERI:** Muslims cannot challenge the large fundamentalist institutions right now because of the vast differences in their size and influence, but I don't even like to see it as a challenge because our role needs to be different. I want to see the reform movement taking place outside of the mosque. We need to define the role of the mosque rather than try to limit it or challenge it or have mosques be service points in the community where everything has to happen through the mosque and remain at the nerve center for Muslim activity. Muslims need to be given the space to fulfill their other social needs outside of the mosque while limiting the mosques to religious and ritualistic obligations. So rather than invite a guest Muslim speaker into the mosque, invite them to another center outside the mosque.

Churches have opened up in terms of giving voices to other people. They are not necessarily limiting or stifling dissent of opinion, which seems to be happening in our own community.

**CHRISTINE:** What is your view of the larger organizations that say they represent all Muslims, such as the previously referred to CAIR and ISNA and the like? Do they speak for you and in your opinion for the majority of Muslims?

**DR. ZUBERI:** The larger organizations in existence like CAIR and ISNA speak for Muslims by default rather than having any official sanction by Muslims. They have taken advantage that there is no other group that has emerged with a similar role.

But yet CAIR and such groups have taken this issue of victimization to an extreme level, and they support Hamas and the Muslim Brotherhood. We do not need to support extreme positions, but to have organizations in the Western context that could take up legitimate concerns of discriminations and human rights. Muslims need to have a place to go. My hope and desire is for alternatives.

## CHAPTER EIGHT

# SHIREEN QUDOSI

### Activist for Reform and Freelance Writer

Shireen Qudosi is a freelance writer and passionate activist for reform. In her "Qudosi Chronicles" on her website, she states her convictions:

> "To really understand Islam, you would have to master theology, sciences, and history to start…and, toughest of all, of course, you have to master yourself. Hence my skepticism of experts who usually lack one or two of these prerequisites. But you can start with your gut, and my gut always told me something wasn't right in the way we understood Islam—and it wasn't acceptable to just leave it at that. And real spirituality, I feel, starts with your intuition."

Shireen is a trailblazer for her generation, particularly for young Muslim women. Her passion, authenticity, and genuineness for the cause of reform were immediately apparent and encouraging as she discussed in her interview some of the personal obstacles she overcame.

## INTERVIEW WITH SHIREEN QUDOSI

**CHRISTINE:** Who has influenced and motivated you?

**SHIREEN:** There are people who elevate my perspective. Robert Reilly is one. What he writes I learn from in refining my own thinking. Another is Daniel Pipes, who has encouraged me to research my peer group and to learn the background. Also, ever since I was little I fought for what was right, even though it might be to my own detriment. I just have to. It is a trait.

**CHRISTINE: As a Muslim who is dedicated to your country, America, tell me about your own personal journey, which includes experiences and lessons learned as a reformer.**

**SHIREEN:** You will have troubles in everything worth doing. You're attacked, you're not taken seriously. You wonder if anyone is reading your work or listening to you, but you have to have faith. You have to keep in the back of your mind the divine perspective that you are doing something important, and remember that you are not alone. It can feel like an isolating road that you are on, but I think of the billions of people that have passed and the billions that will come and will be affected by the small number of people who do the right thing. Even if you fail and don't do what you wanted to do, from a divine perspective you still did the right thing, and if at the very least you have inspired someone to do a little more, you have succeeded.

Muslims have to hang in there. There are times where you will debate someone, and even though they get angry or hostile, you might notice that spark of thought in their expression, or they might say they never thought of it that way. Others might curse you and move on, only to come back later and ask you a question, which shows they were thinking about what you said. That to me is victory. It shows you have initiated an action that sparked a thought for someone. Our society today is based on statistics and [is] success-based, but this is damaging, in that you cannot think about money, status, career, and comparisons; instead, you have to think about what is important, that you are not in it for yourself but for a greater cause, and you must stick it out. Sometimes you have a lapse and take a break from it, but if you're doing the right thing, you get pushed back into it. If you are on the course you are supposed to be on, you will find your way back to it. The inspiration for me is the famous leaders in history. They all had to make sacrifices to their quality of life.

This has been a divine grace for me. I am not educated enough like my peers who can speak Arabic with a PhD, so there is much working against me, but I have been given insight to see things as they are and to use the faculty of thought and pair it with spirituality to move forward, to evolve, and to bring those around me to a progressive level. I am doing this for human civilization. People talk about the Arab world and the Muslim world, but it's about one civilization. We are in a globalized society, so we are all affected as a civilization by all of our peers. It is a human problem, and Muslims must reform.

Another issue I have encountered are problems with both right-wing groups and left-wing groups. A lot of the right-wing groups have a problem with Muslims. Anything you say is interpreted in a wrong way. They don't realize that I am just like them and share their views. Then you have the left-wing liberal groups, who are overly politically correct and apologetic. So Muslims try to find a balance. They go from being overly aggressive on an issue regarding Muslims to being overly defensive about their faith. It relates to the public perception, which is always shifting. We have not reached any balance yet and the media does not help, because they cater to the victim ideology.

A reporter reached out to me about Muslims in America since 9/11, and absolutely nothing I said was in that interview. It was highlighting and catering to CAIR, discussing how America should make special concessions to Muslims to make them feel included. So this reporter spoke to a moderate, but did not give me a voice. Instead, my perspective did not get featured, as well as the many who think like me. The media damages our goals, which are for a greater society. Our fundamental principles need to be secured, but the challenges continue, both within and not helped by the media.

**CHRISTINE: How did you confront and resolve issues about your faith?**

**SHIREEN:** I sort of just put my faith to the side for a time. I didn't know what I would do. It was a journey that I stumbled on. I read the Koran three times and the first time I was extremely depressed. So I read it again and then a third time. I decided to explore Christianity, did Bible study, kept myself open. I wish more people would do that. There were questions I couldn't get answered about my faith that I wasn't able to get answered by anyone, including imams and respected individuals. They tell you it will come to you when you are ready, which really means they don't know, either. If you need to address the problems of a faith, you need to be part of the faith, so I came back, but I questioned the Koran.

**CHRISTINE: What is your view on the state of Muslim youth in assimilating in America?**

**SHIREEN:** Terrible. The group between 20 and 30 is reaching out and creating art, publications, films, and blogs for a Muslim voice. We don't need a Muslim media, a Muslim play, a Muslim movie. I would like to see Muslims adapt and assimilate.

The other problem with Muslim youth is that they assimilate culturally in terms of dress and pop music, but as time goes on and they become of marrying age, they revert to old traditions and don't break out of the mold. They settle into expectations of parents, which shows no progress.

**CHRISTINE: Are there plans for reaching this young demographic?**

**SHIREEN:** It's difficult. Because I am aggressive in my approach, this audience doesn't want to hear it, but persistence is necessary. They are active in dialogue online, and as long as you try to maintain a level of diplomacy, some of them come around. A movement is only as powerful as it is seen. So if it's seen as gaining legitimacy through the reformers and moderates, then it will be better.

## ISLAMISM

**CHRISTINE: How would you define an Islamist?**

**SHIREEN:** There is no stereotype in how they dress, walk, and live among us. They are savvy, well-spoken, discreet, unrecognizable, but they use the political and social system to push the Jihadi agenda through the back door, which is to topple our Western system and replace it with their idea of a perfect Islamic state.

They want a political and social system in accordance with Sharia law, Islamic culture and structure, like stoning, female genital mutilation, and honor killings. People say that such things are not a part of Islam, but the culture is at play. Another example is in Britain. The Muslim British Council filed a report and sent it into the school districts. It was on how to make Muslim students feel more comfortable. It was a list to basically turn an English–British school system into something that mirrors a Saudi system, like hijabs, time for prayer, you can't eat pork, you have to fast, and to celebrate Ramadan. It is a mistake because these are little steps. Others include free speech, where we can't criticize or offend Muslims. We have to be politically correct, and that's what the Islamist agenda is. It makes our society a cocoon, enabling Islamic doctrines to creep in over our own Western principles.

**CHRISTINE:** How would you compare "peaceful" Islamists vis-a-vis violent ones?

**SHIREEN:** They have the same aim, even though one is more outright. Yet Islamists are more deceiving and dangerous, even though not outright aggressive. They are like the wolf in sheep's clothing, where they appear to be part of the democratic political structure, but they are not. They use diplomacy and diplomatic ties to achieve the same ends. They have legal grounds to manipulate people, where the more aggressive Jihadists use religious grounds, but they are the same. At the end of the day you have to look at their objectives and goals, and they are not that different.

**CHRISTINE:** In your opinion, do problems with Muslim integration in the West fuel Islamism, particularly among young Jihadists?

**SHIREEN:** Yes. Islam is superior for Islamists. From that, you get hatred toward a culture and race. On the other side, many Americans are misinformed and ignorant. For example, I have been asked, "Where is your hijab?" They were not being racist, but didn't know that not all Muslim women wear a hijab. Muslims don't help, either. They are generally not friendly, and for some Americans who encounter a Muslim, this might be the only one they met or would meet, so what impression did that Muslim leave? A lot of Muslims are not interacting and not adapting. The blame could be shifted everywhere, but more on us as Muslims. If we are going to claim victimization, then the responsibility falls on us to rise to the challenge. Groups like CAIR don't help.

We have to take accountability as Muslims first. Maybe there are issues about America, like an imperialist attitude and insensitivity, but we have to look at ourselves first before pointing fingers. We don't have a right to say it is America's fault, because what have we done to change ourselves first?

**CHRISTINE: How has Western ignorance facilitated the advancement of the Islamist Project?**

**SHIREEN:** It was never just a war on diversity and tolerance, which is what Islamists say, but really a war on ideas and faith. If you want the Islamist agenda to change, you need Muslims who can make the change you want. Take, for example, the King hearings on Homeland Security and radical Islam: A petition signed by some 50 leading organizations made the claim that it was McCarthyism all over again. You see accusations of fascism, which is not the case. Since 9/11, there is actually more Muslim outreach and more Muslim dialogue. At the end of the day, it is a Muslim problem.

On a local level, at the LA County Sheriff's Department, one of the Arab officers started a Muslim community relations project to reach out to the Muslim community. He invited me to the first roundtable about terrorism with other Muslims of different stripes: CAIR, Egyptian Muslims, etc., plus there was an FBI expert. We spent about an hour talking about terrorism, yet Islamic terrorism was avoided. When I raised the issue, I got the looks, and the expert tried to wriggle out of it, and people became reactive. Those present pointed to the IRA, Christian evangelical terrorism. I replied that is fine, but you don't see those people sitting at this roundtable. We're all here of a certain demographic background for a reason. But it was the avoided elephant in the room. This whole issue is not about victimization. It is about flat-out denial, which goes back to Imam Rauf, where he talks about America having a part to play in 9/11. If we don't move in the area of reform, America will lose. The focus on diversity and tolerance are not the issues.

There is also a huge failure in the intelligence community, because they are not taking seriously the ideas presented by reformers. Their major use of Muslims in the War on Terror is as informants. It's degrading, delegitimizes us in the community, and is a waste of our resources.

## PROBLEMATIC TEXTS

**CHRISTINE:** There are texts in the Koran that advocate violence, supremacy, and marriage to underage girls by our definition. How do you come to terms with those?

**SHIREEN:** You must challenge the Koran. You have to. If you don't challenge that, you can't challenge the faith, which is the biggest problem we have. A reformist was talking about a committee willing to interpret passages in the Koran. I think it is great that someone is doing it, but I don't think that is enough. It's not about interpretation in my view, because that's what Jihadists did. They interpreted it to their extreme. If you can't challenge the verses and admit there is a problem with it, how can you reform anything?

People don't want to change the Koran or to address Muhammad, and I am not saying that to attack him, but to treat him as a human being, not as a divine being. The problem is, not many people want to do that.

**CHRISTINE:** Do you have some personal doubts or questions about Muhammad as a model to Muslims today?

**SHIREEN:** I do. I think he was not perfect and I don't expect him to be perfect. There are hundreds of prophets, and not all of them were perfect. Islam sees Muhammad as infallible, but I don't. Muhammad himself said in the Koran that he was God's messenger, and the Koran says don't follow the prophet but follow God. He's just the messenger and died like everyone else, and I think we turn him into a demigod. We idolize him, and that is what we see in the Hadiths: Everything from basic etiquette to civil matters or in Sharia law, we follow what he said. Why are we following what he ate or what his wife wore, like the hijab, if we are not supposed to be following him, but following God's law instead of man's law? With Muslims, we confuse human law with divine law.

**CHRISTINE:** How does a moderate Muslim view the compatibility of their faith with a modern era?

**SHIREEN:** It's not even a matter of modernity, but a question of whether certain texts in the Koran are compatible with a divine perspective. As Muslims, we are people who devoutly believe in God and his edicts, and if you go past Muhammad, the seed of it is God. So we need to look at natural law and man's law to understand what God wants for us. What we are doing as Muslims is not compatible with God's view of how we should be.

## ISLAMIC REFORM

**CHRISTINE:** How would you describe a Muslim reformer?

**SHIREEN:** Someone who actively aims to change Islam. That has been tricky even with moderate and academic Muslims, because they believe Islam should not be reformed. A leading thinker said the word "reform" is offensive to him, that I should not use the word reform, that Wahhabis use the word reform, but why should I not use the word reform? Why should we let them have that right to take our language away? Why should we give up our right and let them tell us what words we can and cannot use? He also said that to even suggest that Islam needs to be reformed is offensive, because that is a justice law. Someone like that, as brilliant as they are, is a moderate. They are not a reformer. A reformer is someone actively seeking to change Islam, to change Muslims, and to change perceptions.

Even among those who call themselves reformers, many don't think the Koran or Muhammad has any faults. In their view, it is how the Koran gets interpreted. They see that reform is needed among the people, but not Islam; I don't agree.

**CHRISTINE:** How do you refute or justify many arguments by moderates that further the view that Muhammad and Islam were justified in the seventh century to kill, as Islam faced an existential threat?

**SHIREEN:** If you are a moderate, you are essentially disagreeing with a lot of elements within the faith. A lot of it got twisted around over the centuries and there are also distortions, but there are key elements in the faith—fundamental grievances within the time of the prophet, and my biggest issue is the fact he raised the sword. He should have never done that. It was not about protecting your people at that time or surviving at that time. It is about the bigger picture, and a person of God thinks that way. He thinks, how are my actions going to affect billions of people to come? If it means that by not raising the sword your people don't exist tomorrow, then so be it, because at the end of the day, you are doing it in God's name. You have to look at the wrongs, the core of what he said when he was alive, and what he said God said. You have to change and reinterpret that. If you don't, then the Jihadis are justified by just looking at the Koran. People say it's historical, that you can take it or leave it, but you are still justifying it. If this book came from God and it's divine and perfect, then the Jihadis are justified. You don't need to be an academic to see what's in the Koran. It's black and white.

**CHRISTINE:  How is the reform movement faring now in your opinion?**

**SHIREEN:** The fact that I am talking to you now is progress, a huge progress, and we need more people like you, people who are willing to listen to a Muslim voice, and people like Daniel Pipes, who makes the time. Also, I see more willingness between reformers and moderates to interact with one another. We may not always agree, and we don't need to, but we need to see and recognize the willingness that we ultimately have the same goal, and those elements to me show progress.

**CHRISTINE:  What more could reformers do to bring change?**

**SHIREEN:** We need to organize and be collective. As individuals, we have no collective voice and are not powerful enough. There needs to be a counter to groups like CAIR, and the American public needs to see this. The media ignores us, we don't get published. We get interviewed, but much of what we say does not get published, so we need a collective clout to be taken seriously and on a platform that is reaching people.

# PART TWO

## CHAPTER NINE

# ISLAM AND ISLAMISM
*Identifying the Enemy*

Erdogan is peaceful in his means along the adage you can't get people with vinegar but with honey. It's an evangelical Islamic thing. Islamists don't want to acknowledge that al Qaeda is a natural offshoot of their ideology.

—DR. ZUHDI JASSER

Essentially their [al Qaeda and the Muslim Brotherhood] goals are the same to establish Sharia but their methods differ. One is a civilized veneer; the other is a crude one.

—RAHEEL RAZA

Islamists are like the wolf in sheep's clothing where they appear to be part of the democratic political structure but they are not. They use diplomacy and diplomatic ties to achieve the same ends. They have legal grounds to manipulate people where the more aggressive Jihadists use religious grounds but they are the same.

—SHIREEN QUDOSI

ACCORDING TO THE DISTINGUISHED ISLAMIC SCHOLAR, Dr. Daniel Pipes, "Islamism is an ideology that demands man's complete adherence to the sacred [written] law of Islam and rejects as much as possible outside influence, with some exceptions (such as access to military and medical technology). It is imbued with a deep antagonism towards non-Muslims and has a particular hostility towards the West. It amounts to an effort to turn Islam, a religion and civilization, into an ideology."[1]

Dr. Pipes's words were written prior to 9/11. The term "Islamism" can be likened to other isms, such as fascism, socialism, and Marxism. It is a political ideology similar to Marxism, as it consists of a "radical utopian scheme" and aims to control powers over the state and every element of society.[2]

## CALLING ISLAM THE PROBLEM: THE KILLING OF A PROFESSOR

Many argue that there is no distinction between Islam and Islamism, that Islamic supremacy, violent and stealth Jihad, the ills apparent in Sharia states such as systemic misogyny, black slavery, child brides, the subjugation of non-Muslims or infidels, the murder of apostates, persecution of minorities, are all inherent in the religion of Islam.

One of the foremost proponents of this argument is Dr. Wafa Sultan, a Syrian-born psychiatrist and co-founder of the American human rights group Former Muslims United (FMU). Sultan states that her life changed in 1979 when she was a medical student at the University of Aleppo, in northern Syria.[3] At that time, the Muslim Brotherhood was using terrorism to try to undermine the government of President Hafez al-Assad.[4] She witnessed firsthand Muslim Brotherhood gunmen bursting into a classroom at the university and killing her professor as they shouted, "Allah is Great!"[5] This was a turning point in her life that caused her to abandon the religion altogether in search of "another God."[6]

Sultan's current focus, and that of Former Muslims United, is to educate the public about the threats posed to civil, political, and human rights under Islamic Sharia law, which she warns is being forced upon non-Muslim majority countries and poses a dire threat to Western civilization.[7] Her mission is to preserve democratic and open societies in the West, and she has earned considerable influence. In 2006, *TIME* magazine voted Sultan among the world's 100 most influential people.[8]

"I believe our people are hostages to our own beliefs and teachings....Only the Muslims defend their beliefs by burning down churches, killing people, and destroying embassies. This path will not yield any results. The Muslims must ask themselves what they can do for humankind, before they demand that humankind respect them."[9]

Her writings expose her to millions of devout Muslims in the Arab world and beyond, and she reports receiving daily death threats. She was also forced into hiding in 2009 before the release of her book, *A God Who Hates: The Courageous Woman Who Inflamed the Muslim World Speaks Out Against the Evils of Islam.*[10]

In October 2010, Sultan was called as an expert witness to give testimony at the Geert Wilders trial. Wilders faced five counts of hate speech and discrimination for public remarks he allegedly made between 2006 and 2008 that were considered insulting to religious and ethnic groups and were also in his controversial short film, *Fitna.*[11] Sultan testified about meeting Wilders, seeing his film, *Fitna*, and agreeing with his views about Islam.[12] The treatment of Sultan and Wilders by Islamists further supports their position that Islam is not a religion of peace currently, even though there are peaceful Muslims, and this notion is exemplified in an excerpt from a speech delivered by Wilders:

"Like the specter of Communism in the past, the danger of Islam is political. Islam is mainly a political ideology because its aim is political. What the London and Boston killers, Boko Haram, al-Shabaab, the Muslim Brotherhood, Hamas, Hezbollah, al Qaeda, and other individuals and groups, causing pain and misery all over the globe, have in common is that, inspired by the Koran, they want to impose Islamic Sharia law on the whole world."[13]

The works of Sultan and Wilders are compelling and invaluable in educating Westerners about the Islamist threat. It is futile to assert that there are no texts in the Koran that support the violence and hatred about which Sultan and Wilders warn the West, but there are Muslims, as interviewed in Part One, who do not subscribe to the literal understanding of such texts. They denounce the notion of a political Islam, and instead choose to embrace what they see as the spiritual message and peaceful inspiration of the Koran, found mostly in the earlier parts of the Muslim holy book, while Muhammad was in Mecca.

When I interviewed Wilders about moderate Muslims in May

2011, he acknowledged peaceful Muslims and made a key distinction between the Muslim individual and the ideologies of Islam. "The more moderates the better," he said, and "we should support them in any way possible."[14] He also made the point that the Koran regards such Muslims as apostates worthy of death, yet maintained that if they see themselves as Muslims, we must support them.

Wilders does not believe that Islam can be changed, but he noted that people can change. This notion is key in garnering support for reform. As revealed in Part One, moderates have various explanations for the problematic texts in the Koran, ranging from consigning particular verses to a specific context or era, to asserting that violent interpretations are incorrect, and even to discarding the belief that Muhammad was the perfect model for emulation, but an inspired yet imperfect human being; yet common to all was that Islamic adherents need to abandon the literal interpretation and practice of difficult texts that are better left in the seventh century.

## THE PLURALISM OF ISLAM

Reformer Dr. Subhy Mansour, founder of the Koranist sect, teaches that a Koran-based Islam has two meanings: "One is the innermost belief in and interacting with Almighty God,"[15] and the other is "peace in dealing and interacting with others.[16] He affirms the belief of reformists in "separation of church and state" and states "human rights slogans should be adopted," as should the principles of "justice for all, freedom for all, and equality among and for all."[17] Mansour rejects the Sunnah and the Hadiths, and asserts that mainstream Koranic interpretations have been, and continue to be, distorted by Wahhabists.

The Koranist sect and those Muslims who advocate peace make the personal choice to practice their faith in private, contrary to Muslims who espouse political Islam or Islamism, hence the necessity of separating the terms Islam from Islamism. It is erroneous to brand all of the world's 1.6 billion Muslims as enemies to our democracy.

As Dr. Zuhdi Jasser stated, "Normative Islam is what comes out of Al-Azhar University and Saudi schools, which is the majority of what is being taught. It needs tons of reform as it involves being anti-women, cutting of limbs, killing people that leave Islam, oppression of minorities, etc." Given that normative Islam *is* Islamism, the solution is Islamic reform in which Muslims practice their faith personally and privately however they deem fit, and question it or even leave it, without risking death threats from Islamists and verbal opposition by non-Muslims, judging whether or not they are Muslims at all.

## STEALTH ISLAMISTS BENEFIT FROM NOT SEPARATING ISLAM FROM ISLAMISM

Failing to make a distinction between Islam and Islamism is an advantage to stealth Islamists of the Muslim Brotherhood, as it abets their efforts to conceal and disguise their identity and ambitions. In Canada, a handbook entitled "United Against Terrorism," putatively aimed at preventing youth radicalization, was released at a mosque in Winnipeg, Manitoba.[18] It was completed in consultation with the National Council of Canadian Muslims (NCCM), formerly CAIR-CAN—now conveniently renamed—which has connections to terrorists organizations, since CAIR-CAN is the Canadian branch of CAIR (Council on American–Islamic Relations), which was designated an "unindicted co-conspirator" in the Holy Land Foundation Trial, the largest terrorist financing trial in US history.[19] The handbook recommended avoiding the use of important identifying words like "Jihad," "terrorism," and "moderate" to describe Muslims, stating that "we never hear the term 'moderate Christians' or 'moderate Jews' or 'moderate atheists.' Why is this adjective then attached so frequently to the word 'Muslim?'"[20]

As established in the interviews in Part One, there is an important distinction between moderates and Islamists; the latter term also includes crypto-moderates, since they are the most deceptive among Islamists. It is imperative that Westerners grasp such distinctions, given the strategy of Islamists to remain untracked and undetected in order to pursue their quest for dominion over Western constitutions. As Sheikh Subhy Mansour stated earlier, "Salafists are like untamed animals, saying what's in their hearts, but the Muslim Brotherhood is very cunning, intelligent, and they know what to say and what to conceal, but they have the same ideas of the Salafis."[21]

## WESTERNERS AND THE ISLAMIST AGENDA

The Obama administration adopted a policy of not separating Islam from Islamism by refusing to acknowledge any relationship between violent Jihad and Islam and avoiding the use of terms like "Islamist" and "Jihadist," reasoning, "Islamic terrorists are simply extremists."[22] In 2009, the White House ordered a removal of any training materials that "Islamic groups" deemed offensive. According to the *Washington Times*, "some analysts are asking whether the 2009 edict and others that followed have dampened law enforcement's appetite to thoroughly investigate terrorism suspects for fear of offending higher-ups or the American Muslim lobby."[23] Political correctness, and the fear of being branded racist or Islamophobic, has enabled the Islamist agenda by providing Islamists with the ability to operate covertly while publicly invoking grievances of history, such as colonialism and the Crusades.

The Islamist agenda is also strengthened by the fear, panic, and chaos that erupts after a fateful terrorist strike, such as the *Charlie Hebdo* attacks on January 7, 2015, in Paris, France, over the publication of cartoons insulting to Muhammad and Islam.[24] Two masked gunmen armed with assault rifles burst into the offices of the French satirical weekly newspaper and went on a shooting spree, killing 11 people and injuring others while shouting "Allahu Akbar."[25] Two police officers were also killed. Several other related terrorist outbreaks followed in the next two days. By the end of the rampage, 17 people were murdered by Islamic terrorists and 22 others injured, some critically. Al Qaeda in the Arabian Peninsula claimed responsibility.[26] The terror continued, with Islamist cyber attacks on France and outbreaks in Pakistan, where police authorities and crowds clashed in a nationwide rally against the Muhammad images featured in *Charlie Hebdo*.[27] The protest was called by Jamaat-e-Islami, the country's largest Islamist party.[28]

This barbaric ideology that encourages the murder of all who insult Muhammad too often escapes being subjected to scrutiny in the public square. Instead, mass media reports often dilute the issue out of fear for their safety or of being branded racist, and thus the Islamist goal of subjugating the West is concealed and protected. In the case of the *Charlie Hebdo* massacre, the predictable narratives followed.

**I. Diverting attention away from Islamists.** There has been an insistence that the *Charlie Hebdo* massacre was an issue of the sacred right to free speech, with little mention as to who is threatening this fundamental freedom and how we go about fixing the problem. Fox News's Bill O'Reilly was one of the few who did mention the perpetrators, delivering an important commentary following the *Charlie Hebdo* killings. He stated, "There is no question it's another terror attack by Muslim fanatics who are waging war against nearly everybody. Every country on earth is being impacted by the Jihad. Yet we still will not admit the truth about this ongoing war."[29] O'Reilly criticized President Obama's statement: "One thing I am very confident about is the values that we share with the French people: a universal belief in the freedom of expression is something that can't be silenced because of the senseless violence of a few."[30] O'Reilly accurately pointed out that it isn't "just the few," but that the "Jihadists have strongholds in at least a dozen countries" and "have killed thousands of American military people [and] tens of thousands of civilians."[31]

**II. It is Israel's fault, the victims' fault, or the West's.** The typical narrative in this scenario is that we should not provoke terrorists; that it is immoral to make fun of another's sacred deity. Russia's Council of Muftis stated, "Attacks may be unavoidable unless satirists stop 'provoking' the faithful."[32] There are conspiracy theorists who have implicated Israel, such as former President Jimmy Carter, who blamed Muslim anger festering over the Palestinian–Israeli conflict.[33] US Green Party politician Jack Lindblad, a member of the Los Angeles County Council, claimed that the killings were by "US and Mossad to keep Israel's Netanyahu in power."[34] Turkish President Recep Tayyip Erdogan accused Israel of orchestrating the attacks and blamed the West for "playing games with the Islamic world," warning fellow Muslims to be "aware."[35]

**III. Denial: claiming that the fanatics that did this atrocity were not practicing Islam at all, and within every group there are fanatics.** A report in *The Economist* exculpated, if not denied outright, the reality of Jihadi war, stating, "If there is a common thread among those who become Jihadists, it seems to be the quest to transform small, angry lives into powerful ones."[36] French President François Hollande said, "Those who committed these acts, these fanatics, have nothing to do with the Muslim faith,"[37] while France's Prime Minister Manuel Valls identified and targeted the problem cogently in stating, "France is at war against terrorism, Jihadism, and radical Islamism…. France is not at war against a religion. France is not at war against Islam and the Muslims."[38]

## THE PROLIFERATION OF ISLAMISM

Islamism is so pervasive and global it can no longer be ignored. But the primitive and rigid nature of Islamist theology is a perversion of an ancient pluralistic faith. The majority of Muslims in the twenty-first century are living in increasingly globalized environments where information technology has proliferated across national and cultural boundaries, allowing more personal choice and expression. As Dr. Daniel Pipes has indicated, "you can take what you want out of the Koran."[39]

Dr. Pipes also states that those who focus on the Islamic faith as the problem, such as Wafa Sultan, whom he has debated publicly, reach the conclusion that a moderate form of Islam is impossible; they point to Muhammad's life and contents of the Koran to establish the existence of Islamic Jihad, Muslim supremacism, and misogyny.[40] Yet as mentioned in the Introduction, Ayaan Hirsi Ali, who has often denied the possibility of a moderate Islam, stated in her speech "Here is What I Would Have Said at Brandeis," after Brandeis University revoked its invitation to her to receive an honorary degree at its commencement ceremonies following protests by students, faculty, and outside groups: "Both Christianity and Judaism have had their eras of reform. I would argue that the time has come for a Muslim Reformation."[41] Ali subsequently followed up by writing a book, *Heretic*, in which she argues "ordinary Muslims are ready for change," a significant modification from her earlier stance that "the best thing for religious believers in Islam to do was to pick another faith."[42] In *Heretic*, Ali uses the metaphor of a house to illustrate how Islam can be reformed. She calls for a "gut renovation" that would result in making "the outside look a lot like the original, but changes the house radically from the inside, equipping it with the latest amenities,"[43] a complex task indeed of which Ali encourages a religious revolution.[44]

While Dr. Pipes acknowledges that Islamists follow the Koran and Hadith literally, he asserts that moderate Muslims who provide a modernized vision of Islam lack the Islamists' near-hegemonic power.[45] As a historian, he further asserts that Islam is a fourteenth-century-old faith of more than a billion believers that includes everyone from quietist Sufis to violent Jihadis.[46] He goes on to detail Islam's historic achievements and notes the point at which a "dissonance" entered into the equation, resulting in the development of a virulent form of Islamism:

> "Muslims achieved remarkable military, economic, and cultural success between roughly 600 and 1200 CE. Being a Muslim then meant belonging to a winning team, a fact that broadly inspired Muslims to associate their faith with mundane success. Those memories of medieval glory remain not just alive but central to believers' confidence in Islam and in themselves as Muslims."[47]

The idea that "being a Muslim then meant belonging to a winning team" is also founded upon the Koran itself, which tells believers: "Whoever does righteousness, whether male or female, while he is a believer—We will surely cause him to live a good life, and We will surely give them their reward [in the Hereafter] according to the best of what they used to do" (16:97)[48] and "And as for those who disbelieved, I will punish them with a severe punishment in this world and the Hereafter, and they will have no helpers" (3:56).[49] Thus the righteous will live "a good life" while the unrighteous will be punished "in this world." In other words, piety is fully equated with worldly success.

Pipes continues:

> "Major dissonance began around 1800, when Muslims unexpectedly lost wars, markets, and cultural leadership to Western Europeans. It continues today, as Muslims bunch toward the bottom of nearly every index of achievement. This shift has caused massive confusion and anger. What went wrong, why did God seemingly abandon His faithful? The unbearable divergence between pre-modern accomplishment and modern failure brought about trauma."[50]

When George W. Bush declared the War on Terror, this raised the question: at war with whom?[51] Jonathan Schanzer, a Middle East scholar and vice president of research at the Foundation for Defense of Democracies, answered unequivocally that we are not at a war with Islam because there are too many sects, offshoots, and branches of Islam among the world's most recent count of 1.6 billion Muslims.[52] While Schanzer acknowledges that the 9/11 hijackers were all Muslims, that the FBI's most wanted terrorists are Muslims, that almost all groups and individuals listed in President Bush's executive order blocking terrorist funds were Muslims, he still insists that the free world is not at war with Islam, but rather at war with a militant Islam that is a minority outgrowth of the faith, characterized by a bitter hatred for Western values of individualism and capitalism, and seeks to replace these values with a strict interpretation of the Koran and Sharia law.[53]

## ISLAMIST DECEPTIONS: BEWARE

Modernized Islamist movements are frequently called "moderate" movements, which is both a misnomer and misleading. Such movements are comprised of crypto-moderates and are deceptively invisible to the average Westerner, as they appear democratic but are in fact Islamist. They claim to renounce violence and advance their goals politically through a public show of ardent support for democracy. They are sophisticated enough to realize that they cannot be politically successful through a brazen advancement of Sharia law, nor through their silence about the crude methods displayed by their co-religionists, such as the Islamic State of Iraq and Syria. They posture publicly, gain media coverage, and the naïve Western population assumes that their motives are sincere.

Nearly a hundred Edmonton Muslims came to the Alberta, Canada, legislature to offer prayers for the victims and their families of terrorist attacks that took place in Ottawa and Quebec in the space of a week in October 2014. It was an emotional event, organized by the Muslim Association of Canada, and an open declaration of solidarity with Canada.[54] Imam Bassam Fares said, "When these types of attacks happen, we all, as Canadians, stand against them....We want to offer our condolences and show our solidarity with these families."[55] While it is impolitic to question the sincerity of his language, it is necessary, as

Fares is an Executive Director with the Muslim Association of Canada (MAC), one of the only Muslim organizations in the world that openly admits roots and ties to the Muslim Brotherhood and to Hamas.[56]

The motives behind these public pro-democracy displays and solidarity with Westerners are rarely questioned. The Muslim Brotherhood has managed to gain huge inroads globally, including on our continent. Its plans and strategies for the West include avoiding open alliances with known terrorist organizations, in order to maintain the appearance of being moderate, and using deception to mask their goals.[57] Their existing networks on North American soil will be further examined in the chapter, "Who Speaks for Muslims?"

The Muslim Brotherhood exists in more than 70 nations in the world. Its founder was an Egyptian named Hassan al-Banna, who wanted to create an ideal government, based on Islamic law and society of the seventh century.[58] As revealed by Sheikh Subhy Mansour in Part One, al-Banna was an agent of Saudi Arabia, who argued that before this ideal Islamist state could be achieved, the Muslim masses "would have to be gradually brought back to a fundamentalist Islam that was unpolluted by Western ideas."[59] Al-Banna's Muslim Brotherhood preached the seemingly harmless values that can be observed in any traditional Western family: self-help, generosity, family values, and restricting women to their traditional role in the home. The Brotherhood also provided hospitals, schools, and other services for the poor.[60] Al-Banna was a gifted visionary, and many of his democratic notions and goals have appealed to Westerners, yet the goal of the Muslim Brotherhood and al Qaeda remain fundamentally the same: the united objective of attaining a global caliphate.[61] Astute Western critics warn that when the Muslim Brotherhood gets enough power, it will become more radical.[62]

## ERDOGAN AND AL QAEDA: A MODEL IDEOLOGICAL INTERSECTION BETWEEN VIOLENT AND STEALTH ISLAMISTS

Many of the moderates interviewed in Part One stated that Islamists, both stealth and violent, hold Salafi and Wahhabi ideologies with the end goal of global conquest and Sharia law. It follows that the ideologies of Turkish President Recep Tayyip Erdogan, ISIS, and al Qaeda are one in the same, despite differences in methods. It is no secret that the state of Turkey has been a key funder of ISIS.[63] Turkey has tried to cover up its role by claiming that it is impossible to control its 566-mile border with Syria, while failing to explain its collaboration with ISIS at the highest regime levels.[64] On January 10, London's *The Guardian* newspaper ran an article: "Isis 'ran sophisticated immigration operation on Turkey–Syria border,'" which stated that passenger documents which were seized by Kurdish forces between December 2014 and March 2015 indicated a formalized relationship between Turkey and ISIS. Passengers were found to be carrying the stamps of ISIS's "department of immigration" and "department of transport;" and furthermore it was revealed that ISIS fighters freely moved back and forth through the Turkish–Syrian border areas.[65]

Turkey has offered easy border crossings, medical aid, funds, logistics, training, and arms to ISIS, according to eyewitnesses, journalists, and even CNN, which ran the clip "The Secret Jihadi Smuggling Route Through Turkey."[66]

The shared hatred of the West and Israel among violent and stealth Islamists manifests in spreading propaganda and hate to indoctrinate Muslim adherents. Returning to the *Charlie Hebdo* killings, and Erdogan's accusation that the West and Israel were behind the attacks and deliberately blamed Muslims, he also invoked the victimhood propaganda as he cited "racism, hate speech, and 'Islamophobia.'"[67]

Farid Benyettou, the former Imam and "recruiter of Jihadists," the man who is said to have helped radicalize the brothers Saïd and Chérif Kouachi, the *Charlie Hebdo* murderers, condemned the killings, stating that, "Whatever was done, whether it be the cowardly and monstrous murder of the journalists, or of the police and members of the Jewish community, it should not be attributed to Islam...if you are murderers then that's your business."[68] Yet Benyettou is a radical whom the brothers met at a mosque in northeast Paris; the "janitor-turned-preacher set up a pipeline for young French Muslims to join Abu Musab al-Zarqawi's al Qaeda network in Iraq."[69] While Benyettou defends Islam verbally, his actions support Islamic Jihad, while many Westerners echo his views that violent Jihad committed in the name of Islam should not be attributed to Islam. Never mind the *Charlie Hebdo* murders—consider the routine slaughter of apostates globally, the persecution of Christians by Islamists, the Darfur genocide, and Muslim-on-Muslim sectarian violence that has killed about 10 million people since 1948.[70]

## CONCLUSION: AN ENEMY NECESSITATES IDENTIFICATION

There is a turf war raging between seventh century Islam and a twenty-first century reformation. A modernized, peaceful, and private practice of Islam that is consistent with the Universal Declaration of Human Rights and is supported by a fledgling moderate and reformist movement needs to be fully supported. It is in the interests of Western powers to do so, especially in light of the fact that there have been historic movements for reform of Islam that were violently squelched by ruling Islamic despots and theocrats. Labeling of the vast, multiethnic, and multilingual Islamic world as a monoculture fails to recognize the plurality of the faith in how it is practiced. It is counterproductive to antagonize the world's 1.6 billion Muslims by labeling them enemies to the West due to their faith. It is how Muslims choose to practice their faith that determines their status as Muslim friends or Islamist antagonists. Failing to separate and identify Islamists blurs the focus of the West and allows them to operate covertly in their quest to establish global Sharia.

## CHAPTER TEN

# MODERATES AND REFORMISTS

Islam is being reformed. Who is making the reformation? No
single individual. It is a cycle process, a historical process. There
will be casualties. America was founded upon the Republican
principle that men were created equal, and they had to fight a
civil war and they had to fight a civil rights movement in our
lifetime. Nothing is static because the process of reaching one's
fullness is a struggle that goes on.

—Dr. Salim Mansur

A litmus test for being a moderate is acceptance of another
opinion without labeling them an apostate, a kafir, and such
terms. Criticism is the opening of that watershed that will lead
to the real change to take place.

—Dr. Jalal Zuberi

The terms "moderate" and "reformist" have different connotations depending on who is using them. For this reason, it is essential to
define them and be able to recognize the ways in which these words
are commonly used, including the ways that Islamists use them in order
to confuse Westerners. As a summation of the collective viewpoints of
those interviewed in Part One of this book, reformists seek a full reinterpretation of Koranic verses to be consistent with modernity, whereas
moderates ignore problematic verses, deeming them to be antiquated
or limited to particular contexts, and so live in accordance with the
peaceful texts, mostly contained within the teachings of Muhammad in
Mecca before his flight to Medina; the latter can be viewed as Meccan

moderates. Dr. Qanta Ahmed stated in her interview: "I don't consider myself a reformer as I don't see what there needs to be reformed in Islam. But I am a moderate."

This chapter explains the various usages of the terms "moderates" and "reformists."

## WHAT KIND OF REFORM?

There are Islamist movements today that seek a kind of puritanical "reform" in the opposite direction of that of modernization. Such movements strive to pull Muslims back to the seventh-century teachings of the Koran, in accord with Wahhabism, a form of Sunni Islam practiced in Saudi Arabia and Qatar that has spread globally, with petrodollars.[1]

Wahhabism was named after Muhammad ibn Abd al-Wahhab, who led a religious movement in the 1700s to restore the purity of Islam in Arabia, considered the Muslim holy land where Muhammad lived and died. Wahhab believed in the strict, literal interpretation of the Koran, and joined with the Saudi family of Arabia to violently suppress all Arab Muslims who resisted him.[2] After two centuries of conflict, the Saudis and their Wahhabi allies established the Kingdom of Saudi Arabia in 1932, with the Saudi royal family handing over all religious governance to Wahhabi clergy.[3] Today Saudi Arabia has no elected government and has little regard for human rights. The hands of thieves are cut off, and floggings, stonings, beheadings, and eye-gougings are still practiced in accordance with Wahhabism, which strictly opposes any variations in the fundamentalist definitions of Islamic religious practices.[4]

Another puritanical "reformist" movement is Salafism, which is not formally unified, but appeals to a large number of Muslims who seek a conservative religious renewal to resist modernity. The term is often used interchangeably with Wahhabism, but Wahhabism is a more specific reference to the version of Islam practiced within and energetically propagated by Saudi Arabia. All Wahhabis are Salafis, but not all Salafis are Wahhabis. Salafis generally believe that the Koran and the Hadiths are the ultimate religious authority in Islam.[5]

Here is a list of some of today's prominent and revered Islamist leaders who push puritanical reform and calls to Jihad:

Egyptian Islamic theologian and Muslim Brotherhood leader Dr. Yusuf al-Qaradawi, who is one of the most influential Islamic clerics in the world:

"If you believe that Muhammad is the messenger of Allah, then you must obey him—for he does not command except that which is good. So, even if he tells you to kill, you must...let the people be satisfied with the Truth [Sharia teachings], not the false."[6]

The Taliban's supreme leader, Mullah Mohammed Omar:

"The plan [to destroy America] is going ahead and God willing it is being implemented, but it is a huge task beyond the will and comprehension of human beings. If God's help is with us, this will happen within a short period of time."[7]

Palestinian Mufti Sheikh Ikrima Sabri said in a radio sermon broadcast in 1997:

"Oh Allah, destroy America, her agents, and her allies! Cast them into their own traps, and cover the White House with black!"[8]

Iran's religious leader, Ayatollah Ali Khamenei, in 1998:

"The American regime is the enemy of [Iran's] Islamic government and our revolution....It is the enemy of your revolution, your Islam, and your resistance to American bullying."[9]

Hezbollah leader Hassan Nasrallah, in 2005:

"How can death become joyous? How can death become happiness? When Al-Hussein asked his nephew Al-Qassem, when he had not yet reached puberty: 'How do you like the taste of death, son?' He answered that it was sweeter than honey. How can the foul taste of death become sweeter than honey? Only through conviction, ideology, and faith, through belief, and devotion.

"We do not want to...leave our homeland to Israel....Therefore, we are not interested in our own personal security. On the contrary, each of us lives his days and nights hoping more than anything to be killed for the sake of Allah."[10]

Despite Islamist calls to Jihad and an urge for puritanical reform by prominent Salafists in the name of Islam, it is an erroneous assumption that these radical elements represent the majority of the world's Muslims, as many do not follow the Salafist doctrine. Muslim moderates and reformers believe that the answer is to be found in working with anti-Islamist Muslims to modernize Islam.[11] Take, for example, the book *Reforming Islam: Progressive Voices from the Arab Muslim World*, a compilation of viewpoints of Arab Muslim intellectual voices taken from the website Almuslih. Collectively, they challenge the strident voices of Islamism as they make the case for Muslim reform. They call for an urgent "intellectual rehabilitation" of a "Bedouin culture that is fundamentally xenophobic." Jordanian-Arab scholar Shaker al-Nabulsi further notes that the Koran has been distorted by Arab scholars to reflect an Arab bravado in which the literalism of the text is the central axis, thus rendering human intellect, ethical judgments, and experience meaningless or inferior to the text, while marginalizing discourse and spawning a culture of violence and backwardness. The authors posit that Islamic heritage is accountable for the psychological problems of contemporary Arabs, which include a "predilection for the absolute," suspicions about external conspiracies, and the "exoneration of Muslims of any criminality." They conclude that any attempt at reforming Islam "requires a process of de-sanctification," and they demonstrate the inability of the tyrannical sentinels of Islamism to stifle truth and progress.[12]

## MODERATES, CRYPTO-MODERATES, AND REFORMERS: WHO'S WHO?

It is imperative to clarify nuances between a moderate, a crypto-moderate, and a reformist. Militant groups like the Taliban, al Qaeda, and the Islamic State of Iraq and Syria (ISIS) are overtly Islamist, but their stealth Jihadist counterparts, who advance similar ideologies of political Islam or Sharia and conquest, are routinely and incorrectly referred to as "moderate" in Western news reports and discourse. Stealth

Islamists have finessed their presentation and can appear thoroughly Westernized, which makes them more dangerous, as they are routinely accepted by mainstream society as moderate Muslims.

According to William Kilpatrick, author of *Christianity, Islam and Atheism*, stealth Jihad is much more difficult to detect and resist than armed Jihad, and the army is not trained to engage with it. He gives the example of Major Stephen Coughlin, who was the US military's top expert on Islamic law until he made the "mistake" of stating, "Islamic law obliges Muslims to wage Jihad."[13] Coughlin was subsequently fired from his position. Kilpatrick says that the official attitude was captured by an admiral who, upon hearing Coughlin's appraisal of the incident, replied that he would first have to check with his imam on that.[14] This attitude has become commonplace with Westerners who are timorous of potentially offending stealth Islamists, deemed moderate Muslims, even if that offense arises simply from telling difficult truths. Kilpatrick adds that similarly, a manual for US troops in Afghanistan directed troops to avoid "any criticism of pedophilia," or of "anything related to Islam."[15] Genuine moderates have no problem with criticism of Islam and pluralistic viewpoints that they may disagree with.

Political correctness strips Westerners of their rights to free speech, particularly the right even to question Islam in the face of pressure coming from Islamist leaders in the Muslim community who are accepted as "moderates," but who are in reality crypto-moderates. Mass media have been tricked by these crypto-moderate leaders, who swiftly and intentionally brand Westerners as racists and "Islamophobes." Imam Syed Soharwardy, founder of the Islamic Supreme Council of Canada (ISCC), is known for his pacifist sermons. He has called the Islamic State of Syria and Iraq (ISIS) un-Islamic, and warned that ISIS was actively recruiting in Canada, claiming also that one member issued him a death threat.[16] This earned him much popularity among mainstream Canadian citizens for appearing to stand up for democratic values. Soharwardy began a 48-hour hunger strike to raise awareness about the danger of ISIS and pay homage to American journalist James Foley, who was beheaded by ISIS captors.[17] Imam Soharwardy then led 38 imams to sign a formal edict (fatwa) against Canadian recruitment by ISIS. The six-page document mentioned the human rights brutalities by ISIS, which included mutilations and civilian murders, of which Soharwardy referred to as "violations of Islamic jurisprudence, teachings of the holy Koran, and teachings of the holy prophet."[18]

Since most Westerners take altruistic gestures as genuine, and are unfamiliar with the stealth Islamist mindset, it renders them more susceptible to strategies of deception. On further investigation, Soharwardy has a history that should call into question his reputation as a moderate. He once dragged outspoken human rights lawyer Ezra Levant to the Alberta Human Rights Commission for republishing the notorious Danish cartoons of Muhammad, which were deemed insulting to Muhammad, thus contesting the Western right to free speech.[19] Soharwardy eventually dropped his complaint to the Commission and admitted, "Over the two years that we have gone through the process, I understand that most Canadians see this as an issue of freedom of speech, that that principle is sacred and holy in our society." Levant, however, did not take Soharwardy's self-correction as sincere, accusing Soharwardy of chickening out of an unexpected battle and calling his values "out of sync" with those of Canada.[20]

Soharwardy then argued in an email to the *Calgary Herald* that Levant was portraying him as a "hate-mongering, anti-Semitic, Wahhabi radical who wants to see Canada governed under Sharia law. Nothing could be further from the truth."[21] Soharwardy outed himself when he stated, "Presently, what Israeli forces are doing to Palestinians is worse than the Holocaust of World War II."[22] Canwest's library system showed that Soharwardy wrote in a column "Sharia cannot be customized for specific countries. These universal, divine laws are for all people of all countries for all times."[23] Soharwardy also boasts that he is one of the founding members of the Islamic Institute of Civil Justice, and "the mandate of the institute is to resolve disputes within existing Canadian laws by using the principles of conflict resolution from Islamic Law, or Sharia."[24]

Soharwardy's case is not isolated, and it exposes the duplicity of crypto-moderates who disguise their real agenda. They openly condemn their fellow violent co-religionists to win public confidence, while plotting global Sharia dominance. The strategies employed in service of this agenda, and the persistence and patience in their execution, will be addressed in the chapter, "Who Speaks for Muslims?"

Just like the term "moderate," the word "reform," as referred to at the start of this chapter, does not have a universal definition, but can also refer to ultra-conservative, puritanical "reform." In recognition of the Wahhabi use of the term "reform," Stephen Schwartz, a convert to Islam and the founder of the Center for Islamic Pluralism (CIP), stipulated:

"CIP supports social reform in Islamic countries, but most of us do not use the idiom of 'religious reform.' There is an important reason for this: Although it is counterintuitive to non-Muslims, the radicals—and I mean the very worst radicals, like al Qaeda and the Taliban—have appropriated the terms 'Islamic reform,' 'reform of Islam,' and 'Islamic reformation' to identify themselves. They especially oppose spiritual Sufi and Shia Islam for practices they say are 'backward,' like praying at tombs, and they claim to be 'reforming the religion by returning to its roots,' i.e., through a fantasy of Islamic purity in the early Muslim period.

"Most of us in CIP therefore refer to ourselves as moderate, traditional, conventional Muslim believers who do not see any need for changes in the religion per se, but for changes in the way the religion is interpreted as applying to people's lives. One argument for the lack of a need to change the religion itself is that radical Islam as we know it is new; Wahhabism is only 250 years old, Khomenism has been in power for 30 years, the Muslim Brotherhood only 83 years old, and the Taliban only 15 years old. Radical Islam is an expression of a distorted attempt to create a 'cleansed,' simplified, and ideological Islam for the needs of modern people who do not have time to dedicate to the serious study of the religion that was upheld by the traditionalists. The fact that we are mainly Sufis reflects in this position.

"Daniel Pipes pointed out to me that when he was studying Islam in Egypt in the 1970s it was taken for granted that Islam was modernizing; few non-Muslims grasped that the modernization would be diverted into neo-fundamentalism, as it was after the Khomeini revolution.

"Most ordinary Muslims around the world associate the idea of 'reforming Islam' with radicalism, extremism, and violent 'purification.'"[25]

While Schwartz highlights important facts and adheres to the view that Islam does not need reform, other moderates do state that Islam needs a kind of reform that is rooted in Islamic traditions, but also consistent with human rights and equality. In their book, *Reforming Islam*, Stephen Ulph and Patrick Sookhdeo focus upon numerous Muslim reformists who challenge the strident language of Islamism. Their collection of translated essays demonstrates the inability of the tyrannical sentinels of Islamism to stifle truth and progress, and serves as a reference guide to the work of Muslims who aim to "establish and legitimize the discussion of Islamist political agitation and militant violence as manifestations of a religiously defined problem with modernity" that has serious repercussions for the future of Western civilization.[26]

Despite Schwartz's reluctance to use the word "reform," he has acknowledged the possibility of a modernized reform in his writings: "Reformation movements have always had two alternative paths they may follow: the fundamentalist purge or the adaptation to the passage of history[27].... I do not call for reform of our religion, but for restoration of pluralism. Once pluralism and debate are restored, with the end of the Wahhabi monopoly in the Haramain, we can discuss the legitimacy of reform and of issues that may need new interpretations. But first we must re-establish pluralism."[28]

Prominent Egyptian reformer and author Tarek Heggy argues that pluralism is the prerequisite for reform. He states that "there can be no progress for peoples who do not believe in pluralism or who fail to construct their culture and general climate upon the acceptance of what pluralism achieves."[29]

While many Muslims reject the term "moderate" and/or "reformist" as used in this book, it is their right to hash these terms out among themselves. But it is imperative that Westerners have identifiable benchmarks to enable them to differentiate between an Islamist, a moderate, and a reformist. When clearly defined, such terms head off quarrels over semantics that distort the Islamist problem and distract Westerners from focusing on targeting and stemming Islamism.

## IRSHAD MANJI'S FEATURED PROBLEM WITH THE WORD "MODERATE"

Renowned Canadian reformist, author, and educator Irshad Manji illustrates an important perspective of debate within the Muslim community on the identity of reformists and moderates. In her book, *Allah, Liberty and Love*, Manji embraces and advances a pluralistic approach among fellow Muslims that encourages unbridled freedom of expression without fear of offending others in a "multicultural world."[30] Manji also struggles with the term "moderate," and believes that a truly modernized Muslim can only be a reformist. She asks the question: "How can each of us embark on a personal journey towards moral courage, the willingness to speak up when everyone else wants to shut you up?"[31] She rebukes "moderate" Muslims as being part of the problem for not advocating reform, stating that Muslims must reinterpret the troubling passages of their scriptures "just as Christians and Jews" have done. She rails against the widespread fear that Muslims have of speaking out, and condemns the tolerance of what she refers to as intolerable customs like female genital mutilation, honor killings, and stonings, decrying moderates for putting "awkward Koranic verses in context."[32] Manji refers disparagingly to well-known writer and renowned Swiss–French academic Tariq Ramadan, who is often referred to as a "moderate," to highlight her disdain for the term.[33]

Manji describes a British documentary in which Ramadan discusses a Koranic verse that is frequently pointed out as proof that Islam is a religion of hate:[34] "Fight and slay the pagans wherever you find them, and seize them and beleaguer them (Sura 9:5)."[35] In the documentary, Ramadan asserts that passages like these should not be taken out of context, but refer to a situation leading up to battle that was a threat to the survival of the first Muslim community. Therefore, given this existential threat, he argues that this passage cannot be viewed as admonishing Muslims to kill all non-Muslims in any era.[36]

This is where Manji asks a valid question: How does this line of reasoning differ from that of terrorists? She cites Ahmed Nasser in Yemen, who told her that wars of Western imperialism have victimized the twenty-first-century Ummah, which is why he has committed himself to protect Muslims everywhere, and she states that he was obeying the verse to "fight those who fight you in the path of Allah."[37] Manji further asserts that such a verse could be and should be reinterpreted and reformed. She also notes that more Muslims are being tortured, killed, imprisoned, and maimed by fellow Muslims than by anyone else, so that in order to "fight those who fight you in the path of Allah," she says that Muslims would have to "repel the colonizing schemes of fellow Muslims" by "anti-imperialist Jihadis."[38]

Manji likewise underscores another Koranic verse that is regularly cited to prove that the Koran displays value for human life: Sura 5:32, which states, "Whoever kills a human being, it is as if he has killed all mankind."[39] According to Manji, this frequently quoted passage is incomplete, and the rest is being concealed. The complete passage states, "Whoever kills a human being, except as punishment for murder or other villainy in the land, shall be regarded as having killed all mankind."[40] For the London Jihadis, Manji explains that "villainy in the land" describes US soldiers on Iraqi soil. She warns that this Koranic verse gives Jihadis their justification to kill.[41]

In continuing this debate, Irshad Manji reveals her own inner struggle with moderates. She states in *Allah, Liberty and Love* that there will always be suspicions about reform-minded Muslims, which leads them to question themselves, even to the point of asking, "Is there something wrong with me?"[42] Manji looks to the inspiration of Martin Luther King Jr., to whom she refers to as a "reformer." She states that even before he faced off against white segregationists, King had to battle against the "abrasive prejudices" of his own father, as "daddy tried to prevent his son from joining a new interracial council of students from Atlanta's white and Negro colleges, arguing that King should stay among his own and not risk betrayals from the white students." Manji points out King's biggest decision, which now faces modern-day reformists, was that he had to choose "between his father and his conscience."[43] In Manji's view, Islam does not need more "moderates," but more self-conscious "reformists."[44] She concludes that it is reformists who will bring to Islam the "debate, dissent, and reinterpretation that have carried Judaism and Christianity into the modern world."[45]

As a formidable reformer, Manji makes a cogent case for her definition of reform, but an important lesson comes from her usage of the terms "reform," which she correctly identifies as reinterpretations of Koranic texts, and "moderate," which she uses to include stealth Islamist apologists. Why refer to the latter as "moderate" at all? They are crypto-moderates and should be defined as such. As Schwartz explained, many moderates "do not see any need for changes in the religion per se, but for changes in the way the religion is interpreted as applying to people's lives." Such moderates should not be lumped with the crypto-moderates, as they genuinely seek change in the direction of modernity, while rejecting all aspects of the Sharia. Despite the moderate's resistance to altering Koranic texts, they have adapted their personal practice of the religion from the traditionalism and puritanism of the seventh century to modernity, compatible with Western constitutional law and the UN Declaration of Human Rights.

A guideline to differentiating a genuine moderate from a crypto-moderate is one's attitude toward pluralism, which is foundational, as pluralist Muslims are focused on peace with the world around them and diversity of thought, as opposed to the rigidity of Wahhabism, Salafism, and the promotion of political Islam.

## A SYMBIOTIC RELATIONSHIP

When Dr. Tawfik Hamid was asked whether he believed that moderates were important players in the reformist movement, he replied that moderates and reformists share a symbiotic relationship, and that moderates "are extremely important because the reformers provide the theory but the moderates are the ones who show others that the theory could be practiced and can be followed also. They are the role models for others. It's like a crystallization phenomenon. You have the reformers at the theoretical level, and then you have the moderates who join the rest of the people to follow the movement. Without the moderates to follow, there will be a big gap."

Dr. Hamid states that one of his goals as a reformist is to provide a modern interpretation of the Koran—which he has indeed written and published—in order to diminish the level of hatred and violence that derives from traditional interpretations of the Koranic text.[46] He has also pushed for the revival of ijtihad, an important historic concept that was practiced by Muhammad and other leaders in early Islam whenever difficult questions arose. Ijtihad was an instrumental exercise of reasoning and judgment, but after about 400 years Sunni Muslim leaders considered all major questions settled by consensus (ijma), and closed the "Gates of Ijtihad," so that if a seemingly new difficult problem arose that appeared to have no answer, analogies were drawn from earlier scholars and that same ruling was applied to the problem.[47] From the tenth century onward, Sunni Muslim leaders forbade followers from the practice of ijtihad, which inhibited the evolution of Islam toward any form of modernity.[48]

Muslim leaders today, not unexpectedly, reject opening the gates of ijtihad, since challenging the Koran, Hadiths, and older interpretations of Islamic jurisprudence (as expressed in Islamic schools of thought) poses the risk of upsetting the established order and bringing down "the autocracies and despotic regimes which rule most of the Muslim world."[49]

Egyptian Muslim reformer Sayed el-Qemany argues that the challenge to reform lies not in the Islamic religion, or any religion, but in the way any given religion is utilized.[50] He acknowledges the fear of criticizing Islam caused by Salafist antipathy to progressive thought, as well as the issuing of fatwas against modern innovators who they deem apostates and heretics.[51] A further challenge to reform that el-Qemany notes is the reluctance of Western scholars to sufficiently enter into the classical study of Orientalism, an arena from which Orientalists are "still struggling to emerge from Edward Said's damaging legacy."[52] Said was a Palestinian-American academic and the author of *Orientalism*, a foundational text for the field of post-colonial studies, which ascribed any criticism of Islam to Western colonialism and imperialism.[53] Writer Joshua Muravchik, a fellow at the Foreign Policy Institute of the Johns Hopkins University School for Advanced International Studies and formerly a resident scholar at the American Enterprise Institute, referenced Said as "an unlikely symbol of the wretched of the earth" who misrepresented his subject and managed to transform the West's "perception of the Israel–Arab conflict" by rolling "American racism and European colonialism into one *mélange* of white oppression of darker-skinned peoples." Muravchik also states that Said paved the way toward "a new, post-socialist life for leftism."[54]

## CHAMPIONING REFORM

There should be no argument that divergence of opinion is a value to be encouraged among moderates and reformers alike, as they engage in valuable ijtihad in the collective process of engendering a new contemporary Islam that is consistent with human rights, modernity and Western constitutions. There are many nuances and dissensions in using the terms moderate and reformer among Muslims, as shown in this chapter. The terms as defined in this book leave no ambiguity, as they refer to Muslims who advance a modernized Islam with the centrality of human rights, the rejection of political Islam and Sharia law, a celebration of pluralism and the encouragement of free speech, and dialogue and plurality.

As reformer Zuhdi Jasser states, Islam needs to have its own reformation similar to the Catholic Reformation, which began centuries ago and resulted in the separation of church and state. He asserts that the Islamic faith has not yet gone through that process.

Progressing toward the modernization of Islam requires the championing of an expansive reform movement that encourages adherents of the faith to practice it in peace, to freely critique Koranic texts, and to challenge what Jasser referred to in Part One as normative Islam, of which he stated "comes out of Al-Azhar University and Saudi schools" and of which "involves being anti-women, cutting of limbs, killing people that leave Islam, oppression of minorities, etc.," which is rooted in Islamic law.

Moderate Muslims cannot ignore difficult Koranic texts and the influence of Salafist adherents of Islam who invoke them. In response to ISIS, Boko Haram, Al Shabbab, and the like, many moderates have publicly stated that violence in the name of Islam is un-Islamic. Yet according to historian Bernard Lewis, "the overwhelming majority of classical theologians, jurists, and traditionalists understood the obligation of Jihad in a military sense."[55] Any attempt to reform Islam requires acknowledging problematic texts and how Islamists utilize them, while offering modern interpretations of such texts.

Upon arriving to America after being exiled from Egypt, Sheikh Subhy Mansour was shocked to discover that the same fanatical Sharia injunctions that he suffered under in Egypt were being taught in American mosques. Reformists collectively support the separation of mosque and state, the practice of the Muslim faith in peace, and encouragement of adherents to embrace the right to question the faith, texts, and their religious authorities. It is reformists who have taken unto themselves the ultimate burden of challenging and defying the rigidity of Islamic jurisprudence and providing peaceful alternatives to problematic texts, which the next chapter addresses.

## CHAPTER ELEVEN

# PROBLEMATIC ISLAMIC TEXTS

Most of the translations that exist today have been fueled by
the Saudi petrodollars and include interpretations that are very
supremacist.

—Dr. Zuhdi Jasser

The word of God is eternal and God is speaking to me in the
twenty-first century, not the seventh century. The Koran is no
more static than any other culture or society.

—Dr. Salim Mansur

We have enough trouble trying to figure out what happened in
Afghanistan, let alone in the times when the prophet Muhammad demanded that certain tribes be beheaded. Literalists take
everything black and white.

—Dr. Jalal Zuberi

ISLAMIST GROUPS SUCH AS AL QAEDA, its offshoot ISIS, and al-Shabaab
invoke Koranic texts to justify odious acts of violence, prompting
Western debates about the very existence of a moderate Islam. After
9/11, Osama bin Laden and his associates decreed an open death fatwa
requiring the killing of Americans, both civilian and military.[1] Part of
this decree referred to the duty of all Muslim adherents to wage violent
Jihad in the name of their religion:

"The ruling to kill the Americans and their allies, civilians, and
military, is an individual duty for every Muslim who can do it in any
country in which it is possible to do it.…[E]very Muslim who believes

in Allah and wishes to be rewarded to comply with Allah's order to kill the Americans and plunder their money wherever and whenever they find it."[2]

Koranic and/or Islamic religious texts from the Sunnah and Hadith that dictate violence and advocate supremacy based on gender and religion, or Hadiths about Muhammad taking a prepubescent girl as a wife, are difficult for many Muslims, as shown in the interviews in Part One. Yet it is the collective human practice of a faith that defines it, and determines its place in the world and its future course. The solution to Islamism is in either reforming problematic texts with modernized interpretations or ignoring them altogether as a document better left in the seventh century. I concur it is the reform movement that offers the greatest promise in influencing the collective future course of how Islam is practiced.

This chapter investigates "problematic texts" and the various ways they are observed or regarded by Islamists, and by moderates and reformists who vehemently reject such texts as antiquated and archaic.

## AMBITIOUS JIHADIS INVOKE THE KORAN AND HADITH

In examining the historical underpinnings of modern day Islamism, it was the fall of the Ottoman Empire and European expansion that produced the reactionary movement Pan-Islamism, which was intended to "shore up the ramparts against economic and ideological penetration."[3] Yet post-Ottoman states met with one failure upon another. In 1928, Hassan al-Banna formed the Muslim Brotherhood, which provided a needed paradigm that married an indigenous religious conservatism to political activism with the goal of restoring the "lapsed fortunes" of the Islamic world. The Muslim Brotherhood was, and remains, cunning in its presentation of a democratic structure. What appears to be a willingness to employ democratic systems does not indicate a real belief in them. In al-Banna's view, if one doesn't win at the ballot, one resorts to military revolution, just as Hitler came to power by the ballot box in 1933, but dismantled the system from within, to become Europe's most savage and genocidal dictator.[4]

Al-Banna instructed in his treatise about Jihad that it is the duty of all Muslims to make Jihad. He stated:

"Jihad is an obligation from Allah on every Muslim and cannot be ignored nor evaded. Allah has ascribed great importance to Jihad and has made the reward of the martyrs and the fighters in His way a splendid one. Only those who have acted similarly and who have modeled themselves upon the martyrs in their performance of Jihad can join them in this reward. Furthermore, Allah has specifically honored the Mujahideen (those who wage Jihad) with certain exceptional qualities, both spiritual and practical, to benefit them in this world and the next. Their pure blood is a symbol of victory in this world and the mark of success and felicity in the world to come."[5]

Arab Egyptian scholar Tarek Heggy discusses how Islamists traditionally divide the world in two: the Abode of Islam and the Abode of War, in which the non-Muslim enemy is held responsible for all the Islamic world's problems from colonialism until present day.[6] Despite leftist Western sympathies toward Islamism, there are abiding words in the religion of Islam that have historically perpetuated violence through conquest and subjugation of women, and are invoked today to commit violence:

### Bukhari Volume 4, Book 52, Number 53:

The Prophet said, "Nobody who dies and finds good from Allah (in the Hereafter) would wish to come back to this world even if he were given the whole world and whatever is in it, except the martyr who, on seeing the superiority of martyrdom, would like to come back to the world and get killed again (in Allah's Cause)."[7]

### Bukhari Volume 1, Book 3, Number 125:

The Prophet raised his head (as the questioner was standing) and said, "He who fights so that Allah's Word (Islam) should be superior, then he fights in Allah's cause."[8]

### Book 31, Number 5917: (Re: the attack on the peaceful Jewish tribe at Khaibar)

Allah's Messenger, on what issue should I fight with the people? Thereupon he (the Prophet) said: "Fight with them until they bear testimony to the fact that there is no god but Allah and Muhammad is his Messenger, and when they do that then their blood and their riches are inviolable from your hands but what is justified by law and their reckoning is with Allah."[9]

**Koran 9:5:**
"Kill the idolaters wherever you find them and take them prisoners, and beleaguer them, and lie in wait for them at every place of ambush. But if they repent and observe Prayer and pay the Zakat, then leave their way free.[10]

## JUSTIFICATION AND INVOCATION OF RELIGIOUS BRUTALITY

In addition to the invocation of problematic texts, Islamists justify their brutality and supremacism by indicting the West and/or Israel for past and present "wrongs" such as colonialism and racism. In doing so, the violence and human rights violations rampantly committed by Islamists who obey problematic texts are manipulated by the victimhood narrative. Violence perpetrated by Islamists is then viewed by sympathizers as reactions to the "sins" of the West and of Israel. This narrative is reinforced by far leftists in the West, and has become well engrained among the mainstream left. Middle East scholar Efraim Karsh observes, "The sight of Arabs killing Jews (or other Arabs for that matter) is hardly news, while the sight of Jews killing Arabs is a man-bites-dog anomaly that cannot be tolerated."[11]

What is deemed acceptable is the violent language of Yusuf al-Qaradawi, an Egyptian Islamic scholar, spiritual leader to the Muslim Brotherhood, and a highly influential force among Muslims worldwide: "Throughout history, Allah has imposed upon the [Jews] people who would punish them for their corruption. The last punishment was carried out by Hitler."[12]

The following examples illustrate how Islamists employ the victim narrative and leftist Western sympathizers enable the Islamist agenda:

I. Sheikh Ahmed al-Tayeb, the Grand Imam of Al-Azhar University in Cairo, the foremost source of religious authority in Islam, spoke at a counterterrorism conference in Mecca, Saudi Arabia, aimed to encourage all Muslims to join forces against terrorism. He blamed Israel and America for the chaos in the Arab world, stating, "We face major international plots targeting Arabs and Muslims...in a way that agrees with the dreams of the new world colonialism that is allied with world Zionism, hand in hand and shoulder to shoulder. We must not forget that the only method used by new colonialism now, is the same that was used by colonialism in the past century, and its deadly slogan is 'divide and conquer.'"[13]

II. Senior theologian Karen Armstrong, one of 18 leading group members of the Alliance of Civilizations, an initiative of the former UN General Secretary Kofi Annan, blames the West for the violence and problems of the Muslim world, including 9/11.[14] As an Islamist apologist, her exaggerations disregard the pervasive suffering induced by the ancient and modern day Islamist practices of amputations for stealing, child brides, honor killings, murdering apostates, stonings, slavery, mass rapes, and persecution of Christians and other religious sects. Armstrong chides that, "Western people have a responsibility for everybody who is suffering in the world," and that "modernity did not come with independence but with colonial subjugation, and Muslims are not free because Western powers often control their politics behind the scenes to secure the oil supply or other resources."[15] Armstrong overlooks the history of the caliphate and the current agenda of Islamist despots and clerics; even worse, as a professing Christian, she ignores the suffering of persecuted Christians in Islamic states. As Pope Francis said, "Today we are dismayed to see how in the Middle East and elsewhere in the world many of our brothers and sisters are persecuted, tortured, and killed for their faith in Jesus.... this Third World War, waged piecemeal, which we are now experiencing, is a form of genocide taking place."[16] He was referring to the extermination of Middle Eastern Christians by ISIS.

## A PROBLEMATIC HISTORY

The victimization of Christians in Jihadist warfare is historically established: Following Muhammad's death, Palestine, Syria, and Egypt, once the most heavily populated Christian areas in the world, quickly succumbed to Islamic invasions, and by the eighth century, Muslim armies had conquered all of Christian North Africa and Spain. Three centuries later came the Muslim conquest of present-day Turkey, which had been

Christian since the time of St. Paul. The old Roman Empire, known as the Byzantine Empire, was reduced to little more than Greece.[17]

In Chapter Three, Sheikh Dr. Subhy Mansour stated that he "stood against the Saudi influence and suffered. Establishing the Koranic intellectual trend is a story of agony and a severe peaceful struggle against Al-Azhar and the dictators of Egypt and the Saudi regime." We see no Western colonialist influence in the history of Islamic Caliphates, nor in Mansour's description of his own suffering. Rather, we see an aggressive Islamist agenda fueled by Saudi Arabia's petrodollars and polemicists from Al-Azhar. Armstrong's assertion is popular in the West, but fraudulent, and it serves to promote and justify the Islamists' victimology narrative.

In removing Western "sins" from the equation, Muslims have invoked and applied problematic religious texts for fourteen centuries, and have slaughtered over 10 million fellow Muslims since 1948 in the name of sectarian theology, fueled on both sides by Koranic literalism, which is ongoing.[18]

Some examples: On June 29, 2014, the Islamic State, formerly known as the Islamic State of Iraq and the Levant, declared the establishment of an Islamic Caliphate, with its leader Abu Bakr al-Baghdadi, as the Caliph.[19] The ideology of the Islamic State is that of Sunni Salafist-Jihadism, a hardline interpretation of Sharia law, validated by problematic texts. The ISIS interpretation of Sharia law is ruthlessly enforced in the areas controlled by the Islamic State, which it sought to expand.[20] ISIS militants outlined a chilling five-year plan for global domination, and they indiscriminately massacred civilian populations as they advanced into new territory.[21] Their victims have included Shiites, viewed by ISIS as heretics worthy of death.[22] They have aggressively solicited foreign fighters, including women to marry and support the militants, with promises of material rewards in this world and paradise in the next, and enjoin attacks on Western soil.[23]

ISIS advertised its practices of forced impregnation, rape, the sexual enslavement of teen girls, dismemberment of body parts in city squares, public beheadings, amputation of limbs for smoking cigarettes, and stealing. A panel of independent UN human rights investigators concluded that ISIS "actively promotes their abuses and crimes to demonstrate its control and to reinforce its ideology."[24] It has done so through its own publications and social media; in one publication, 153 detained Kurdish boys between 14 and 16 were forced to watch videos of beheadings and attacks and to study the militant ideology of ISIS.[25]

The atrocities committed by Boko Haram in Nigeria are another example of invoking Islam to justify sadistic violence. Boko Haram leaders consistently invoke religious rhetoric in telling stories about what it means to be a Muslim in Nigeria to "activate fears that pious Muslims are losing grounds to the forces of immorality."[26]

Amnesty International described an attack that killed 2,000 civilians as the "deadliest massacre" in the history of Boko Haram.[27] Most of the victims were reportedly children, women, and the elderly who were unable to run fast enough to escape insurgents who drove into the Nigerian town of Baga, firing rocket-propelled grenades and assault rifles on local residents.[28]

Contrary to the claims of Islamist apologists such as Armstrong, obscene human rights abuses were routinely inflicted upon victims in Islamic states throughout Islamic history, long before colonialism, and long before the Christian Crusades. "The history of Islam's imperialism and the persistence of the Ottoman imperialist dream outlasted World War I to haunt Islamic and Middle Eastern politics to the present day. The House of Islam's war for world mastery is traditional."[29]

American author and researcher Raymond Ibrahim, the son of Egyptian Coptic immigrants, refers to the Encyclopedia of Islam's entry for "Jihad" by Emile Tyan, which states that the "spread of Islam by arms is a religious duty upon Muslims in general....Jihad must continue to be done until the whole world is under the rule of Islam....Islam must completely be made over before the doctrine of Jihad [warfare to spread Islam] can be eliminated."[30] Ibrahim also quotes Iraqi jurist Majid Khadduri, who wrote that Jihad "is regarded by all jurists, with almost no exception, as a collective obligation of the whole Muslim community."[31]

## A MATTER OF INTERPRETATION

It is also fallacious to mitigate the depredations of Islamism by stating that violence committed in the name of Islam is un-Islamic; those who oppose this Wahhabi-Salafist agenda are considered apostates from

Islam. Dr. Zuhdi Jasser identifies this agenda as "normative Islam." Dr. Daniel Pipes stated that it is fundamental for anti-Islamists to confront the violence and supremacy within the religion. He states:

> "We know there is an aggressive Jihadi sentiment, an Islamic suprema-cist ambition that is the hallmark of Muslim life over 1,400 years. I think it's absolutely crucial that Muslims acknowledge this. They can-not pretend it didn't take place and advance that there wasn't a Jihad or in some cases there wasn't slavery. You get mind-boggling assertions that are completely contrary to historical fact. If you start that way, you're not going to get anywhere. You have to acknowledge that there was Jihad, slavery, oppression of women, and so forth, and once you've done that, then you can build anew. Now we can take the Koranic texts, Hadiths, the term Jihad, and understand them in a more allegori-cal form or we see certain texts as abrogated. Whatever you might do as an Islamic scholar, you have to start by recognizing the facts and if you deny them then you're not going to get anywhere."[32]

There are innumerable Muslims who have rejected "normative Islam" and who dispute the evolution of Islam over the past 1,400 years. Before addressing this history, it is important to note the differences between the Koran, Hadith, and Sunnah.

The Koran is deemed to be the word of God, the cornerstone of every believer's faith, and the oldest and most sacred text of Islam. The Sunnah is the second source of Islamic jurisprudence after the Koran, and it is derived from how Muhammad lived his life. The Hadiths, or "reports," present narrations from Muhammad's life: They tell what he approved of, his deeds, his sayings, his physical appearance, and a great deal more that is normative for Islamic law, since Muhammad is designated in the Koran as an "excellent example" for Muslims (33:21). The Sunnah, or accepted practice, is derived by Islamic jurists from the Koran and Hadith. During the proliferation of Islam in the seventh and eighth centuries, Islamic scholars were left with the task of pre-serving the message of the various interpretations of the Sunnah, and what began as an oral tradition was codified at that time, amid some disagreement.[33]

Given Islam's primary focus upon the Koran, its authenticity is of cardinal importance. It was addressed by scholar Said Nachid, who articulates a strong case against the Muslim holy book's infallibility, noting the many variations in recording the contents of the Koranic "revelations" and uncertainty about preserving the original contents of those revelations following the death of Muhammad.[34] The Koran Muhammad left behind was not in the form it is today; portions were scattered among various people who had memorized particular sections, and the book in its entirety was formulated at a time before the Arab language was even standardized.[35] By the time of the third Caliph, Uthman ibn Affan, some of the verses were obscure and interpreted arbitrarily or by consensus. According to scholar Hasan Mohsen Ramadan, there was also an observable weaving together of Muhammad's life events with events from the Torah.[36] Arab scholar Shaker al-Nabulsi further posits that the Koran has been distorted by both Sunnis and Shias to reflect Arab heroism, in which the literal understanding of the text is the central axis, thus rendering human intellect, ethical judgments, and experience as meaningless or inferior, marginalizing discourse and spawning a primitive culture of violence.[37] This has been exploited by Muslim leaders and clerics for hefty monetary gain and power, including Egypt's famed Al-Azhar University.[38]

Muslim views of Koranic texts range from puritanical literalism to modernist interpretations. Many moderates argue that problematic verses of the Koran are incompatible with the twenty-first-century laws and norms, but were appropriate to the context of the time when Islam faced existential threats. Others, such as Shireen Qudosi, interviewed in Chapter Eight, strip away any justification whatsoever for the difficult texts.

## THE TWO FACES OF THE KORAN

Certain Muslims and scholars hold to the belief that there are virtually "two Korans," reflecting the change in Muhammad's character from Mecca to Medina; from Mecca, when his community of followers was weak and more inclined to compromise, to Medina, where Muhammad's "strength grew"[39] and he created a new society, but faced opposition and ultimately declared war, and the message of the Koran grew less tolerant and more violent. When the Jews of Medina rejected Muhammad and refused to convert, he expelled two of the major Jewish tribes from the city, and "in 627 Muhammad and his followers killed between 600 and 900 Jewish men, and divided the surviving Jewish women and children amongst themselves."[40]

The Koran therefore reveals a changed focus from the spiritual to that of conquest and war, as well as community building and lawmaking. Many Muslims today hold that Muhammad drafted the Constitution of Medina, the principles of which formed the foundation of the first Islamic State, and included people of different religions and cultures, now together comprising the Ummah, the Arabic term for community or nation.[41]

## THE LAW OF ABROGATION

The change in Muhammad's teachings between Mecca and Medina, and the lack of chronological order of Koranic verses, lead to confusion among many readers of the book and disagreement among scholars. Many jurists and scholars acknowledge inconsistencies and differences between the Meccan and Medinan period, but they also accept the traditional view that the later verses of the Koran take precedence over the verses revealed earlier, in accordance with the doctrine of abrogation. This means that the violent verses have replaced the peaceful ones, hence the peaceful texts no longer apply (unless, according to some scholars, the circumstances of their revelation are replicated), or they were negated in accordance with Koran 2:106, which depicts Allah stating that his later pronouncements supersede his earlier ones.[42]

Those who do not accept the law of abrogation are considered to be outside the mainstream of Islamic belief. The Ahmadiyah sect, concentrated in Pakistan, consistently rejects abrogation because it believes that the Koran is free from errors.[43] Mainstream Muslims also consider the Koran to be without fault, and some consign the principle of abrogation to the Hadith only, maintaining that Koran verses cannot be abrogated. Others accept the possibility of abrogation in Koran verses, arguing that this fact doesn't render the Koran not free of error, but only shows that Allah reveals the truth in stages, rather than all at once, replacing incomplete formulations with more complete ones.

According to Daniel Pipes, in the mainstream Muslim view, Muslims can reconcile problematic Koranic texts through the doctrine of abrogation:

"There is abrogation. There are plenty of contradictions in the Koran and standard Islamic interpretation privileges some verses over others, which tend to be the worst verses because the early verses tend to be abrogated in favor of the later verses and the later verses tend to be far more aggressive. You can abrogate the more aggressive in favor of the less aggressive. There is plenty of room for interpretation. One of my favorite quotes about Islam is from an Egyptian philosopher by the name of Hassan Hanafi, who said the Koran is like a supermarket. You can take from it what you will."[44]

Those who have abrogated the more aggressive passages in favor of the less aggressive have faced formidable obstacles. Mahmoud Muhammad Taha, a Sudanese Muslim theologian who argued that the Meccan passages should take precedence over the Medinan instead of the reverse, was executed in 1985 by the Sudanese government for heresy and apostasy. Sheikh Subhy Mansour recounted, "If these Muslim Brotherhood people had the chance, they would have killed me according to their punishment for apostasy, plus they claim I'll go to hell." Tawfik Hamid noted, "The reformists were killed throughout history, including those who rejected the Sunnah."

Statements that stem from Muhammad in Mecca or when he first arrived in Medina, such as the Koranic passage "There is no compulsion in religion" (Koran 2:256), and the Hadith that depicts him saying that Jihad is primarily about internal struggle and only secondarily about holy war, may be applauded, but those who place too much emphasis on them misunderstand abrogation in the context of Islamic theology. It is important to acknowledge that what university scholars believe, and what most Muslims, or more extreme Muslims, believe are two different things. For many Islamists and radical Muslims, abrogation of the peaceful verses from Mecca is real, and what the West calls terror is considered to be just.[45]

## REFORMING PROBLEMATIC TEXTS THROUGH IJTIHAD

Reformists support the contention that Islam must undergo a transformation through the process of critical thinking and independent judgment, which is "ijtihad," to create a modernized translation or interpretation of the Koran.[46] This means abrogating the violent or problematic texts of the Koran in favor of peaceful verses and new interpretations, as Taha advocated. These reformers regard the Koran as divine, inspired, and an ultimate authority, but argue that traditional interpretations are useful as historical and scholarly reference resources, but are not acceptable in a modern context. They have thus rejected "the right of the clergy" to determine the meaning of difficult passages.

Reformer Dr. Tawfik Hamid authored one such work, *A Modern Interpretation of the Quran.*[47] Hamid's motivation was to counterbalance radical interpretations with those that are consistent with modernity, and to shape the impressionable minds of the younger generation of Muslims. His style delivers the traditional Koranic text with his interpretation beneath it, which offers the reader a comparative study.[48] *A Modern Interpretation of the Quran* also contextualizes problematic Koranic texts, while emphasizing the more peaceful ones.[49]

## WHY KORANIST REFORMISTS REJECT HADITH AND SUNNAH

There are reformists who identify themselves as Koranists and leaders of the "Islamic Reformation" which has gained momentum over the last 15 years.[50] As with all moderates, they do not believe in religiously mandated violence, nor in the notion of a global caliphate.[51] They contend that such beliefs fail to acknowledge the diversity of the Muslim world, and do not distinguish between the various streams of thought within Islam, historically and currently. The Koranist movement in Egypt was founded during the 1980s, and was headed by theologian and reformer Dr. Subhy Mansour, who was interviewed in Part One.[52] Al-Azhar is the most reputable Islamic university in the world; inside it, ideological and theological battles can be ferocious.[53] Koranists are non-political, and their aim is to influence Muslims to think logically, rather than to resort to violence.[54] This group does not depend on the Hadiths or Sunnah, since the belief of Koranists is that the Hadiths were "subjected to falsification by some crook theologians" and were not recorded until over 200 years after the death of Muhammad.[55] They also regard Hadiths as being at times irrational and contrary to normal reasoning.[56]

Koranists were deemed heretical in Egypt and became victims of repression by extremists and even the government of Egypt. Mansour explains, speaking from personal experience, that the first wave of attacks happened in 1987, when many Koranists were detained by the Egyptian government and tortured.[57] In 2000, Dr. Mansour was exiled to the US, where he is emphatic about his vision for Islam.[58]

Contrary to the rejection of the Hadiths and Sunnah by Koranists, most traditional Muslims assert that the Hadiths and Sunnah are indispensable, and that one cannot practice Islam without consulting both sources.[59] The late Islamic scholar Muhammad Nasir-ul-Deen al-Albani stated, "There is no way to understand the Koran correctly except in association with the interpretation of the Sunnah."[60] It is interesting to note that al-Albani did not believe that Western thinking or constitutions are compatible with Islam. Al-Albani declared in an interview that the lifestyle of "true Muslims" is incompatible with life in America. He advised his US-based Muslim interviewer to move back to a Muslim country, stating that a Muslim should live in a non-Muslim country only for the practice of dawah (propagating Islam), and to do so effectively there are certain criteria which he must possess: the da'ee (one who devotes himself to dawah) must be married, and raise his children according to "Islamic manners and from a Muslim surrounding that is more like a Muslim country, and that it is also imperative to possess the 'correct knowledge and a good amount of it in Islam.'"[61] Even under such required conditions, al-Albani states that a Muslim should aim to leave the non-Muslim country as soon as possible, or "when his task or project is completed."[62] He states further that "one should not have the intention of residing or investing on living there for many years to come or for the rest of their lives because "you don't want to go to a non-Muslim society to give dawah and it is you and your family that now needs the dawah."[63] In reference to the Muslim sects that do not accept the Sunnah, al-Albani advised Muslims not to pay attention to them, as to "refute them you need knowledge and a big tongue because they only argue a lot."[64] Instead, he gave the explicit instructions to "just leave it to the scholars and knowledgeable brothers to deal with."[65] Al-Albani is not the exception; he exemplifies the current state of normative Islam today, which reveals the extent of the turf war between puritanical traditionalists who strive to maintain their strongholds, and Muslim moderates and reformists who seek to advance modernity and the Universal Declaration of Human Rights.

After the death of Muhammad in 632 CE, the Islamic community broke into numerous sects. The two main sects are the Sunni and the Shia, which make up approximately 80 percent and 15 percent of the world's 1.6 billion Muslims respectively, each claiming to have its own collections of "authentic" Hadith.[66] There are numerous contradictions between these collections, and even within collections, and with regard to "problematic texts" of the Koran. Although much of the Hadith is in agreement with the Koran, there are many sayings that are regarded as appalling and even perverse by many Muslims, as they delve into details about Muhammad's sex life and generate heated controversies.[67] Some defenders of the Hadith assert that the "private details of the prophet's life were intended to remain private, and not become the subject of conjecture in the form of Hadith."[68]

## REFORMING PROBLEMATIC TEXTS THROUGH PLURALISM

In addition to questions about the authenticity of the Hadiths and outright rejection by some reformers, there are also texts in the Koran that are inconsistent with the modern definition and practice of equal rights. Stephen Schwartz, Executive Director of the Center for Islamic Pluralism, notes that, "the form of the Koran as it is now written and read did not exist in the time of Muhammad. As all Muslims are aware, Muhammad was illiterate, and the text of the Koran was typically recited in his lifetime."[69]

In a post-9/11 modern world, torn by Islamic terrorism, Wahhabi influences, the Arab Spring, and the reformist drive toward a more pluralistic and modernized version of Islam, Muslims face the challenge of how Islam will evolve within competing sects. According to Khaleel Mohammed, Assistant Professor in the Department of Religious Studies at San Diego State University, "Islam faces more than just the hurdle of a proper English translation of its main document. Until Muslims learn to question the reliability of the Muslim oral traditions, or divorce themselves from medieval exegetical constructs, they will be living in a world much apart from the Judeo–Christian entity that has known reformation and enlightenment."[70]

Dr. Jalal Zuberi pointed out that, "after accepting criticism, then the journey becomes easier. Most Muslims have not crossed that threshold, but feel victimized by forces that they see as demonizing Islam and Muslims. They cannot cut through that and see that some of these criticisms have some validity. Muslims have not gone through this phase of evolution as other religious faiths and races have. This will make a very big difference."

Dr. Tawfik Hamid blames a Muslim "impulse to violence" on the "mainstream sources of Islamic law," which establish the principle "that anyone who insults the prophet Muhammad must be killed without even giving them a chance to repent."[71] Citing the Muslim reaction to the film, *Innocence of Muslims,* that denigrated Muhammad and sparked widespread violence throughout many Islamic countries, Hamid asserts that such laws justify Muslim violence against those who are perceived to insult Muhammad, and even to those who provide the freedom to do this.[72] Many Muslims thus see America as a co-conspirator to insulting the founder of Islam. Hamid also rejects and denounces the Hadiths (which are found in the Hadith collection that Muslims consider most reliable, Sahih Bukhari) pertaining to Muhammad's relationship with his wife Aisha, whom Hadiths record as his having married when she was six and consummated the marriage when she was nine. Hamid referred to Bukhari's accounts as in themselves "insulting to Islam" and to Muhammad, by representing him as a pedophile.

Khaleel Mohammed asserts that the Koran is a difficult document, given its archaic language and verse structure, and says that translation only accentuates the complexity. He states that over time, translators have lost much of the Koran's Judeo–Christian cultural references, as medieval Muslim scholars sought to abandon such references.[73] This is a critical point, as such relatively tolerant references during Muhammad's Meccan experience provided the template for Islamic pluralism. There is another reference to a black Ethiopian, Bilal ibn Rabah, who was born in Mecca and became one of the first inhabitants of Mecca to accept Muhammad's message. After becoming Muhammad's close and trusted companion, Bilal was the first person to be asked to chant the Muslim call to prayer.[74]

Khaleel Mohammed notes that for most Muslims who are unaware of the evolution of Islamic scholarship, the Koran is "immutable and uncreated, even though the Koran never makes such a proclamation." The traditional Sunni view, however, is that the Koran is indeed uncreated, as it is a perfect copy of the "Mother of the Book" that has existed forever with Allah: "Indeed, We have made it an Arabic Koran that you might understand. And indeed it is, in the Mother of the Book with Us, exalted and full of wisdom" (Koran 43:3–4). Khaleel Mohammed criticizes the failure of mainstream Muslim scholars to place the Koran into historical context, and asserts "such a failure facilitates the use of the Koran by governments that support chauvinism and incite hate and by terrorists such as those who brought down the World Trade Centers."[75]

Sheikh Dr. Subhy Mansour discusses lost elements in Koranic interpretation, stating that "Egyptians recast their old religious traditions in Arabic under the title of Islam, but these traditions had nothing to do with the Islam of the Prophet Muhammad," and that "all Egyptians—Muslim and Christian—share the same rituals with different names, and all of these religious observances grew out of ancient Egyptian civilization."

There are compelling reasons to question the normative interpretations of the modern-day Koran, and the degree to which it has been manipulated over time. The complexity of ancient Arab interpretations is best thrashed out among Islamic jurists, scholars, and reformers. In dealing with problematic texts, one can acknowledge the role of reformists in challenging the very authenticity of these texts through the passage of time. A process of desanctification thus occurs which causes questions to be asked, questions which are strictly discouraged by the Salafist mindset that strives to maintain textual rigidity to further a Puritanical agenda.

Reform lies in relaxing this rigidity and giving way to the right to choose how to practice one's faith according to free will. It is this freedom of thought that Salafists fear most, as it is the direction out from under the repressive strictures of Islamism. Reform will bring freedom of expression to the Islamic world, and pluralism beyond its borders, which includes the acceptance of Western free speech and collectively adapting to the norms of free democracies. Moreover, reform will facilitate a necessary assimilation of Muslims in the West to become equal citizens under the law, not a group that expects special treatment as supremacists, which is demonstrated through a victimology narrative and bogus "Islamophobia" drives, to be examined in the next chapter. Westerners need to understand and support the efforts of reformists to win the turf war against the Salafi and Wahhabi ideology, which has spread to the West and is now infecting Western constitutions through the manipulation of the victimology narrative and the fear of being politically incorrect in expressing warranted criticisms of Islamists.

## CHAPTER TWELVE

# THE "ISLAMOPHOBIA" DECEPTION

Islamists claim they are being persecuted and they claim they are being silenced when underneath, they are stealthily advancing their own mission.

—Dr. Qanta Ahmed

Islamists bring children up with a sense of arrogance and superiority. This brainwashing takes place at a very young age so you find a whole generation of young people who have grown up with a set of ideologies that teaches hatred toward others, intolerance of others, and disrespect toward others, and that could easily transform into violence.

—Raheel Raza

THE WORD "Islamophobe" is frequently used to brand those who offer any critique of Islam, inciting the fear of being labeled a racist. The misuse of this word prevents a candid and productive dialogue about all matters relating to Islam, and creates a safety net for Islamists who invoke "Islamophobia" to escape censure and scrutiny.

## A CLOAK OF INVISIBILITY

Perhaps the most significant and shocking case to date that demonstrates how fear of being called racist or "Islamophobic" has been imprinted into Western non-Muslims is the sex abuse scandal in

Rotherham, England, that sent shockwaves through media outlets. Fourteen hundred children, some as young as 11, were raped by gangs of Pakistani men over a 16-year period from 1997 to 2013, while the Labour-run council and child protection services deliberately ignored what was going on and police protected the perpetrators. Muhbeen Hussain, founder of Rotherham Muslim Youth Group, commented, "Race, religion, or political correctness should never provide a cloak of invisibility to such grotesque crimes."[1]

A council-commissioned independent review into child protection was created and a report was released that described children being threatened with guns, doused in petrol and threatened to be lit ablaze, forced to witness violent rapes, and told they would be next if they opened their mouths.[2]

The report also revealed that police deemed child victims as "undesirables not worthy of protection," and that some fathers who tried to rescue their children were arrested themselves when police arrived.[3] The inquiry team noted fears among council staff of being labeled "racist" if they focused on the victims' descriptions of the majority of abusers.[4]

Labour Member of Parliament Simon Danczuk, who helped expose a pattern of "grooming of white teenage girls by men from a Pakistani background in Rochdale," said that "Asian councilors were under constant pressure from the community to conform and other politicians acquiesced for fear of being accused of racism" and that "elements of Pakistani political culture itself were partly to blame for the cover-up."[5] He stated that "politics are done differently in Pakistan," and described "a looking after your own" within the Asian community which other politicians accepted.[6]

The appalling failure of a system to protect the most vulnerable against gangs of rapists, and the cover-up, exposed how the fear of being branded "Islamophobes" and racists hindered authorities from doing their job.[7]

Western laws, constitutions, and safety are at risk if "peaceful Islamists" can so readily wield the "Islamophobia" weapon, if and when it suits them, along with other deceptions and intimidation tactics using victimology and "taqiyya," which will be described later, to escape accountability for criminal and seditious activities.

In another case, Canada's RCMP (Royal Canadian Mounted Police) once issued an apology to the Muslim community for making terrorism-related arrests during Ramadan.[8] Calling an emergency meeting of the cultural diversity consultative committee to apologize, RCMP Corporal Wayne Russett went one step further, commanding that in support for "Muslim brothers and sisters during Ramadan, there will be no food or drink during this most important meeting."[9]

He also restricted the meeting to one hour only, so that Muslims could "observe prayer time and the breaking of the fast during Ramadan."[10]

Right after the arrests, Corporal Russett also held over a dozen meetings with Muslim groups in Ottawa, including visits to mosques, Muslim community centers, and several meals to break the Ramadan fast.[11]

Canada's Prime Minister at the time, Stephen Harper, responded to this shameless kowtowing by the RCMP in stating, "In fairness this is an operational matter for the RCMP and I wouldn't pretend to know all the details and aspects of the story.[12] But the general approach that this government would expect to see (from law enforcement agencies) is that the law, our important laws, are enforced every day of the year."[13] Members of the moderate Muslim Canadian Congress applauded Harper's remarks. Its founding member, Tarek Fatah, stated, "The notion that in Ramadan you can't arrest people is so foolish";[14] while Salma Siddiqui, vice president of the congress, called the RCMP patronizing and condescending, stating, "We have one law in Canada and it applies to everybody. We need to stop all this political correctness."[15] She further asks, "Would you apologize to other Canadians if you arrested someone on Christmas?," and recommends that police diversity committees be dismantled because they have been "taken over by Islamists."[16]

It is critical to note that moderate Muslims in all Western countries welcome open dialogue as a two-way street. This is a marker of their identity as moderates. They do not engage in stifling questions pertaining to their religion nor do they levy accusations of racism to mask wrongdoings by their fellow co-religionists. "Islamophobia" is a word they shun.

## TAQIYYA: THE LAW OF DISSIMULATION

Islamists have refined a practice called "taqiyya" or dissimulation, and "kitman," which is the deliberate omission of important facts so as to mislead. These concepts originated in Shia Islam, and are still used as tools to promote Islam to "unbelievers" or "infidels."[17] It is essentially an allowance for the deception of non-Muslims. Taqiyya permits Muslims to conceal their beliefs, convictions, emotions, opinions, and strategies if they perceive present or future danger to their religious identity and/or to save themselves from what they perceive as mental and/or physical persecution.[18]

This practice is encouraged in Muslims in "dar al-harb" (countries where Muslims are in the minority which are considered the Houses of War) and encouraged by the Koran (Koran 3:28, 16:106). It permits Muslims to conform outwardly to the requirements of the non-Islamic state, while inwardly "remaining faithful" to whatever one believes to be Islamic, and to do this while waiting for the tide to turn in one's favor.[19] Taqiyya is in effect an active form of deceit when waging Jihad and is deemed to be among military virtues, such as courage, fortitude, or self-sacrifice.[20]

In his "stealth analysis" about the home grown terror threat to America, Walid Phares of the National Defense University indicates that America is penetrated by Jihadists who are operating freely on American soil due to their practice of taqiyya, and asks, "Does our government know what this doctrine is all about and, more importantly, are authorities educating the body of our defense apparatus regarding this stealthy threat dormant among us?"[21] The notion of taqiyya is difficult for Westerners to grasp, and so the deception most often goes undetected. Under this veiling of the truth, in accordance with taqiyya and kitman, many Islamist objectives are allowed to ripen. There are no restrictions on how taqiyya can be used; negotiations, dialogues, and conflict resolution are environments where people are accustomed to the rule of law and are inclined to trust those with a warm smile, who display willingness to compromise and give a promise and a handshake. The current level of sophistication of taqiyya and kitman will be addressed in the chapter, "Who Speaks for Muslims?," along with the comprehensive Islamist Project.

## "ISLAMOPHOBIA" AND VICTIMOLOGY

When a society has a predilection toward guilt, this provides fuel for taqiyya objectives. The word "Islamophobia," for instance, has been used to intimidate critics of Islamism so frequently that when Western-ers merely question Islam, or its role in terrorism, they generally know that they risk being branded as "Islamophobes" or "racists."[22] The prac-tice of victimology, that is, perpetually portraying Muslims as victims of racism, colonialism, or imperialism, has also generated impressive results in vanquishing the infidel and providing Islam with immunity from criticism, even from satire or comedy, which other religious groups tolerate. As a result, whenever the subject of Islam is raised, open dia-logue ends, and media and public discourse are restricted or shut down out of fear of being branded "Islamophobic" or "racist," even when no such sentiments may be present or expressed.[23]

Dr. Zuhdi Jasser states, "CAIR, the Islamic Society of North Amer-ica (ISNA), and all of the other Muslim Brotherhood front groups based in D.C." are pretending to speak for all American Muslims and "do not show the true diversity of the American Muslim popula-tion."[24] Instead, Dr. Jasser says they are of a "victimology mindset and only looked at terrorism as a problematic tactic rather than looking at the core problem, the root cause, which was an ideology that was pre-modern, that had not gone through a phase of enlightenment as we had in the West."[25]

Following the terror attacks in Paris in November 2015 that left 129 people dead and over 350 injured, many American state gover-nors declared that they would refuse to accept Syrian refugees in their home states, which prompted immediate cries of "Islamophobia."[26] ISIS claimed responsibility for the Paris attacks, and reports revealed that a Syrian passport was found near the body of one of the suspected terrorists who was killed during the rampage.[27]

Secretary of State John Kerry stated that the number of Syrian refugees that the US accepted could rise to 100,000.[28] The generally positive public response to the American governors refusal to cooperate in the resettling of Syrian refugees prompted CAIR to issue a state-ment claiming that the governors' announcements were "indicative of growing Islamophobia among many in the US."[29]

CAIR dismissed valid concerns about the potential dangers of exposing American citizens to an influx of Syrian refugees, where ISIS fighters and other Jihadist warriors could easily hide. It was later revealed that the Islamic State had smuggled thousands of extremists into Europe.[30]

## ISLAMIST APOLOGIST POLITICIAN CHRIS CHRISTIE FURTHERS THE "ISLAMOPHOBIA" DECEPTION

In keeping with a victimology mindset routinely deployed by Islamists, CAIR released a report on Islamophobia and its impact in the United States entitled "Legislating Fear."[31] Zuhdi Jasser and Daniel Pipes are listed among those individuals in the "inner core" of "Islamophobes," whose primary purpose is to "promote prejudice against or hatred of Islam and Muslims and whose work regularly demonstrates Islamophobic themes."[32]

In this same report, CAIR praises individuals for "their outstanding contributions to pushing back against Islamophobic trends in 2011 and 2012."[33] Named second on that list is New Jersey Governor Chris Christie. First on the list was Rais Bhuiyan, who was tragically shot in the face by a deranged person, Mark Stroman, while working at a store.[34] Stroman had decided to go on a shooting spree and "hunt Arabs" following 9/11. Since Bhuiyan was simply a victim who really had contributed nothing to "pushing back against Islamophobic trends," it was actually Christie who was effectively highest on CAIR's list; he serves as an example of how Western leaders embrace and assist the Islamist agenda, and are manipulated by Islamist groups as they do so.

CAIR applauded Christie's August 2011 warnings about Islamists introducing Sharia law in the US legal system: "This Sharia law business," Christie declared, "is just crap. It's just crazy, and I'm tired of dealing with the crazies."[35]

This was an inaccurate and misleading statement, certainly to voters in Oklahoma, Ontario, and elsewhere who approved of measures designed to stop the implementation of aspects of Sharia law. In November 2010, Oklahoma voters overwhelmingly approved a ballot initiative to create a statute that prohibited judges from applying

Sharia law in their rulings.[36] Shortly after passage of the Save Our State Amendment, Muneer Awad, the Executive Director of the Oklahoma chapter of CAIR, filed a lawsuit in federal district court, claiming that the Oklahoma vote was a violation of his constitutional right to religious liberty.[37] A panel of judges from the 10th Circuit Court of Appeals in Denver convened to decide whether a lower court judge was correct in blocking the initiative to forbid Oklahoma courts from considering applying Sharia laws in their decisions, but upheld the ruling striking down the anti-Sharia law.[38]

The outcome was different in Ontario, Canada, when the idea of arbitrating family matters in accordance with Sharia law was introduced.[39] When Toronto lawyer Syed Mumba Ali announced in 2004 that an Islamic Institute of Civil Justice would shortly begin arbitrating family matters on the basis of Sharia law, accompanied by a warning that Muslims who did not submit cases to Islamic arbitration panels were not "good Muslims," a heated controversy pitted moderates who opposed Sharia against Islamists who favored it.[40]

Many women's groups, including Muslims, opposed implementing Sharia laws, and the Muslim Canadian Congress argued that Sharia does not view women as equals and therefore cannot provide equal justice to all parties in a dispute, especially on matters of divorce, child custody, and division of property.[41] Founder Tarek Fatah stated, "The weakest within the Muslim community, namely the women, will be coerced by their community."[42] Ontario Premier Dalton McGuinty finally declared, "There will be no Sharia law in Ontario. There will be no religious arbitration in Ontario. There will be one law for all Ontarians."[43] Since 1991, arbitration decisions were being made according to religious laws and were enforceable in Ontario courts, but the Premier rescinded the Arbitration Act that settled disputes related to commerce, religion, and civil issues.[44]

Chris Christie's comment about this "Sharia law business" being "crap" no doubt pleased his Islamist bedfellows. The FBI's former chief of counterterrorism, Steven Pomerantz, notes that CAIR has given aid to international terrorist groups, while counterterrorism expert Steven Emerson calls CAIR "a radical fundamentalist front group for Hamas."[45] CAIR has consistently defended, protected and supported, accused, and even convicted radical Islamic terrorists; for instance, in

October 1998, after Osama bin Laden issued his first declaration of war against the United States and had been named the chief suspect in the bombings of two US embassies in Africa, CAIR demanded the removal of a Los Angeles billboard that described Osama bin Laden as "the sworn enemy," claiming that this depiction was offensive to Muslims.[46]

Christie has also long defended Imam Mohammad Qatanani, a Hamas-linked cleric whom the Department of Homeland Security has been trying to deport from the country.[47] Qatanani's attorney, Sohail Mohammed, was appointed by Christie to serve as a state Superior Court Judge.[48] In 2012, the Clarion Project, a non-profit organization dedicated to exposing the dangers of Islamic extremism while providing a platform for the voices of moderation and promoting grassroots activism, broke the news that four Islamists, including Qatanani, sit on Christie's Muslim outreach committee.[49] Christie's Attorney General, Jeffrey Chiesa, who oversees the committee, was appointed by Christie to serve as an interim state senator.[50] The Clarion Project also reported that these Islamists continued to meet with the top brass of New Jersey's law enforcement.[51] A fifth member was also identified as a convicted felon who sat on Christie's Muslim outreach committee while its members were briefed on how non-profit organizations can win Homeland Security grants.[52]

Following a Ramadan dinner held by Chris Christie on July 24, 2012, at his Governor's Mansion in New Jersey, where Imam Mohammad Qatanani was in attendance, Christie railed against denunciations of his Islamist ties.[53] Before a Muslim audience, Christie insulted his critics and those of Qatanani as "bigots," stating, "You'll all be fascinated to learn that in many publications around the country, I'm called an Islamist....These are the kind of red herrings that people put up who are bigots, who want to judge people based upon their religious beliefs, want to judge people with a broad brush." He continued that the criticism was a manifestation of an "intolerance that's going around our country that's disturbing."[54]

## ISLAMOPHOBIA AND CIVILIZATIONAL JIHAD

Senator Dick Durbin (D-IL) was also praised in CAIR's "Islamophobia Report" and honored for his criticism of the House Homeland

Security hearings on homegrown Islamic terrorism.[55] Durbin held a counter-hearing on "Islamophobia" in March 2011. Billed as the first-ever congressional hearing on the civil rights of American Muslims, Durbin said he convened the hearing because of "rising Islamophobia, manifested by Koran burnings, hate speech, and restrictions on mosque construction."[56] Durbin focused on crimes committed against American Muslims while ignoring those committed by Muslims and Muslim groups' network of radical ties.

Islamism has influenced political figures looking for the Muslim vote, encouraging them to be mouthpieces for the "Islamophobia" deception. The US Muslim Brotherhood strategic memorandum detailing its plans for "eliminating and destroying Western civilization from within" listed CAIR's predecessor, the Islamic Association for Palestine, as one of its fronts.[57] The Islamic Association for Palestine was established in 1981 by Hamas operative Mousa Abu Marzook, founder of the Holy Land Foundation for Relief and Development.[58]

Given the reputation and associations of CAIR, its endorsement is confirmation that Christie and others are abetting the goals of Islamists. Western authorities would do well to steer clear of any Muslim groups that are found to have terrorist associations.

According to Dr. Qanta Ahmed, a Templeton-Cambridge Journalism Fellow in Science and Religion, interviewed in this book, Islamists claim to represent official Islam, concealing their totalitarian ideologies in a veil of faith.[59] Through stealth or violent Jihad, they wage war from what she calls an "entrenched position of anti-Western de-secularization.[60] They claim ownership of the public space by divine right, suffocating everyone else,"[61] and they do it by purposefully labeling critics of Islamism as "Islamophobes" and/or "racists."[62]

This victimology subterfuge is effective in the West, as Westerners value dialogue and acceptance, and are inclined to be solicitous of those who appear to be disadvantaged. Ahmed goes on to explain the Islamist's mastery at manipulating the Western masses, by "preying on the ignorance of Islam" to advance an "anti-Western, anti-Zionist, anti-Semitic, anti-secular propaganda."[63]

Turkey's Prime Minister, Ahmet Davutoğlu, visited Ottawa in September 2012 when he was foreign minister, and called on the West to fight "Islamophobia."[64] "Islamophobia" he said, "should be declared a crime against humanity."[65] He commended Canada's multicultural identity while condemning what he called the profiling of Muslims at US airports. He referred to this alleged profiling as a provocation that can alter the psychological atmosphere of an entire country;[66] yet he made no reference to how global Islamic terrorism can have the same, or worse, impact.

In the same week as Davutoğlu's visit to Ottawa, Turkish President Recep Tayyip Erdogan, who was Prime Minister at the time, also pronounced "Islamophobia" a "crime against humanity"[67] in the wake of the film, *Innocence of Muslims*, which the Obama administration blamed for the murders in Libya of US Ambassador Christopher Stevens and three other American diplomats.[68]

There have been numerous instances of intimidation and death threats, as well as murders and attempted murders by Muslim extremists against those who are deemed to have insulted Islam. In addition to the massacre at the offices of satirical magazine *Charlie Hebdo*, there was the famous Iranian death fatwa against Indian novelist Salman Rushdie, the murder of Theo van Gogh on an Amsterdam street in 2004, the attempt on the life of Danish Islam critic Lars Hedegaard, and threats against such critics of Islamism as Ayaan Hirsi Ali, Magdi Allam, Kurt Westergaard, Geert Wilders, Dr. Wafa Sultan, and even Gillian Gibbons, a kindergarten teacher in the Sudan whose students named a toy teddy bear Muhammad.[69] Westerners who witness intimidation and bullying by Islamists are often given the impression that if anyone ever felt that he or she may have insulted Muhammad, or Islam, he or she as a freedom-loving individual could expect to be never left in peace again.[70]

The Danish cartoonist Kurt Westergaard, who barely escaped death at the hands of an axe-wielding Somali Muslim, recently warned that the West cannot retreat into silence for fear of offending Islamist sensibilities.[71]

Another case of "Islamophobia" appeared with the release of the documentary, *Honor Diaries,* in tribute of International Women's Day in 2014.[72] The Council on American Islamic Relations (CAIR) launched a vehement attack on the film and sought to shut down screenings at many college campuses, including the University of Michigan and Illinois.[73]

Ayaan Hirsi Ali, a prominent and heroic defender of women's rights in the Islamic world, was involved in making *Honor Diaries*, as were two moderate Muslim women who are interviewed in this book: Raheel Raza and Dr. Qanta Ahmed. The documentary presents the personal stories of nine women with roots in the Islamic world. Many are devout practicing Muslims, but share a passion to expose the heinous abuses of women and girls in many Muslim countries that are committed in the name of family honor. These women defied the political correctness that exonerates the perpetrators of such abuses and encourages the untold sufferings of innocents. As these nine brave women tell their stories in *Honor Diaries*, they also defy the intimidation and bullying of powerful lobbies like CAIR that have cowed Westerners into believing that any light shone on the darkest corners of Islamism is "Islamophobic."

Dr. Zuhdi Jasser has repeatedly discussed how prominent Muslim groups such as CAIR and ISNA use the concept of victimology, and try to convince Muslim communities that they are in fact being victimized. These groups fuel the false notion that American Muslims are in perpetual danger at the hands of "racists" and "Islamophobes," while they practice the tactical deception of taqiyya in their promotion of the extremist rhetoric of their radical agenda.

Abdur-Rahman Muhammad, a former member of the International Institute for Islamic Thought (IIIT), was with IIIT when the word "Islamophobia" was formally branded, and has since then rejected the ideology of the IIIT.[74] He revealed the original intent behind the concept of "Islamophobia," stating, "[t]his loathsome term is nothing more than a thought-terminating cliché conceived in the bowels of Muslim think tanks for the purpose of beating down critics."[75] He explained that "Muslims are everywhere in this country, doing practically everything. There are Muslim doctors, lawyers, and businessmen like Park 51 developer Sharif El-Gamal, who went from waiting tables just a few years ago to being a multimillionaire. There are Muslim soldiers and CIA agents. Could this be possible if America were Islamophobic?"[76]

There are those who try to put forth the argument that "Islamophobia" is not a post-9/11 term or phenomenon and claim that it was deeply rooted in Europe's essentialist orientalist perception of non-European cultures, especially Islam,[77] but the reality is this: Who had heard of this term prior to 9/11? It was virtually, if not wholly, non-existent as a conventional Western term until after 9/11, when it became fashionable to use it to shut down any legitimate criticism of Islam.

## MULTICULTURAL CANADA VULNERABLE TO "ISLAMOPHOBIA"

Canada, which functions under a Multicultural Act, is particularly vulnerable to Islamists' use of "Islamophobia," taqiyya, and victimology in their assaults on free speech. The Islamist tactic of "lawfare" involves exploiting the courts (and in Canada, the Human Rights Commissions) as weapons, by filing or threatening to file costly, frivolous, and malicious lawsuits to discourage anyone from criticizing Islam. The moderate Muslim Canadian Congress (MCC) stated in a lawfare case that was launched by the Canadian Islamic Congress against *Maclean's* magazine that the Ontario Human Rights Commission (OHRC) had "become the virtual organ of Canada's Islamist organizations and that it has taken sides in the bitter struggle within Canada's Muslim community where Sharia-supporting Islamists are pitted against liberal and secular Muslims."[78] A main criticism that the MCC leveled against the OHRC was that it was "perpetuating the Islamist myth that Muslims in Canada are a persecuted group."[79]

Looking at persecuted groups in the US, in 2013 the FBI released their annual crime statistics report on hate crimes. It showed that hate crimes against Muslims remain rare. In looking at the 1,663 hate offenses reported by law enforcement, 14.2 percent of hate crimes motivated by religious bias were against Muslims, while 59.2 percent were against Jews.[80]

In an attempt to protect free speech against the multifaceted challenge of the "Islamophobia" ploy, in the autumn of 2011, Conservative Member of Parliament Brian Storseth introduced a ground breaking Private Members Bill (C-304) to repeal Section 13 of the Canadian Human Rights Act, which banned hate speech over the Internet or by telephone.[81] The bill in effect stripped the authority of Canada's Human Rights Commissions to investigate online hate speech, as well as the commissions' authority to remove these websites if they were found in violation. Storseth, in his presentation to the House of Commons, called freedom of speech "a fundamental principle in our democracy and one which Canadians have fought and died for, for over a century," as well as a freedom on which all other freedoms are built.[82] He continued a step further in a call to all his countrymen: "This is not a fight that one Canadian can take on himself, but rather an issue that all Canadians must engage in vigorously."[83]

Bruce Bawer contends in his book, *While Europe Slept,* that the Islamization of Europe is being implemented largely without violence and without any effective response from European leaders, who are blind to the ambitions of Sharia supremacists.[84] [85]

Nina Shea, a former commissioner on the US Commission on International Religious Freedom, notes that for over 20 years, the OIC has been pressuring the West to restrict free speech in accordance with its charter to "to combat defamation of Islam."[86] Shea also cites the 2009 fatwas issued by an official OIC organization, the International Islamic Fiqh (Jurisprudence) Academy calling for bans on free speech, legislation to protect Islamic interests, and judicial punishment for public expressions of apostasy.[87] Shea highlights the demands to ban free speech by such groups as Egypt's Salafist Nour party, Iran's theocrats, Hezbollah, and al Qaeda–linked groups.[88]

In Canada, a video created by a member of the Canadian military mocking terrorist mastermind Osama bin Laden was deemed "Islamophobic."[89] The video, shown during an event, was a satire of the brutalities practiced within Islamic regimes, which freedom-loving Muslims themselves rail against. A lieutenant general issued an apology to those who were offended, and stated that the military has "zero tolerance for acts that do not reflect our Canadian values, especially the respect we owe to other cultures and religions."[90] A full military investigation was also launched, with a promise to follow through with disciplinary action against those involved. CAIR-CAN called it "tragic that an ignorant prank threatens to cast a shadow on our heritage."[91] The real tragedy, however, was the intimidation and attempt at censorship, which the West continually encounters in the face of Islamism.

## THE FREE SPEECH ANTIDOTE

Irshad Manji once told Canada's *Globe and Mail* that "offending people may be the only way to achieving a pluralistic society."[92] In opposition to this is the social advancement of Muslim victimology: The Islamophobia Research and Documentation Project, which is promoted by the Center for Research and Gender at the University of California, Berkeley, "focuses on a systematic and empirical approach to the study of 'Islamophobia' and its impact on the American Muslim community."[93] The study claims that Muslims are feared, demonized, and discriminated against in the West. It refers to "Islamophobia" taking "center stage" at the "highest levels of political discourse," because the first black president was feared to be a "closet Muslim" by a "sizeable number of Americans."[94] The Islamophobia Research and Documentation Project also focused on the usual clichés of the "dominant culture," and how the War on Terror was used to reintroduce "long-discredited Eurocentric paradigms," while claiming that the War on Terror had had devastating effects upon the Muslim community.[95]

Racism is alive and well, and "Islamophobia" is a term that was invented for a specific purpose: advancing the goals of the Muslim Brotherhood in the West by haranguing and intimidating critics of Islam. The "Islamophobia" deception has served as a brilliant tool to disarm the West from fighting the necessary ideological war against Islamism. By attempting to force a blackout of any spoken or written word that questions or critiques Islam, the West is unwittingly capitulating to Islamism. The best defense against the "Islamophobia" ploy is the active defense of our constitutions that are based on human rights, defending free speech, even when offensive, and encouraging pluralism within Islam. To criticize or insult Islam—or any religion for that matter—is neither racist nor an act of incitement; in fact, the reverse is true: Smothering public discourse creates fertile ground for toxic emotions to fester against all Muslims, and exacerbate frustrations about Islamism seeping across our Western borders. I was in attendance at a speech delivered by a Swedish Democrat politician, which addressed some troubling ills stemming from the influx of Muslim immigrants and refugees to Western countries, when a polite, level-headed lady applauded the shooting of an innocent Muslim. The speaker immediately admonished her applause, which was motivated by unaddressed concern and impatience. Free speech is the weapon that vanquishes the spread of ideological Jihad that is in turn fueling anger and retaliation in Western citizens.

## CHAPTER THIRTEEN

# THE ISRAEL FACTOR

If I say I support the existence of Israel, which is part of the whole reform idea, then I am a Zionist agent, or I and other reformists/moderates are not Muslims. The uneducated village guy in Pakistan will burn his shirt and give his life for Palestine, and if you ask him where it is on the map, he has no clue.

—Raheel Raza

This is a key litmus test. Even though to me, the Palestinian–Israeli issue is not an Islamic one, [it is] the geo politics of the Palestinians....

—Dr. Zuhdi Jasser

The moment I find a Muslim who is anti-Semitic—either overtly or covertly, I would question whether they have Islamist sympathies....Even those Muslims who are among the most educated can be Islamists who are astonishingly anti-Semitic and who deny the Holocaust.

—Dr. Qanta Ahmed

THE MAJORITY OF MODERATES INTERVIEWED in Part One of this book noted that belief in the right of Israel to exist is a straightforward litmus test in separating moderates from Islamists. Dr. Tawfik Hamid indicated that Islamists can lie about their belief in Israel's right to exist and that a better litmus test is their justification for attacking innocent Israeli civilians: "I am a typical Arab Egyptian with a Muslim background. As any Arab, I was brought up on hating Israel and the Jews. When I was four years old, the dehumanization of the Jews everywhere around me led me to imagine them as green ugly people, full of evil."[1]

Dr. Daniel Pipes points out that sentiments about Israel are not necessarily a litmus test in identifying an Islamist from a moderate, as one need not be a Muslim to oppose Israel's right to exist. This chapter explores the historic and current sentiments among Islamists toward the Jewish people. The Koran says that Jews are the worst enemies of the Muslims (5:82) and under Allah's curse (9:30). It will be noted that Islamists have a common disdain for Jews and do not support the Jewish State, as Dr. Pipes pointed out in a *Fox News* interview *On the Record with Greta Van Susteren* in June 2002. Van Susteren asked, "How central is Muslim anti-Semitism?" Pipes answered, "In many ways, the Muslim world today is comparable to Nazi Germany in the extent to which one finds anti-Semitic themes found pervasively throughout the culture."[2] Even though one cannot unequivocally conclude that any Muslim who does not support the State of Israel's right to exist is an Islamist, such sentiments should at least prompt an observer to suspect Islamist sympathies.

## "WHY MUSLIMS MUST HATE JEWS"

Nonie Darwish, an Egyptian-American human rights activist, ex-Muslim, author of *The Devil We Don't Know*, and well-known critic of Islam, explains "why Muslims must hate Jews."[3] She discusses the routine preaching by clerics and politicians across the Muslim world that exemplify what Pakistani religious leader, Pirzada Muhammad Raza Saqib Mustafai, stated, "When the Jews are wiped out...the sun of peace would begin to rise on the entire world." Darwish points out that few people in the Western media are alarmed or even care to expose this "dreadful dark side of Islam's obsession with Jew hatred," that she calls a pathology and atrocity against Jewish people.[4]

Darwish also states that Muslims justify hating Jews because they claim that Jews betrayed Muhammad. This is so deeply ingrained that even when she was no longer a Muslim, she said she initially continued to believe that Jews deserved to be killed, terrorized, and even lied to and victimized with propaganda. Even more astonishing is her claim that "to the average Muslim, routinely cursing Jews in mosques feels normal and even holy."[5]

Darwish states that the foremost duty of the faithful is to protect Islam's reputation, which overrides even the life of its followers, so that it does not matter how many Muslims die in the process of preserving Islam's reputation. In addition to this pride in Islam's reputation, Darwish states that the roots of Islamic hatred of the Jews can be traced back to Muhammad.[6]

When Muhammad embarked on his mission to spread Islam, he sought legitimacy and support from the two Abrahamic religions: Judaism and Christianity, to which the Koran refers to as "People of the Book."[7] During a period of fierce persecution against the Muslims, Muhammad encouraged his beleaguered followers with a message of patience and perseverance, virtues demonstrated by Moses and the Jews who were persecuted in Egypt. Thus there are friendly references to Jews in the first Mecca part of the Koran, in which the Torah was described as containing "guidance and light" (5:44) and Jews were called a "righteous" people (6:153–154), who "excelled the nations" (45:16).[8] After the death of his respected and affluent wife Khadijah, who encouraged him to follow his path and is in fact considered to be the "first Muslim," Islamic tradition forced Muhammad to suffer rejection and ridicule from his own tribe. He fled to Medina, where he expected Jews to welcome him.[9] When the Jews did not do so and refused to convert to Islam, the Jews became, in his view and that of the Koran, the "most intense of the people in animosity" toward Muslims (Sura 5:82).[10]

This is where some adherents of Islam contend that Muhammad faced an existential threat to his religion and that he was defending it from hostile opposition as he waged a war in self-defense, against the Jews of Medina and Arab tribes. According to Darwish's explanation of history, "Muhammad never got over his anger, humiliation, and rejection by 'the people of the book' and went to his grave tormented and obsessed that some Jews were still alive, even commanding Muslims to 'kill them wherever you find them,'" as stated in Sura 2:191–193.[11] Darwish's views of Muhammad's intent and character will remain a point of discussion and disagreement among Muslims of all perspectives, including moderates, but the abiding hatred of the Jews by Islamists is disturbing evidence of the deeply ingrained nature of Islamic anti-Semitism.[12]

## AN UNQUENCHABLE JEW HATRED

On November 23, 1937, Saudi Arabia's King Ibn Saud told British Colonel H.R.P. Dickson:

> "Our hatred for the Jews dates from God's condemnation of them for their persecution and rejection of Isa (Jesus) and their subsequent rejection of His chosen Prophet."[13] He continued that "for a Muslim to kill a Jew, or for him to be killed by a Jew, ensures him an immediate entry into Heaven and into the august presence of God Almighty."[14]

When Hitler introduced the Nuremberg Laws in 1935, he received congratulatory telegrams from throughout the Arab world. The Nuremberg Laws were anti-Jewish statutes that determined racial policy and removed Jewish influences from Aryan society. They were intended to ostracize, discriminate, and expel Jews from Germany,[15] depriving Jews of German citizenship. Germans were forbidden from marrying Jews, and sexual relations between Jews and Germans were criminalized.[16] During the Holocaust, one of Hitler's most ardent supporters was the Grand Mufti of Jerusalem, Haj Amin al-Husseini. Under the Mufti's direction, Arab Muslims adopted laws patterned after those of the Nazis. Jews were never permitted to live in Jordan according to Civil Law No. 6, which stated explicitly: "Any man will be a Jordanian subject if he is not Jewish. The Jews spare no effort to deceive us, deny our Prophet, incite against us, and distort the holy scriptures."[17] An Arabic translation of Adolf Hitler's *Mein Kampf* has become a bestseller in the Palestinian territories.[18] In 2005, the official Palestinian Authority information website, Al-Nakba, which was directly connected to Palestinian Authority President Mahmoud Abbas, published a copy of the Protocols of the Elders of Zion in Arabic, while in its English section, the copy is notably absent.[19]

According to *Palestinian Media Watch*, Abbas' vicious anti-Jewish libel is being taught to grade 10 students in the Palestinian Authority (PA), with a history book that was published in 2004 by the Palestinian

Ministry of Education.[20] It teaches students that Zionism is a global danger and the foundations of Zionism were created at the First Zionist Congress; "The Protocols of the Elders of Zion" is supposedly a transcript of the proceedings, the goal of which was global domination. Despite extensive archeological evidence of the Jewish roots in Israel, PA curricula teaches that the Jewish claim to the Holy Land was invented, and that the land of Israel is really Arab Islamic "Palestine," with no Jewish roots.[21] Palestinian children are further taught hatred of Jews. Grade 9 students study from official textbooks that assert: "Treachery and disloyalty are character traits of the Jews and therefore one should beware of them."[22] Jews are deemed Satanic, violent, and cunning, "thieving conquerors" who have stolen Arab land and must be fought and defeated, while Jihad is encouraged and glorified as a means to liberate "Palestine."[23] Even children's poetry contains Jihadist indoctrination.[24] Grade 5 students memorize such lines as, "I shall take my soul in my hand and hurl it into the abyss of death."[25] Children on official Palestinian television have recited those same verses. Grade 6 children read about a young boy who grew up with "the love of Jihad flowing through his veins and filling every fiber of his being"; and that "joy" comes only at "the sight of the enemy lying dead" or "fleeing for their lives."[26] This culture of death and enmity toward Jews is engrained in children, and "Palestine" replaces Israel on all maps in PA textbooks. Jews are cast as enemies of Islam, along with European colonizers.[27] In this invented history, students are taught that Arabs lived in "Palestine" before the Jews, Palestinian Arabs are deemed the descendants of Canaanites, and Jerusalem is depicted as an ancient Arab city built before Islam.[28] Jews are therefore depicted as illegitimate thieves of Palestinian lands, foreign invaders, and an evil and unwelcome presence in the land of Palestine, to be uprooted.

Following the 1967 Six Day War, Israelis discovered public school textbooks used in the West Bank that were filled with racist and hateful portrayals of Jews. Syrian textbooks have also been studied, and they, too, were replete with promoting hatred against Israel, Jews, and Zionism.[29]

Anti-Semitism in the Muslim world is so normalized that the most absurd claims can be made against Jews without query. The late King Faisal of Saudi Arabia once said that Jews "have a certain day on which they mix the blood of non-Jews into their bread and eat it."[30] He proceeded with a tale that while in Paris visiting, police discovered five murdered children whose blood had been drained, and "it turned out that some Jews had murdered them in order to take their blood and mix it with the bread that they eat on this day."[31]

In 1999, when then–First Lady Hillary Clinton visited Gaza, the late PA Chairman Yasser Arafat's wife Suha said that "our people have been subjected to the daily and extensive use of poisonous gas by the Israeli forces, which has led to an increase in cancer cases among women and children."[32] Other outrageous allegations have been made by other Palestinian officials about Israel: dumping toxic waste in the West Bank, marketing carcinogenic juice to Palestinians, releasing wild pigs in the West Bank to destroy crops. Israel has also been accused of infecting Palestinians with AIDS and dropping poison candy from planes for children in Gaza.[33]

According to an Arab media review by the Anti-Defamation League investigating anti-Semitism, vicious anti-Semitic articles and malicious cartoons are published daily across Arab media that include menacing depictions of Jews with big noses, black coats and hats, and large skull caps.[34] Many Jews are shown promoting global dominance and implicated in conspiracy theories; there are also numerous blood libels. Images that portray Israel include scorpions, snakes, and Nazi symbols. Such sinister and mocking themes are incorporated with news reports about the "Israeli settlements," Iran's nuclear ambitions, and the new relationship between Israel and South Sudan that was condemned in a Sudanese news report as a "threat to Sudan's national security" because Israel was and will always be "the sole mortal enemy to Sudan."[35]

Robert Wistrich, Neuburger Professor of European and Jewish history at the Hebrew University of Jerusalem, expresses an important historic point in his article "Islamic Judeophobia: An Existential Threat" —an excerpt from the book, *Muhammad's Monsters*:[36]

"On November 18, 1947, Hitler's closest confidante, Albert Speer, wrote down the following recollection in his Spandau prison diary which today sounds eerily prophetic:

'I recall how [Hitler] would have films shown in the Reich Chancellory about London burning, about the sea of fire over Warsaw, about exploding convoys, and the kind of ravenous joy that would then seize him every time. But I never saw him so beside himself as when, in a delirium, he pictured New York going down in flames. He described how the skyscrapers would be transformed into gigantic burning torches, how they would collapse in confusion, how the bursting city's reflection would stand against the dark sky....' "[37]

According to Wistrich, this "frenzied imagery" became manifested itself on 9/11 by Islamists, who were filled with the same "unquenchable hatred" that the Nazis and fascists had against the Jews of that era, and that hatred is not only for America and the West, but also for Jews and the State of Israel.[38]

## MODERN DAY JEW-HATRED

I. Hezbollah leader Hassan Nasrallah referred to the State of Israel as a "cancerous entity" of "ultimate evil" whose "annihilation... is a definite matter," and says, "if we searched the entire world for a person more cowardly, despicable, weak, and feeble in psyche, mind, ideology and religion, we would not find anyone like *the Jew*. Notice, I do not say the Israeli"; and also, "If they [Jews] all gather in Israel, it will save us the trouble of going after them worldwide."[39]

II. The Grand Mufti of Jerusalem, Haj Amin al-Husseini, collaborated with Adolf Hitler and Adolf Eichmann during World War II to kill the Jews. Al-Husseini so despised Jews that when he learned that Eichmann intended to swap thousands of Jewish children for German POWs, he protested vehemently, forcing Eichmann to cancel the swap. This cancellation resulted in those Jewish children being sent to death camps in Poland. Germans, acting upon the exhortations of al-Husseini, also slaughtered 90 percent of Bosnia's Jews.[40]

III. CAIR's New York chapter Advocacy Director Cyrus McGoldrick vilifies Israel and does not believe in the right of Israel to exist, according to a statement he made in a Twitter post: "Supporters of a '2-state solution' in Palestine will share a page of history with the defenders of apartheid in South Africa." McGoldrick also supports the anti-Israel, Iranian-inspired Al Quds rally.[41] When the Muslim Brotherhood was poised to take control of the Egyptian parliament in January 2011, a leading member of the MB, Mohammed Ghannam, told the Arabic-language Iranian news network *Al-Alam*: "The people should be prepared for war against Israel. The Egyptian people are prepared for anything to get rid of this regime."[42] Muslim Brotherhood Deputy Leader Dr. Rashad Bayoumi stated in an interview published in the Arabic daily *al-Hayat* that his organization would not recognize Israel "under any circumstances."[43] His comments came shortly after the Muslim Brotherhood, of which Hamas is an offshoot, welcomed and hosted Hamas's Gaza leader Ismail Haniyeh at the Muslim Brotherhood's Cairo-area headquarters, where Haniyeh was greeted by the Muslim Brotherhood's Supreme Guide Mohamed ElBaradei.[44] It was Haniyeh's first trip outside of Gaza since Hamas took over Gaza in 2007, and he boasted that his visit to the Brotherhood center in Cairo would confuse and frighten Israel and that "our presence with the Brotherhood threatens the Israeli entity." In article 15 under Hamas's Covenant of the Islamic Resistance Movement, Jihad for the Liberation of Palestine is an Individual Duty.[45] In a speech in Gaza, the senior leader of Hamas, Khaled Meshaal, stated that "Israel is illegitimate, and will remain so....The liberation of Palestine—all of Palestine—is a duty, a right, a goal, and a purpose....Jihad and armed resistance are the proper and true path to liberation and to the restoration of our rights, along with all other forms of struggle....All these forms of struggle, however, are worthless without resistance....How wonderful was your shelling of Tel Aviv."[46] In response to this speech, Senior Fatah official Azzam al-Ahmad welcomed it as "very positive" and urged implementation of a unity government deal drafted by Fatah and Hamas, which finally came to fruition.[47] Meshaal has also said, "Before Israel dies, it must be humiliated and degraded. Allah willing...we will make them lose their eyesight, we will make them lose their brains."[48]

IV. The Palestinian Authority (PA), continues its promotion of martyrdom and cultural hate propaganda against Jews and Israel in open events and arts broadcasts. A December 2013 event broadcast live on PA official TV under the auspices of PA leader Mahmoud Abbas featured the participation of the PA Minister of Culture Anwar Abu Aisha. Abu Aisha opened the event, which was hosted by Ramallah's Youth Club and called "5th Festival of the Heritage of the Fathers."[49] The event awarded plaques of honor to two terrorists on stage, who had been freed two months earlier as a "gesture" for peace talks. On the plaques was a map of "Palestine," wiping out Israel altogether.[50] During the event, a play was performed by PA youth that portrayed divided Hamas and Fatah supporters. A female actress then unites the groups with calls to "blot out" Israel. Upon unifying, the actors shoot and kill all the "Israeli" actors. A PA Arab spy is discovered among them, and as he pleads for pardon, the group's lead shooter shoots him in the head, saying, "He's a traitor, a damn spy. In life, it's either victory or martyrdom, death for Allah." Upon his execution, the audience erupts in applause.[51]

V. David Matas, senior legal counsel for B'nai Brith Canada, created a report on the "B'nai B'rith International Mission to the 25th session of the United Nations Human Rights Council" in March 2014. He refers to the link between the Palestinian leadership and the Organization of Islamic Cooperation (OIC).[52] In the report, he states, "The Organization of Islamic Conference (which was renamed the Organization of Islamic Cooperation in 2011) was created after the Six Day War, in September 1969, in large measure to promote accusations against Israel of occupation and settlements." He points out what the OIC Charter states as one of its purposes: "to support the struggle of the Palestinian people, who are presently under foreign occupation, and to empower them to attain their inalienable rights, including the right to self-determination, and to establish their sovereign state with Al-Quds Al-Sharif as its capital, while safeguarding its historic and Islamic character, and the holy places therein."[53] Matas further points out that this means that the Palestinian leadership has been able to exercise not one, but 57 votes in the United Nations General Assembly, which have been used to attack the existence of Israel, in the PA's overriding determination to obliterate Israel.[54]

VI. Yusuf al-Qaradawi, who is an Egyptian Islamic scholar, spiritual leader to the Muslim Brotherhood, and a highly influential force among Muslims worldwide, has stated, "Throughout history, Allah has imposed upon the [Jews] people who would punish them for their corruption. The last punishment was carried out by Hitler. By means of all the things he did to them—even though they exaggerated this issue—he managed to put them in their place. This was divine punishment for them. Allah willing, the next time will be at the hand of the believers."[55]

It can be argued that being an anti-Semite does not make one an Islamist, it can also be argued that extreme Israel and Jew-hatred is endemic among Islamists. Most of the moderates interviewed in Part One identified the right of Israel to exist as an easy litmus test to distinguish moderates from Islamists, or as a means to ascertain the presence of Islamist sympathies. The interviewees also exposed the Islamist intensity of sentiment with regards to Israel. As Nonie Darwish noted, this antipathy is not based on rational thought, or Israeli and Palestinian history; rather, it is fueled and reinforced by a propaganda machine rooted in the belief that Jews betrayed Muhammad.

## CHAPTER FOURTEEN

# WHO SPEAKS FOR MUSLIMS?

CAIR, the Islamic Society of North America (ISNA), the International Institute of Islamic Thought (IIIT), the Muslim Student Associations (MSA), and these groups are Wahhabis. They uphold the same Wahhabi culture of ISIS and al Qaeda. According to their innermost Wahhabi faith, they are dividing the world into two camps: the camp of believers and the camp of war. It is needed for them to have the fifth column inside the enemy camp.

—SHEIKH SUBHY MANSOUR

Most mosques in North America and in Europe and around the world are basically reflecting the argument of Muslim Brotherhood and Jamaat Islam. This has been facilitated by petrodollars. It exerts an influence on the world stage since 1972–73 since oil prices went up.

—DR. SALIM MANSUR

IN THE WEST THERE EXISTS A CLASH between moderate Muslims who seek to educate and forewarn the public about Islamism and atrocities committed under Sharia law, and the Islamists, who claim to represent the interests of Muslim communities in the West while furtively advancing Sharia law.

It has proven to be a difficult task for Westerners, especially authorities, to determine which organizations adequately represent the interests and collective voice of Muslims. Dr. Qanta Ahmed stated in Chapter Six:

"Islamists claim they are being persecuted and they claim they are being silenced when underneath, they are stealthily advancing their own mission. The problem with Islamists is that they become self-appointed advocates for the Muslim communities that never elected them."

Daniel Pipes warns:

"It's a common practice for Islamists to claim to be moderates and reformers and they convince a lot of people. The key is whether they are trying to apply Islamic law in its entirety or not. The key is not how fast they are trying to do it."

In discrediting the word "Islamism" at the behest of CAIR, in April 2013 the *Associated Press* decided to discontinue the word Islamist as a "synonym for Islamic fighters, militants, extremists, or radicals." CAIR Communications Director, Ibrahim Hooper, claimed that Islamism "has become shorthand for 'Muslims we don't like'" and "is currently used in an almost exclusively pejorative context."[1]

This chapter investigates how Westerners are being manipulated in accordance with what will be referred to as the Islamist Project, which is advancing the goal of establishing global Sharia.

CAIR's stated mission is "to enhance understanding of Islam, encourage dialogue, protect civil liberties, empower American Muslims, and build coalitions that promote justice and mutual understanding,"[2] but the FBI's former Chief of Counterterrorism, Steven Pomerantz, noted that CAIR gives aid to international terrorist groups.[3] The group was also deemed an "unindicted co-conspirator" in the Holy Land Foundation Trial—the largest terrorist financing trial in US history—along with two other prominent Muslim organizations that claim to represent the interests of American Muslims: the Islamic Society of North America (ISNA) and the North American Islamic Trust (NAIT).[4]

Abdur-Rahman Muhammad, former member of the International Institute for Islamic Thought (IIIT), emphasized the importance of the US government moving to "stop legitimizing groups" like CAIR, MPAC (the Muslim Public Affairs Council), and ISNA, which he described as a "fifth column" in the United States.[5] In other words, they are the covert Islamists among us.

## A CULTURAL INVASION DISGUISED

According to strategic policy and intelligence expert Clare Lopez, one of the most "mainstream" of Muslim Brotherhood (MB) front groups operating on North American soil is the Islamic Society of North America (ISNA). She cites research from the Center for Security Policy that ISNA "functions as a kind of umbrella organization for many hundreds of offshoot Islamic Societies across North America."[6]

Despite the fact that the Department of Justice views ISNA as a front group for the Muslim Brotherhood, the organization was granted an advisory role with the National Security Council of the Obama administration.[7] The organization's president, Muhammad Magid, was a member of the Department of Homeland Security's "Countering Violent Extremism" Advisory Council, and participated in a CIA training session in 2012 at CIA headquarters in Langley, Virginia, where he spoke about "Building Communities of Trust: A Local Example of a Partnership between the All Dulles Area Muslim Society (ADAMS) and Law Enforcement."[8]

The Egyptian magazine, *Rose El-Youssef*, claimed in December 2012 that six American Islamist activists who worked with the Obama administration were Muslim Brotherhood operatives who strongly influenced US policy, and managed to turn the White House "from a position hostile to Islamic groups and organizations in the world to the largest and most important supporter of the Muslim Brotherhood."[9] The article claimed that they influenced policy development for homeland security, foreign policy toward Israel, and counterterrorism strategies, and suggested that secret materials were leaked.[10]

Here are some additional examples of how a kind of cultural invasion of North America has advanced through Islamists:

I. Attacks on free speech: Islamists have targeted embassies abroad and individuals at home for "insulting" Muhammad. The *Innocence of Muslims* film led to frenzied attacks from Tunisia to Indonesia, beginning in Cairo at the US embassy, where a fanatical mob breached embassy walls and hoisted the black al Qaeda flag.[11] Following the riots, in reference to the putative insults to Muhammad, the newly elected presidents of Egypt and Yemen took to the podium at the UN to demand that blasphemy be outlawed globally.[12] Saudi Arabia went further to call for "international collaboration to address freedom of expression."[13] Yet in the face of such violence, US Secretary of State Hillary Clinton declared in a foreign policy speech that "Muslims are peaceful and tolerant people and have nothing whatsoever to do with terrorism,"[14] perpetuating the myth that Islam has no need of reform and need not conform to laws and rights enshrined in the United Nations Charter and the Universal Declaration of Human Rights.

II. In 2013, while addressing the UN Alliance of Civilizations conference in Vienna, then–Turkish Prime Minister and current President Recep Tayyip Erdogan complained of prejudice against Muslims and declared that "Islamophobia" should be considered a "crime against humanity…just like Zionism, like anti-Semitism, and like fascism."[15] After becoming president, Erdogan said that the European Union "must admit Turkey" as a member if it opposed "Islamophobia."[16]

III. An 89-page report, "Hate Ideology Fills American Mosques," was released in 2006 following a year-long study of over two hundred original documents, collected from over a dozen US mosques.[17] The report found a "totalitarian ideology of hatred that can incite to violence" being propagated in American mosques, and declared that this ideology was "being mainstreamed within our borders through the efforts of a foreign government, namely Saudi Arabia." Dave Gaubatz, counterterrorism agent, researcher, and contributing editor to *Family Security Matters*, states that Muslim children attending mosques, Islamic schools, and centers are also being taught violence and hatred against America, and that children as young as seven are being taught that US assimilation means disrespect and dishonor to Islam. They are also being taught that American military personnel are the enemies of Islam and that it is justifiable to kill anyone who dishonors or opposes the Islamic ideology.[18]

IV. Islamic enclaves have sprouted up, in which police are forbidden entry and women are second-class citizens. According to FBI documents obtained by the Clarion Project, radical Muslims are living in communities across the US that are closed to the public, and many are suspected of being homegrown terrorist training centers.[19] A Jihadist enclave was uncovered in Texas, belonging to the network of Muslims of the Americas (MOA).[20] The enclave is linked to a Pakistani militant organization called Jamaat ul-Fuqra, with a 70-acre headquarters in New York, called Islamberg.[21] In February 2016, a disturbing discovery revealed that CAIR had become "intertwined" with this group.[22]

V. In Dearborn, Michigan, Christian street preachers were accosted by an unruly crowd of dozens of Arab Muslim men, women, and children. They were verbally abusive and then physically violent with the Christians, pushing them and hurling objects at them that included bottles, eggs, and rocks and shouting, "Allahu Akbar—God is Great." The Christians repeatedly asked for protection from Wayne County Sheriff's Department officers who were present during the melee but they were denied, indicating that a sovereign country had now relinquished legal control of portions of its territory.[23]

VI. University campuses across North America have been hijacked by hostile, energized Muslim Student Associations and Palestinian Solidarity Network Groups who promote militant Islamic ideologies while demonizing Israel, especially with "Israel Apartheid Week" initiatives.[24]

VII. In airports, security policy has become most inconvenient to travelers since 9/11, yet research shows that some niqab-wearers are given free passes through airport security.[25]

VIII. Islamic Invasion of US border control: Edward Nelson, Chairman of the US Border Control, blames US immigration policy for aiding the Boston Marathon bombing brothers, 26-year-old Tamerlan Tsarnaev and 19-year-old Dzhokhar Tsarnaev from Cambridge, Massachusetts, through a lax system regularly abused by terrorists.[26] The brothers applied for asylum; to get asylum, they would have had to meet the definition of a refugee. However, unlike refugees, applicants for asylum are already in the United States.[27] During the Boston Marathon on April 15, 2013, two pressure-cooker bombs exploded, killing 3 people and injuring over 260 others.[28] Nelson says that obtaining residence in the country is as easy for terrorists as claiming fear of persecution on at least one of five internationally recognized grounds of race, religion, nationality, or membership in a social group or political opinion.[29] One need only consider the risks associated with the tens of thousands of Syrian refugees resettling into United States and Canada, where an ISIS operative revealed the terror group has already smuggled thousands of covert Jihadists into Europe.[30] There is an Islamic practice called "hijrah" emigration, a form of stealth Jihad. Koran 4:100 states of hijrah: "And whoever emigrates for the cause of Allah will find on the earth many locations and abundance. And whoever leaves his home as an emigrant to Allah and His Messenger and then death overtakes him, his reward has already become incumbent upon Allah. And Allah is ever Forgiving and Merciful."[31]

IX. Infiltration by Iran: This became so severe the Canadian government made the decision to shut down Iran's embassy in Ottawa in 2012, as a network of Iranian infiltrators was establishing a fifth column. *Fox News* released an alarming article about an Iranian official working as a cultural counselor in the Iranian Embassy in Canada; he was using the embassy to mobilize Iranian loyalists to infiltrate the Canadian government and eventually "attack the United States."[32] It was also revealed that the Iranian government commanded Iranian-Canadians to "resist being melted into the dominant Canadian culture," to aspire to "occupy high-level key positions…[and] be of service to our beloved Iran." For its decision to shut down the Iranian embassy, Canada was called an "extremist government" that was serving Israel's "Zionist regime."[33]

X. Muslim men are allowed to immigrate to Ontario with multiple wives and collect welfare payments, even though it is illegal to marry more than one wife in Canada.[34]

XI. In the Canadian school system special treatment for Muslims is being demanded, and some public schools and universities granted Muslim requests for prayer times, prayer rooms, and ritual footbaths.[35] A school in Toronto created a "makeshift Muslim congregation" in the cafeteria, which came to be known as the "Mosqueteria."[36] The case drew an outcry with its full display of sexism where girls were forced to pray behind the boys to maintain "modesty" and where menstruating girls sat in the back and were excused from prayer until their "cleanliness" returned.[37]

Canada's Multicultural Act has unintentionally provided greater opportunities for exploitation by Islamists operating covertly through their lobby groups and those who support their efforts, often unwittingly or from political expediency.

In 2011, many leaders openly declared multiculturalism a failure, including French President Nicolas Sarkozy, German Chancellor Angela Merkel, British Prime Minister David Cameron, Australia's former Prime Minister John Howard, and former Spanish Prime Minister José María Aznar.[38] Sarkozy summed it up nicely, stating that there was too much concern "about the identity of the person who was arriving and not enough about the identity of the country that was receiving him," while calling for an end to "passive tolerance."[39]

XII. Despite the declarations about multiculturalism, in 2015, as the war in Syria continued and grew steadily more devastating, huge numbers of refugees from the Middle East, Africa, and elsewhere began flooding into Europe. One little-noted feature of this influx is its Islamist aspect. The Koran promises reward from Allah for those who "emigrate in the way of Allah" (4:100), which means to immigrate to a new land with the intention of Islamizing it; this is the core Islamic concept of hijrah.

Obviously this is not the motive of all of the refugees, but there were numerous signs that many had come to Europe not simply to escape the Syrian war. The Islamic State was discovered to be infiltrating the refugee stream; in fact, it had threatened in February 2015, shortly before the refugee influx began, to flood Europe with 500,000 refugees.[40] In September 2015, an ISIS Jihadist declared, "It's our dream that there should be a caliphate not only in Syria but in all the world, and we will have it soon, inshallah." He said that Jihadis were going into Europe "like refugees," but were planning Jihad attacks there: "Just wait."[41] On May 10, 2016, French intelligence official Patrick Calvar confirmed that ISIS operatives were entering Europe via migrant routes through the Balkans.[42]

This infiltration was successful: On November 13, 2015, nine Islamic Jihadists attacked at several sites in Paris, murdering 130 people. All of the attackers had entered Europe in 2015 as refugees.[43] Besides violent attacks, refugees were responsible for a sharp rise in crime, particularly rape.[44] Unrest seemed inevitable as refugees with values derived from Sharia flooded into a Europe built on Judeo–Christian values. In August 2016, Professor Abdessamad Belhaj, a Moroccan academic, observed, "In Islamic discourses, migration is seen as a beginning of the Islamization of Europe, the rich land that will change the fate of Islam, from a religion of the poor to a religion of the rich....Furthermore, immigration is justified as victory to the community."

Belhaj warned of upheaval in Europe's future because of the Islamic idea that "state law has no weight compared to the law of God." Nonetheless, he noted that Europe's political leaders "encourage migration and accommodate Islam." He added, "Migration is useful for the neoliberal model of the borderless, minimal, global society, but is calamitous for the European citizens as a whole."[45]

This proved to be true. Barack Obama, Angela Merkel, Justin Trudeau, and other Western leaders encouraged and facilitated this mass Muslim migration, and derided opposition to it as "racist." When Donald Trump was inaugurated President of the United States and moved immediately to restrict immigration in the interests of national security, he encountered fierce resistance and a chorus of global condemnation for his supposedly "racist" plan. Valid concerns about national security, and particularly ISIS threats of infiltration, were ignored. The furious response to Trump's proposal illustrated how deeply rooted Edward Said's notion of white Europeans "otherizing," stigmatizing, and demonizing "brown people" had become.

All this posed unique problems for Muslim moderates and reformers. They were presented with a sudden sharp increase in the numbers of their co-religionists in the West, bringing with them a challenge: Could the moderates and reformers articulate a vision of Islam that could convince their Sharia-adherent brethren to accept the parameters of Western secular pluralism? Or in even attempting to do so, would they themselves be vilified and threatened as heretics and apostates?

These are the ongoing questions and challenges to reformists that are addressed in this project and of which further illustrate the need to partner with reformists in opposition to Islamism.

## VOICES HIJACKING CANADA'S MULTICULTURALISM

Canada is well known for its Multicultural Act, being the first country in the world to officially adopt it. Under the Act it is recognized that "every individual is equal before and under the law" and that "all Canadians, whether by birth or by choice, enjoy equal status, are entitled to the same rights, powers, and privileges and are subject to the same obligations, duties, and liabilities."[46]

America and nations which do not have official multiculturalism policies have concerns that Canada's edict is too liberally applied, allowing immigrants to enter Canada, claim full equality, the right to continue cultural practices, such as polygamy, subjugation of women, and female genital mutilation, which are in conflict with Canadian values. Canada's broad application of multiculturalism, while well-intentioned, was not intended to function this way. The majority of Canada's political class yields to activists who manipulate multiculturalism to attract the immigrant vote, further enabling such manipulations. Liberal Prime Minister Justin Trudeau gave a speech at the Reviving the Islamic Spirit conference in Toronto, whose foremost sponsor was IRFAN-Canada (International Relief Fund for the Afflicted and Needy), which was stripped of its federal charity status for supporting Hamas.[47] According to the Canada Revenue Agency, "findings indicate that IRFAN-Canada provided $14.6 million in resources to operating partners that were run by officials of Hamas, openly supported and provided funding to Hamas, or have been listed by various jurisdictions because of their support for Hamas or other terrorist entitles."[48] Trudeau's attendance drew condemnation from the Friends of Simon Wiesenthal Center; many of its members expressed alarm about "whether the Liberals were aligning themselves with a belief system that is contrary to traditional Liberal values."[49] The moderate Muslim Canadian Congress also sent a letter requesting that Justin Trudeau skip the convention.[50] CAIR condemned attempts to "smear" the gathering, while CAIR-CAN (who changed its name to the National Council of Canadian Muslims) came out in defense of the convention, labeling criticism of IRFAN-Canada's sponsorship of the event as "yet another example of Islamophobic vitriol aimed at marginalizing and vilifying Muslims."[51][52]

Canada's multicultural experiment has become a left-wing/right-wing point of divide, which prevents the implementation of effective policies to combat the manipulation of the multiculturalist ethos by Islamists who are attuned to the powers of the multicultural voting bloc and encourage outreach by politicians to their communities. Competing rights and interests exist in America, even in the absence of a multicultural act, so to focus on blaming the Act, which is likely here to stay, is to divert necessary attention away from confronting Islamist exploitations and creating policies to stem them. The circular debate on the merits and flaws of Canada's commitment to multiculturalism prevents rational discussion of policies to contain Islamist infiltration. Furthermore, the Muslim Brotherhood Plan for North America will be addressed, of which the primary goal is "eliminating and destroying the Western civilization from within and 'sabotaging' its miserable house by their hands...so that...God's religion [Islam] is made victorious over all other religions."[53]

Another case of Canadian authorities partnering with Islamists involves an alliance between the Royal Canadian Mounted Police (RCMP) and the National Council of Canadian Muslims (formerly CAIR-CAN) to create a handbook entitled "United Against Terrorism," which was aimed at preventing youth radicalization. The RCMP appeared to disregard documented facts about this organization, an offshoot of CAIR deemed to be "unindicted co-conspirators" in terrorism, in a misguided attempt to embrace diversity. In other words, the RCMP did not do its homework under its own mandate of security. The handbook was released at a mosque in Winnipeg, Manitoba, in October 2014.[54] RCMP headquarters in Ottawa initially directed Mounties in Manitoba not to attend the unveiling of the handbook because of an "adversarial" tone[55] where no specifics were provided, especially of why the RCMP partnered with NCCM in the first place. A section of the handbook even advised that cooperation with Canadian Security Intelligence Service and the RCMP in investigations was "voluntary," and that there was "no obligation" to answer questions or give personal information about family and friends.[56] The handbook balked at the use of the word "moderate" to describe Muslims, presumably to make the word "Islamism" indistinct and thus harder to target. The term "moderate Muslim," the handbook says, "is an oxymoron. We never hear the term 'moderate Christians' or 'moderate Jews' or 'moderate atheists.' Why is this adjective then attached so frequently to the word 'Muslim'?"[57] The NCCM also recommended in the handbook that using the words "Jihad" and "terrorism" should be stopped, stating that by "labeling terrorists as 'Jihadis,' we are playing into the hands of violent extremists," when in fact, to not call a spade a spade is creating a cover for Islamic extremists and supremacists to operate concealed and unidentified. The handbook goes on to preposterously warn that "by equating terrorism with Jihad and by calling terrorists 'Jihadis,' the media, law enforcement, intelligence agencies, and politicians have confused the discourse, and this has been counterproductive in challenging the extremist narrative in the minds of the young and vulnerable."[58]

The Islamist drive to redefine the word "Jihad" to describe a personal striving or struggle faced by all of mankind is what confuses the discourse, where non-Muslims are presented as phobic and ignorant for regarding the term "Jihad" as a violent waging of holy war against unbelievers.[59] This is patently deceptive since in Hadith collections, Jihad means physical war and for Islamic jurists, Jihad is applied in the context of the world divided into Islamic zones (Dar al-Islam or Abode of Islam) vs. non-Islamic zones (Dar al-Harb or Abode of War),[60] so while the term "Jihad" can indeed reference a personal striving, it also has a specific political usage for Islamists, both violent and stealth.

An article in the *Ottawa Citizen* entitled, "Muslim Group Indulging in Lawfare Jihad?" reported an incident involving the NCCM, when the organization demanded that Rabbi Daniel Korobkin, senior rabbi at Beth Avraham Yoseph Congregation, the largest Orthodox congregation in Canada, be excluded from Prime Minister Stephen Harper's delegation to the Middle East. Korobkin's offense, according to the NCCM, was to introduce two critics of Islam, Robert Spencer and Pamela Geller, during a lecture in Toronto a year earlier.[61] When Harper's chief spokesman, Jason MacDonald, responded to the NCCM stating, "We will not take seriously criticism from an organization with documented ties to a terrorist organization such as Hamas," the NCCM threatened Harper and MacDonald with a libel suit for suggesting the NCCM had links to Hamas.[62] This was a troubling example of "lawfare," the use of frivolous or malicious lawsuits to silence critics and prevent law enforcement from conducting investigations.

In 2011, during Parliamentary Proceedings of the Standing Senate Committee on Social Affairs, Science and Technology, counterterrorism specialist and lawyer David Harris testified that it was "regrettable" to have to talk "in terms of moderates versus others, but there are many individuals and groups who masquerade" as moderates who are really "faux-moderates."[63]

In addressing Canada's Senators, Harris explained:

"Among other organizations, there is also the disturbing Canadian Council on American–Islamic Relations, CAIR-CAN, the Canadian chapter of a Saudi-funded US unindicted co-conspirator organization. CAIR-CAN is known for its divisive, poorly documented insistence that Muslims are subject to broad-ranging persecution in Canada. Under its first chair, Dr. Sheema Khan, CAIR-CAN joined its US mother organization in unsuccessful 'libel-lawfare' court assaults on commentators and constitutional free expression, in an effort to silence questions about CAIR and CAIR-CAN, their origins, and agenda. This record, incidentally, has not stopped the RCMP's Community Outreach Program, and a handful of other government entities, from stumbling into dealings with CAIR-CAN, much to the periodic embarrassment of officials."[64]

Courting diversity initiatives may have been the original intent of the RCMP, but it also highlights the danger of "tolerance "above law and national security, combined with carelessness, given the information revealed in the Holy Land Foundation Trials. Recall from the chapter "The Islamophobia Deception," that the RCMP apologized for arrests made during Ramadan and further made concessions to the Muslim community. Moderates, however, railed against this move. Salma Siddiqui, Vice President of the Muslim Canadian Congress, called the RCMP apology and outreach ghettoizing, condescending, and patronizing, stating that diversity groups have been overtaken by Islamists.[65]

Canada's Multiculturalism Act was intended to be a gesture of generosity designed to advance equality and Canada's diversity as a national asset. It was not intended to favor one special interest group or set of immigrants over another. With equal rights should come equal responsibility in accordance with the Act, but leaders of Western countries that have enshrined multiculturalism have fallen short, fanned the flames of competing interests, and have thrown up their hands and blamed multiculturalism for their own failures.

The state government of Quebec, Canada, in an apparent attempt to resolve the issue of competing interests in a multicultural society, devised a Charter of Values. This legislation sought to prohibit public-sector employees from wearing "objects such as headgear, clothing, jewelry, or other adornments which, by their conspicuous nature, overtly indicate a religious affiliation."[66]

The 2014 Quebec Charter was a violation of fundamental religious rights and freedoms, and did nothing to solve the larger issue of the serious threat of Islamist infiltration in Canada; it provided Islamist groups with a golden opportunity to deploy their customary victimhood strategy. Amnesty International, though careful about identifying any group, stated a valid angle: "For people, and particularly for women, who might be coerced into wearing a religious symbol, prohibiting them from wearing it will not solve the problem....The people who had coerced them will still go unpunished, while the people who have been coerced will be punished in a number of ways, such as losing their jobs and hence their right to work and risking becoming isolated and stigmatized in their communities."[67] The bill eventually died in the 2014 election, which was won by the Quebec Liberal Party.

In December 2016, a Muslim Liberal Member of Canadian Parliament, Iqra Khalid, who has suggested "that terrorism carried out by Muslims 'has no religion,'"[68] tabled an "anti-Islamophobia" motion in Parliament (M-103).[69] The motion was titled "Systemic racism and religious discrimination," but it specified that Canadians must "condemn Islamophobia and all forms of systemic racism and religious discrimination and take note of House of Commons Petition e-411 and the issues raised by it." Motion M-103 was a follow-up of a first Petition e-411 that was forwarded in June, stating that, "We, the undersigned, citizens and residents of Canada, call upon the House of Commons to join us in recognizing that extremist individuals do not represent the religion of Islam, and in condemning all forms of Islamophobia."[70] Conservative government members of Parliament did not support the "anti-Islamophobia" motion when it was first presented for approval in Parliament in October,[71] but it finally passed in November.[72]

The Canadian Charter of Rights and Freedoms already ascribes to multicultural inclusiveness, and there are already widespread anti-racism programs across Canada that advocate for all Canadians, so why were Muslims being awarded the special privilege of separate motions?

When one examines who was behind those motions, more comes to light. Last January, Khalid met with board members of Palestine House in Mississauga (near Toronto) and a "large number of members of the Palestinian community," including Palestinian political activists.[73] Palestine House supports the Palestinian al-Quds Intifada, and its settlement program was defunded by the former Conservative Harper government for allying itself with terrorism.[74] It was also condemned for celebrating the release of terrorists and honoring the founder of the Popular Front for the Liberation of Palestine (PFLP), one of the groups that formed the Palestine Liberation Organization and "in the 1960s and '70s, was responsible for numerous armed attacks and aircraft hijackings."[75]

According to the Canadian Arab newspaper, *Meshwar*, which covered the event at Palestine House in honor of Khalid, "the purpose of the event was to strengthen the relationship between the members of the Palestinian community and the Liberal members of Parliament."[76]

Also at the event for Khalid was *Meshwar* editor Nazih Khatatba, who once advised al-Aqsa Martyrs Brigades, the military wing of the Fatah movement, to change their policy and instead of uttering threats at Israel, to demand from Mahmoud Abbas, the Palestinian President and the leader of the PLO and Fatah movement, to re-arm them.[77] Khatatba openly calls for armed Jihad against the State of Israel, and his position is welcomed and supported by the politics of Palestine House. Yet Iqra Khalid, a member of the Canadian Parliament, was hosted by this Jihad supporting hate organization. During her time as a student at York University, "Khalid was active in student politics," and she served as "president of both the Muslim Student Association and one of the two Pakistani student associations."[78] The Muslim Student Associations are well known for their aggressive "Boycott, Divestment, and Sanctions" on-campus drives to demonize and delegitimize the State of Israel, and for their intimidation of Jewish students.

When Khalid introduced "Islamophobia" motion M-103 in Parliament, it included the intent to "recognize the need to quell the increasing public climate of hate and fear."[79] But how does one possibly go about "quelling" an atmosphere of fear, given the truth about the menacing global violence that is victimizing innocents daily in the name of Islam, even in established Islamic states?

What was most dangerous about these "anti-Islamophobia" motions is that they represented a subtle attack against free speech and foisted upon Canadians a kind of Sharia restriction in challenging discourse that may be critical to Islam.[80]

## PEACEFUL REVOLUTIONARIES

Lorenzo Vidino, former Deputy Director at the Investigative Project and author of *Al Qaeda in Europe*, writes, "Europe faces an enormous challenge from terrorism of Islamist inspiration," to which he refers to as "a tripartite threat from radical Islam, of which the terrorist is only the most immediate and evident, but not necessarily the most dangerous one."[81] Vidino's model is relevant for all Western nations. He describes this tripartite threat as akin to a pyramid; at the top, violent Jihadists instill fear, while their colleagues work in other ways. Beneath them are "peaceful revolutionaries," groups and networks that openly express their opposition to any system of government that does not strictly conform to Sharia law.[82] At the base, which comprises the largest section of the pyramid, are groups that "publicly purport to support democracy and the integration of Muslim communities within the European mainstream, but quietly work to radicalize Europe's Muslim population."[83] Consistent with Vidino's tripartite model, moderates in this book have emphasized that the goals of the Muslim Brotherhood (peaceful revolutionaries) and al Qaeda (violent) are the same; they only differ in their modus operandi. At the base level can be found the Muslim Brotherhood offshoots and front groups that claim to be the legitimate representatives of the Muslim community in our midst, also known as "unindicted co-conspirators."

## THE HOLY LAND FOUNDATION DOCUMENTS THAT BLEW "THEIR" COVER

It seems implausible to the average Westerner that an organized and complex network of peaceful Islamists—routinely called moderates—have been planning and executing a strategy of infiltration for many years, and that they are doing it under the cover of mainstream representatives of Muslims living in the West.

The level of infiltration by the Muslim Brotherhood and its intricate strategy came to light during the Holy Land Foundation (HLF) Trial.[84] The HLF was the largest Islamic charity in the US, but it was designated as a terrorist organization in 2001 by the American government and shut down.[85] Its assets were seized and charges were laid down by a federal grand jury in Dallas, the location of its headquarters. Five former officers and employees were charged with providing material support to Hamas that included conspiracy, money laundering, and providing financial support to a foreign terrorist organization. Prosecutors asserted that the Foundation indirectly helped Hamas to "win the hearts and minds" of the Palestinians.[86]

During the course of the HLF Trial, three incriminating documents were presented as evidence:

### I. "Explanatory Memorandum on the General Strategic Goal for the Group in North America"[87]

Described as most significant was "an explanatory memorandum" of the Muslim Brotherhood's "General Strategic Goal" for the US and Canada, authored by senior Hamas leader and Muslim Brotherhood operative Mohamed Akram.[88] It was discovered in 2004 during a home search of a founder of the Dar Al-Hijrah Mosque in Falls Church, Virginia, Ismail Elbarasse. He was a member of the Palestine Committee, which was created by the Muslim Brotherhood to support Hamas in America. Written in 1987, the memorandum was finally published in 1991. It contained a list of "friends" who shared the common goal of dismantling American institutions and turning the US into an Islamic nation. Akram and the Muslim Brotherhood described these "friends" as those who could best serve as a fifth column and destroy America from within by "sabotaging its miserable house by their hands...so that...God's religion [Islam] is made victorious over all other religions."[89]

Akram's blueprint for the stealth advancement of Islamism emphasized the need to form diverse groups from virtually every sector of society: education; religious and political activism; audio and video production; print media; banking and finance; the physical sciences; the social sciences; professional and business networking; cultural affairs; the publishing and distribution of books; children and teenagers; women's rights; vocational concerns; and the law. Among the groups listed that could destroy America from within effectively were: CAIR, an offshoot of the Islamic Association for Palestine, the Islamic Society of North America (ISNA), the North American Islamic Trust (NAIT), the International Institute of Islamic Thought (IIIT), and the Muslim Student Associations (MSA).[90]

This blueprint suggested that the Muslim Brotherhood in America was far more structured and organized than previously known.

Contained in the "Explanatory Memorandum on the General Strategic Goal for the Group in North America" was a furtive method of gathering all Muslims in the service of one unified goal. Among the "keys and tools" in the process of settlement, the Memorandum indicated as part of the responsibility and mission:

> "Absorbing Muslims and winning them with all of their factions and colors in America and Canada for the settlement project...this issue requires from us to learn 'the art of dealing with the others,' as people are different and people [come] in many colors. We need to adopt the principle which says, 'Take from people ... the best they have,' their best specializations, experiences, arts, energies, and abilities....The policy of 'taking' should be with what achieves the strategic goal and the settlement process. But the big challenge in front of us is: how to connect them all in 'the orbit' of our plan and 'the circle' of our Movement in order to achieve 'the core' of our interest. What matters is bringing people to the level of comprehension of the challenge that is facing us as Muslims in this country, conviction of our settlement project, and understanding the benefit of agreement, cooperation, and alliance. At that time, if we ask for money, a lot of it would come, and if we ask for men, they would come in lines...." [91]

### II. The Project

Among the documents in the hands of federal prosecutors in the HLF terrorism financing trial was a file, simply called "The Project," which outlined methods to invade the West culturally. [92] This document pointed to a possible relationship between Muslim Brotherhood and Hamas entities in the US and that of the defunct Al Taqwa Bank of Lugano, headed by Muslim Brotherhood figures Youssef Nada and Ghaleb Himmat. [93] It was recovered in a raid by Swiss authorities two months after 9/11. The Al Taqwa Bank, based on principles of Islamic finance, had a shareholder list that included many Muslim Brotherhood figures, including the family of global Muslim Brotherhood leader and spiritual advisor Yusuf al-Qaradawi, who also served as the bank's Sharia advisor. [94]

Al-Qaradawi is a prominent Islamic scholar notorious for his militant religious rulings and political commentary. In a 1995 conference held by the Muslim Arab Youth Association (MAYA) in Toledo, Ohio, al-Qaradawi issued an open call for violent Jihad: "Our brothers in Hamas, in Palestine, the Islamic resistance, the Islamic Jihad after all the rest have given up and despaired, the movement of the Jihad brings us back to our faith."[95] He also issued a specific call for stealth Jihad:

> "What remains, then, is to conquer Rome. The second part of the omen, 'The city of Hiraq [once emperor of Constantinople] will be conquered first,' so what remains is to conquer Rome. This means that Islam will come back to Europe for the third time, after it was expelled from it twice....Conquest through Da'wa [proselytizing], that is what we hope for. We will conquer Europe, we will conquer America! Not through sword but through Da'wa."[96]

Youssef Nada, who was also Director of the Al Taqwa Bank of Lugano, admitted to being an international leader of the Muslim Brotherhood, and was active in that organization for more than half a century.[97] Even though American and Swiss investigators scrutinized Al-Taqwa's involvement in money laundering and the funding of terrorist groups (including al Qaeda, Hamas, the Armed Islamic Group of Algeria (GIA), and the Ennahda Party in Tunisia, which is deemed to be moderate), Swiss and Italian prosecutions against Nada and Himmat in connection with terrorism financing were eventually dropped for lack of evidence. Both, however, remain on lists of terrorist entities.[98]

"The Project" demonstrated a "flexible, multi-phased, long-term approach to the 'cultural invasion' of the West," according to counter-terrorism and Muslim Brotherhood expert Patrick Poole.[99]

Its recommendations could easily be dismissed as delusional but the architects of this movement were sophisticated enough to know how fantastical it would be deemed. It was all too easy for Western analysts to dismiss.

Among a few of "The Project's" recommendations:

- Networking and coordinating actions between Islamist organizations.

- Avoiding open alliances with known terrorist organizations—like al Qaeda—to maintain the appearance of "moderation."
- Using deception to mask the intended goals of Islamists, so long as this didn't conflict with Sharia law.
- Avoiding social conflicts with Westerners locally, nationally or globally, that might damage the long-term ability to expand the Islamist powerbase in the West or provoke a backlash against Muslims.
- Establishing financial networks to fund the work of conversion of the West.
- Conducting surveillance, obtaining data, and establishing collection and data storage capabilities.
- Setting up a watchdog system for monitoring Western media to warn Muslims of "international plots fomented against them."
- Cultivating an Islamist intellectual community, including the establishment of think tanks and advocacy groups, publishing "academic" studies, to legitimize Islamist positions and to chronicle the history of Islamist movements.
- Developing a comprehensive 100-year plan to advance the Islamist ideology throughout the world.
- Involving ideologically committed Muslims in democratically elected institutions on all levels in the West, including government, NGOs, private organizations, and labor unions.
- Instrumentally using existing Western institutions until they could be converted and put into service of Islam.
- Drafting Islamic constitutions, laws, and policies for eventual implementation.
- Instituting alliances with Western "progressive" organizations that share Islamist goals.
- Creating autonomous "security forces" to protect Muslims in the West.
- Inflaming violence and keeping Muslims living in the West "in a Jihad frame of mind."
- Supporting Jihad movements across the Muslim world through preaching, propaganda, personnel, funding, and technical and operational support.

- Making the Palestinian cause a global wedge issue for Muslims.
- Adopting the total liberation of Palestine from Israel and the creation of an Islamic state as a keystone in the plan for global Islamic domination.
- Instigating a constant campaign to incite hatred by Muslims against Jews and rejecting any discussions of conciliation or coexistence with them.
- Actively creating Jihad terror cells within Palestine.
- Linking the terrorist activities in Palestine with the global terror movement.
- Collecting sufficient funds to indefinitely perpetuate and support Jihad around the world."[100]

The moderates in this book have accurately identified the parallel goals of the Muslim Brotherhood and al Qaeda in the promotion of political Islam or the Sharia state; they only differ in their modus operandi. Western leaders are courting danger in failing to understand the united, complex stratagems of Islamists.

On June 9, 2014, Iraq's second largest city, Mosul, was taken after four days of fighting by al-Qaeda militants (ISIS, the Islamic State of Iraq and Syria).[101] Osama al-Nujaifi, the speaker of Iraq's parliament, declared, "Everything is fallen. It's a crisis. Having these terrorist groups control a city in the heart of Iraq threatens not only Iraq but the entire region."[102]

In this show of "unexpected strength," according to Dr. Daniel Pipes, the most extreme and violent form of Islamism, as represented by al Qaeda and similar groups, proved their capability of going "beyond terrorism to form guerrilla militias that conquer territory and challenge governments. In this, ISIS joins the Taliban in Afghanistan, Al-Shabaab in Somalia, the Al-Nusra Front in Syria, Ansar Dine in Mali, and Boko Haram in Nigeria."[103] Boko Haram pledged allegiance to ISIS in February 2015.[104]

European and North American policy makers need to acknowledge that along with the violent Islamist surge in the Middle East and its global expansion, there is also a stealth Islamist surge, and a combination of both. There also appears to be a general failure to realize the capabilities and sophistication of al Qaeda ranks, as described above by Dr. Pipes, that they have managed to transcend violent terrorism to a kind of blended entity of organized violence that is unpredictable to Western authorities. Prior to the eruption of ISIS, a strategic document was uncovered in Northern Mali that demonstrated the ability of al Qaeda to form a highly organized structure. It should have served as a preview of al Qaeda's capabilities to organize.

### III. Al Qaeda in the Islamic Maghreb's (AQIM) strategy in northern Mali

The *Associated Press* discovered a document in Timbuktu in January 2013 that revealed al Qaeda in the Islamic Maghreb's (AQIM) strategy in northern Mali. The document calls for a "gentler, kinder" al Qaeda. It was reportedly part of a confidential letter from the Amir of AQIM, Abdelmalek Droukdel, to his lieutenants in the Sahara and to the Islamist militant group Ansar Eddine's leader, Iyad ag Ghaly.[105]

The letter revealed a deep strategic fracture between AQIM's leadership and its lieutenants on the ground, as Droukdel saw a military intervention as inevitable. The letter demonstrated a formidable commitment and a worrisome plan for the future. As part of his strategy, Droukdel states:

> "As for foreign policies, you must adopt mature and moderate rhetoric that reassures and calms. To do so, you must avoid any statements that are provocative to neighboring countries and avoid repeated threats. Better for you to be silent and pretend to be a 'domestic' movement that has its own causes and concerns. There is no call for you to show that we have an expansionary, Jihadi, Qaida, or any other sort of project."[106]

Droukdel carefully monitors the progress of al Qaeda in Mali and calls for adaptation as needed in keeping with such progress. In the process, he demonstrates a watchful eye and careful study of the host society, as he pursues his goal of establishing Sharia.

> "We have tried in a succinct way to treat the general picture and the ideal way of action that we see as suitable for the complicated reality

and quickly changing events connected to this Islamic Jihadi project in Azawad. This project, vital and very important to us and to our Jihad, is in this very sensitive and dangerous phase, which requires us all to give it particular care and to prepare the ground for success and avoid as much as possible the elements."[107]

Most critically, Droukdel makes reference to two specific levels of establishing Sharia: the "Azawad Islamic Project" and the "Global Jihadi Project." His advice is to broaden consultations and collaboration as wide as possible, even making reference to the constitution of Azawad and goals to shift it to suit the AQIM project. Such strategy in the Islamic Meghreb demonstrates the level of sophistication that al Qaeda is engaging in territorially and even globally.[108]

Droukdel talks about planting seeds that will grow in the future, and counsels patience in waiting for the tree to grow, while he rebukes "extreme speed" and hastiness to establish Sharia.

"And if we can achieve this positive thing in even a limited amount, then even if the project fails later, it will be just enough that we will have planted the first, good seed in this fertile soil and put pesticides and fertilizer on it, so that the tree will grow more quickly. We look forward to seeing this tree as it will be: stable and magnificent."[109]

His instructions on how to spread the seeds of Sharia "in a wise way" are devious and stealthy, to ensure that the circumstances are right and ripe.

"So in the first stage, we should have focused on preparing the terrain to apply Sharia, to spread dawah, and to talk and preach to people in order to convince them and educate them."[110]

The document addresses the Islamist goal of "reform" in the context of bringing Muslims into adherence to a Wahhabist ideology. Droukdel emphasizes that "going gradually" is a rule from God that every "reformer" should take into account.[111]

The details of Droukdel's instruction are significant. Westerners have merely witnessed the violent manifestations of al Qaeda through media reports, with a limited understanding of the sophistication, intelligence, and control of al Qaeda's operations.

## NO PLACE FOR ISLAMIST VOICES IN THE WEST

According to Dr. Daniel Pipes:

"It's a common practice for Islamists to claim to be moderates and reformers and they convince a lot of people. The key is whether they are trying to apply Islamic law in its entirety or not.

"The key is not how fast they are trying to do it. For example, Erdogan has been going very slowly and his administration is quite clever. They close down liquor stores, for example, on the basis of health and economics. They don't talk about Sharia. They just closed down liquor on many of the airline flights on the basis of economics, health, the proximity to mosques, and so forth.

"They don't actually invoke Sharia, but if you look at it as a whole, they are the one government that has been taking steps toward Sharia. So that's the key: Are they moving toward Sharia or not? It doesn't have to be exclusive. It can be quite subtle and that is the wave of the future. In the past it was very explicit, proclaimed, enforced. Now it's more careful, and slower, and more implicit."[112]

The advancement, sophistication, and determination of Islamists demand Western leaders' resolve to control immigration and to dutifully take measures to protect their societies from further Islamist infiltration. It is vital to resist any ideology, person, and group discovered with links to the Muslim Brotherhood and other terrorist entities, despite pressures to be politically correct. We need to embrace and protect our right to free speech, which includes criticism of Islam like other faiths, and the identification and exposure of Islamists and Islamist groups without fear of reprisals. The Muslim Brotherhood consists of a gargantuan network of "mainstream" organizations that claim to be moderate, to represent the interests and voices of Muslims everywhere and which readily levy accusations of "Islamophobia" if its motives are questioned. Muslim Brotherhood cells have already infiltrated North America and declare: "Allah's religion is made victorious over all other religions" and that without this understanding Muslims "are not up to this challenge and have not prepared ourselves for Jihad yet. It is the Muslim destiny to perform Jihad and work wherever he lands...." Note the usage of the word "Jihad" contrary to those Muslims who state unequivocally that it refers to a personal, internal struggle. Western leaders and citizens also need to scrutinize and demand accountability from public and private sector diversity groups, and to support Islamic reform by encouraging the efforts of Muslim intellectuals, authorities, and leaders who respect human rights and uphold Western constitutions.

# CONCLUSION

A turf war within Islam rages between those who seek to reform Islam back to the seventh century and those who seek to reform it to modernity.

In advancing the latter, "Reforming Islam: Progressive Voices from the Arab Muslim World," a compilation of viewpoints of Arab Muslim intellectual voices taken from the website, Almuslih, was discussed in Chapter Ten. These reformers collectively challenge the strident voices of Islamism in their calls for an urgent "intellectual rehabilitation" of a "Bedouin culture that is fundamentally xenophobic."

From the Golden Age of Islam, in which economic development, science, and culture flourished and reached its apex in the Ottoman Empire, one of the largest and longest empires in history, Islam has a complex history of both conquest and achievement. The proliferation of Islamism today represents a drive to return to an era in which Islam ruled and was supreme politically, socially, and religiously.

In his 2002 book, *What Went Wrong?,* historian Bernard Lewis notes, "For many centuries the world of Islam was in the forefront of human civilization and achievement."[1] During the Ottoman Empire, when Islamic culture thrived, not without defects, it is well established that Christians and Jews had the Koran-derived legal status of the "People of the Book," which made them "acceptable" in the eyes of the Ottomans. The Ottomans granted them freedom to practice their religions, but they were considered inferior and relegated to dhimmi status. They were guaranteed safety in exchange for paying a special tax called the *jizya,* based on Koran 9:29. Jews and Christians were rarely dealt with on an individual basis; instead, they were placed collectively into a "millet" system, in which they were members of a segregated community, vulnerable to harassment by government officials and neighbors.

According to Middle East historian and author Roderic H. Davison, "millets" managed to play a "significant role in helping to bring about a kind of modernization and reformation in the Ottoman Empire by way of their contact with Europeans."[2]

Those once part of the "millet" system in a modern context offer a hope of again working along with Muslims as full equals to advance modernization and reform, but the Islamist barrier to this united effort stands tightly in place and needs to be opposed. Endemic among Islamists is the enduring characteristic of superiority, which is, sadly, rooted in failure. Due to the Ottoman's "failed imperialist bid for territorial aggrandizement and reassertion of lost glory, the Muslim empire has been portrayed as the hapless victim of European machinations, driven into the world conflict by overbearing powers eager to expedite its demise and gobble up its lands."[3] To this day, Europe and other Western nations bear the stigma of racism foisted upon them by accusations levied by Islamists, stemming from a robust declaration of victimology, as reformists such as Zuhdi Jasser and Abdur-Rahman Muhammad have pointed out. Muhammad, a former member of the International Institute for Islamic Thought, exposed the agenda behind the inception of the word "Islamophobia."

The truth has always been thus: that Islamism has a 1,400-year-long history of conquest, and is driven by zealotry and patriarchal pride. In a review of Eugene Rogan's book, *The Fall of the Ottomans*, Efraim Karsh writes, "If anything, it is the region's tortuous relationship with modernity, most notably the stubborn adherence to its millenarian religiously based imperialist legacy, which has left physical force as the main instrument of political discourse to date. But to acknowledge this would mean abandoning the self-righteous victimization paradigm that has informed Western scholarship for so long, and treating Middle Easterners as equal free agents accountable for their actions, rather than giving them a condescending free pass for political and moral modes of behavior that are not remotely acceptable in Western societies. Sadly, *The Fall of the Ottomans* signals no such paradigm shift."[4] This victimization paradigm has resulted in the demonization of the modern day "millets," evident through aspirations by Islamists to obliterate the Jewish State of Israel and the development of strategies to conquer the Western states, whose constitutions are historically influenced by Judeo-Christian principles of human rights.

The scourge of global Islamism is problematic, but the "millets" have evolved as leaders in their own modern nation states throughout the West and in Israel in their full embrace of human rights and equality for all, enshrined in the constitutions of these states.

Unfortunately, there are contemporary progressives who aid in the backward efforts to move Islam toward a medieval puritanism, whether knowingly or unknowingly. The diversity and anti-racism initiatives have been hijacked by Islamists, as pointed out in the previous chapter, "Who Speaks for Muslims?" Those Islamists have managed to garner sympathy among many citizens and leaders of Western societies, who bear guilt for past colonialist wrongs and who support a victimology narrative for Muslims. Such a philosophy has created an us-versus-them paradigm, which creates a blind spot for many Westerners; any criticism of Islam is deemed to be anti-diversity, racist, and "Islamophobic," thereby inhibiting true efforts toward a genuine, modernized reform of Islam. One must be able to scrutinize and engage in debate in order to address the problem of Islamic supremacy that threatens the very tenets of Western democratic freedoms, including—and most especially—freedom of speech. Any criticism of Islam is strongly resisted by Islamic supremacists, who cleverly propel and manipulate "anti-Islamophobia" campaigns to advance their agenda.

Efforts toward a peaceful resistance against Islamism can and should be encouraged. Muslims who seek pluralism and advance free speech among proponents of their faith and practice their religion peacefully offer a hope of Islamic modernization. Although Western news coverage prioritizes the Western struggle with Islamism, stemming from the troubles in the Middle East, it gives less attention to Islam in the Far East, which includes Indonesia, the largest Muslim country in the world, followed by India, Pakistan, and Bangladesh. Pluralism is the antithesis of the Islamist doctrine of supremacy, and it exists abundantly among adherents of Islam worldwide.

Inayat Khan, founder of the Sufi Order in the West in 1914, "recognized the multi-religious roots of Sufism as well as its contemporary relevance for people of all faiths." He delivered a "message of spiritual liberty" to reflect the universal, inclusive nature of Sufism. He also asserted, "every age of the world has seen awakened souls, and as it is impossible to limit wisdom to any one period or place, so it is impossible to date the origin of Sufism."[5]

One can only imagine how offensive Wahhabis, who regard unbelievers with scorn and dismiss Sufis and other pluralistic Muslims as un-Islamic, would find that statement. Stephen Schwartz, Executive Director of the Center for Islamic Pluralism, who was referenced in an earlier chapter, noted, "In Arab core countries, classic Sufi authors may be praised, while living Sufi teachers are derided as un-Islamic charlatans. And in some places, Sufis are imprisoned and murdered."[6]

On the subject of pluralism, Bernard Lewis has stated, "It is difficult to generalize about Islam....In the one sense, it denotes a religion, a system of belief and worship; in the other, the civilization that grew up and flourished under the aegis of that religion. The word Islam thus denotes more than fourteen centuries of history, a billion and a third people, and a religious and cultural tradition of enormous diversity." He continues, "In space, the realm of Islam extends from Morocco to Indonesia, from Kazakhstan to Senegal. In time it goes back more than fourteen centuries," but since the fall of the Ottoman Empire, Lewis warns that "the Islamic world has lost its dominance and its leadership...has fallen behind both the modern West and the rapidly modernizing Orient. This widening gap poses increasingly acute problems, both practical and emotional, for which the rulers, thinkers, and rebels of Islam have not yet found effective answers."[7]

The West has been infiltrated by Islamist "reformists" through the Muslim Brotherhood, which is in essence an adaptation of Wahhabism, and more broadly, Salafism. There is no difference between violent Jihad and stealth Jihad in terms of the Islamist goal, which is the establishment of global Sharia law. For Islamists, the world is divided into two camps: Dar al-Harb (House of War) and Dar al-Islam (House of Islam); their goal is to subjugate all territories that are non-Islamic or not ruled by Islamic law under the hegemony of Islam, governed by Sharia, in essence, a global caliphate. The urgency of such a challenge is accelerated by the migrant crisis flooding Europe. The vast influx of Muslim refugees has brought a surge in crime, particularly sexual assaults due to repressive cultural attitudes toward women. The challenges of Muslim migrants adapting to Western culture is arduous, and brings with it potential homeland security threats, given the infiltration of the refugee stream by Islamic State Jihadists.

The diversity within Islamic thought, pluralism, and debate needs to be embraced and encouraged for any hope of moderates winning this Muslim turf war against Islamist rebels, especially those who have streamed into Europe and North America with a goal of civilizational Jihad and, ultimately, conquest. Islamists must be resisted socially and politically on Western soil and challenged in Islamic states through the support of reformist movements.

Bernard Lewis expresses his hope that Christians and Jews can once again work toward reform: "Christendom and Islam are in many ways sister civilizations, both drawing on the shared heritage of Jewish revelation and prophecy and Greek philosophy and science, and both nourished by the immemorial traditions of Middle Eastern antiquity."[8] Genuine reformists are accepting of the "People of the Book" as equals, not chiefly as people who have, according to the Hadith and Koran, gone astray (Christians) or been accursed by God (Jews). The foremost targets of Islamists are Christians who are widely persecuted and Jews of whom their state is under unceasing threat.

Modern moderates and reformists who espouse the UN Declaration of Human Rights and the principles enshrined in Western democratic constitutions oppose a radical, politicized Islam with its full range of immutable, medieval decrees, which incites atrocities in Islamic states today, such as: honor killings and the devaluation of women through depriving them of education and forcing them to wear head-to-toe coverings in scorching temperatures; amputation of hands as punishment for theft; Islamic supremacy over non-believers; and propagating the "necessity" to obliterate the State of Israel, a goal enshrined in the Palestinian Authority, Hamas, and Fatah Charters. As highlighted among some of the interviewees, Saudi Arabia is a major funder of radicalism, but so is Iran with its influential proxies and loyalists globally.

Moderates and reformists who are devout Muslims have chosen a peaceful path, as found in the first part of the Koran, when Muhammad laid the groundwork for the faith in Mecca, before he arrived in Medina where his message became more divisive and bellicose. As noted with moderates, some purport that Muhammad faced an existential threat to the religion he was advancing and that other religions have gone to war for the same, while others declare that there is no excuse for violence in their or any religion, and that, whatever happened in the seventh century, it is best left there as this brand of Islam is inconsistent with the values and norms of the twenty-first century. Reformists advance the notion of a redefining Islam in a manner that is consistent with modernity, freedom, pluralism, human rights, and equality.

While normative Islam arises out of Egypt's Al-Azhar University and is largely funded by Saudi Arabia, the small but significant group of reformists offers hope against the violent Islamism advanced by today's extremists, particularly in our digital age, in which modernized interpretations of the Koran can, and are, gaining traction. Such interpretations can serve as a guide for Muslims who aspire to a path of peace, the embracement of freedom, of reasoning, and a personal interpretation and practice of their faith which includes questioning and thus the desanctification of ancient texts.

Reformists seek a modernized Islam in which mosque and state are separated, where diversity and pluralism—including discussions and criticisms of Islam—are collectively accepted, and where adherents of the faith do not risk physical danger if they choose to exercise the freedoms stipulated under the Universal Declaration of Human Rights.

As conveyed throughout in this book, moderates and reformists are vital agents of change. In this information age of social media, enlightenment is but a click away, and many of the followers of reformists are frustrated youth, oppressed by aging despots who would keep them imprisoned in a medieval hierarchy, when they need to be liberated and empowered.

The reformation of Islam bears implications and challenges for Islamic states, as reformists have been killed throughout history for their defiant opposition to the Islamist jurors governing those states, and also for Western nations grappling with the spread of Islamism since 9/11. North America and Western Europe were awakened by the shock of those attacks, which revealed a steadfast enemy force committed to their destruction. Now they must come to grips with the morphing of this enemy force into a stealthy foe that declares global conquest as its goal.

Moderates generally content themselves with living as mainstream non-Muslim Westerners, which is to be applauded; not everyone can be an activist and agent of change. Reformists have taken on the responsibility of modernizing their faith, courageously opposing the aggressive Islamist Project, often paying a high personal cost for their activism, with the hope that more Muslims will support this crucial mission and abandon the violent Islamism that is aggressively propagated in mosques, including those standing on Western soil.

Reformists have served to inform the West about the threat of Islamists to the very structure of our constitutions; many have also faced death threats and marginalization from their own Muslim communities and sidelining from Westerners who kowtow to Islamists for short-sighted political gain. They are frequently criticized for advancing a progressive Islam that is consistent with modernity, being dismissed as "non-Muslims" and disparaged in their efforts to engage in the turf war waging within their faith. Westerners need to rally behind those who challenge what is now considered to be normative Islam, which is in truth Islamism, so that the reformist vision of a new normative Islam consistent with human rights and pluralism can be established and realized.

Given the global threat posed by Islamism, it is imperative that Westerners understand and resist its advance. Free speech and pluralism are hallmarks of Western constitutional law, which both moderates and reformists respect and uphold. Whether or not a country is governed by laws akin to Canada's Multicultural Act or not, it is the duty of all leaders to uphold the equal rights of all its citizens, not to exalt or protect one group over another.

Moderate and reformist Muslims do not seek special treatment. You will not hear them crying out that that they are victims of "Islamophobia"; they simply wish to be respected as equal citizens under the law, and they espouse the universality of individual dignity and protection, as defined by the United Nations Declaration of Human Rights. It is in the interest of the West to support their efforts to modernize their faith and disempower the aggressive surge of Salafism that seeks to take Islam back to the seventh century and usurp the freedoms and liberties enshrined in the rule of law and protected by constitutional democracy, to which so many people in underdeveloped nations aspire.

The battle against Islamism is one of the greatest challenges of the twenty-first century. As author of this book, the cause of Islamic reform galvanized me, as it is critical to the advancement of humanity toward peace and reconciliation. As a journalist, the topic of Islam captured my interest after interviewing reformists in the Toronto region. I was moved and inspired by their zeal, their love for humanity, their commitment to law, liberty, and freedom of religion in particular, which is too often taken for granted in Western democracies.

The immense and necessary mission to modernize Islam is continuously stymied by takfiri mentalities, despotic turf wars, and ambitious radical preachers striving to maintain personal supremacism and world domination. Islamists who infiltrate and stand in the way of progress must be challenged by their so-called apostate co-religionists from the inside and by infidels from the outside. Only when Islam is depoliticized can it collectively join the twenty-first century in peace. I wish reformers every success as they advance human rights, pluralism, the intellectual query of their faith, and their quest for peace and unity with human kind.

# GLOSSARY

**ADL** Anti-Defamation League, with a mission "to stop the defamation of the Jewish people, and to secure justice and fair treatment to all"

**AIFD** American Islamic Forum for Democracy, which started after 9/11 to "provide an American Muslim voice advocating for the preservation of the founding principles of the United States Constitution, liberty and freedom, through the separation of mosque and state"

**Aisha** Muhammad's child wife

**Ashan** call to salat, prayer

**Ahl us-Sunnah** "People of the Accepted Practice," the Sunnah being the practices that are acceptable as per the Koran and Muhammad's example in the Hadiths, the recorded sayings of the prophet

**Al Qaeda** "the base" founded in 1988 by Osama bin Laden Abdullah Azzam to fight against the Soviet invasion of Afghanistan

**Al-Azhar University** located in Cairo, deemed Sunni Islam's most prestigious university

**Allah** the Arabic name of God

**Allahu Akbar** Arabic, meaning "God is Great"

**Baathists** anti-imperial, Arab socialist party founded in Syria

**Blasphemy** the act of insulting or showing irreverence for Muhammad or Islam. In Islamic literature, there are many types of blasphemy, e.g., sabb (to insult) and shatm (to abuse or vilify), takdhib or tajdif (to deny), la`n or la'ana (to curse) and ta`n (to accuse or defame)

**Boko Haram** group of the People of Sunnah for Preaching and Jihad; offshoot of al Qaeda and declared allegiance to the Islamic State in 2015

**Bid'a** a major sin in traditional Islam

**Burka** long, loose outer garment which covers a woman's whole body from head to feet

**Caliph** successor of Muhammad, ruler of an Islamic theocracy
**Caliphate** an Islamic state led by a caliph
**CAIR** Council on American–Islamic Relations, based in Washington, D.C., designated an "unindicted co-conspirator" in the Holy Land Foundation Trial, a Hamas financing case
**Civilization Jihad** a term found in the "Explanatory Memorandum on the General Strategic Goal for the Group in North America" to describe a process of settlement

**Da'ee** one who devotes himself to dawah, propagating Islam
**Dar al-Harb** abode or house of war
**Dar al-Islam** abode or house of Islam
**Dawah** proselytizing or preaching of Islam

**Eid** Muslim festival or celebration, particularly Eid al-Fitr (end of Ramadan) or Eid al-Adha (festival of sacrifice)

**Fatwa** an Islamic legal ruling, edict, or pronouncement issued by an expert in religious law (mufti)

**Hadith** the reported sayings and actions of the prophet Muhammad which serve as a model of behavior for Muslims
**Hajj** pilgrimage to Mecca
**Hamas** acronym for Harakat Al-Muqawama Al-Islamiyya, a militant Islamist "resistance" movement and offshoot of the Muslim Brotherhood, operating in Israel's West Bank and Gaza
**Hakim** ruler, governor, or judge
**Hezbollah** also Hizballah, meaning "party of Allah," a Shia Islamist militant group and political party based in Lebanon, headed by Hassan Nasrallah
**Hijab** headscarf and covering worn by many Muslim women
**Hijrah** flight of Muhammad from Mecca to Medina to escape persecution; jihad by emigration
**Holy Land Foundation** was the largest Islamic charity in America; in 2008 a trial of its charity leaders for providing material support for Hamas earned the reputation of the largest terrorism financing trial in the history of America

**Iftar dinner** the meal eaten by Muslims after sunset during the month of Ramadan

**Ijma** Arabic term for consensus or agreement among Muslim scholars

**Ijtihad** Islamic legal term for independent reasoning in finding a solution to a legal question. The gates of ijtihad were closed by Sunni jurists in the tenth century. Reformists view ijtihad as an exercise of critical thinking and independent judgment and therefore the gates of ijtihad must be opened to encourage modernization and plurality

**Ikwan** members of an Islamic military brotherhood which were prominent in the unification of the Arabian Peninsula under Ibn Saud Guard. Following this tribal army of Ibn Saud came the Saudi Arabian National Guard

**Imam** leader of mosque and Muslim community or of prayer service; in Shia Islam, a Muslim leader and descendant of Muhammad

**Iman** a Muslim's personal belief in the six articles of faith: one God (Allah), the angels of Allah, the books of Allah (especially the Koran), the prophets of Allah (especially Muhammad), the Day of Judgment, the supremacy of Allah's will in predestination

**International Islamic Fiqh (Jurisprudence) Academy** an international body of Muslim experts that promotes the fiqh; based in Jeddah, Saudi Arabia, created in 1988 as an initiative of the Organization of Islamic Cooperation (OIC)—an international organization founded in 1969, consisting of 56 member states; Palestine is often included to make it 57 member states

**International Institute for Islamic Thought (IIIT)** an Islamic think tank which focuses on the Islamization of knowledge; named in "An Explanatory Memorandum on the General Strategic Goal for the Group in North America" as one of the Brotherhood's twenty-nine likeminded "organizations of our friends"

**IRFAN-Canada** (International Relief Fund for the Afflicted and Needy)—a Muslim charity of which its charitable status was revoked by the Canadian Federal Government in 2011 and it was subsequently listed as a terrorist entity in 2014, after being found to be funneling money to Hamas

**Islamic Society of North America (ISNA)** a Muslim umbrella group; designated an "unindicted co-conspirator" in the Holy Land Foundation Trial, a Hamas financing case

**Islamic Circle of North America (ICNA)** a Muslim umbrella group which traces its origins to the Muslim Student Association; named in "An Explanatory Memorandum on the General Strategic Goal for the Group in North America" as one of the Brotherhood's twenty-nine like-minded "organizations of our friends"

**ISIS** Islamic State in Iraq and Syria (also known as the Islamic State of Iraq and the Levant)

**Islamist** one who believes that Islam should influence political systems and strives toward the goal of establishing a Sharia-based Islamic state in the "abode of war"

**Jamia** gathering—at a mosque, community, school, association

**Jamaat Islamiya** conservative Pakistani Islamist party founded in 1941 during the British Raj

**Jihad** struggle, Arabic word meaning "striving in the way of Allah"

**Jihad as-saghir** offensive jihad, military struggle, holy war

**Jihad ad-daf'a** defensive jihad

**Jihad bil-mal** waging jihad using one's finances

**Jihad bil-saif** jihad by the sword

**Jizya** extra tax imposed on non-Muslims (Dhimmis) who live under Muslim rule

**Jumu'ah** Friday prayer

**Ka'bah** black cube-shaped building at the center of Islam's most sacred mosque (Al-Masjid al-Haram) in Mecca; deemed "the house of Allah"

**Kafir** derogatory term to describe non-Muslims, meaning "unbeliever"

**Kalam** "science of discourse"; intended to establish and defend the Islamic faith

**Kitab** book, usually sacred book

**Kitman** action of covering or dissimulation, used alternately with taqiyya

**Koran/Qur'an** "recitation"—the holy scripture of Islam, revered as the literal word of Allah and Allah's revelations to mankind, revealed to the prophet Muhammad in 610 CE in the cave Hira through the angel Jibril (or Gabriel) over a period of 23 years. It contains many teachings, admonitions, and stories of earlier prophets found in Jewish and Christian scriptures

**Kutub al-Sittah** six books containing collections of Hadith (Sahih Bukhari, Sahih Muslim, Sunan Abu Dawood, Jami al-Tirmidhi, Sunan al-Sughra, Sunan ibn Majah/Muwatta Malik)

**Madrassa** Islamic religious school

**Masjid** mosque, place of prayer

**Mecca** Islam's holiest city in Saudi Arabia; the birthplace of Muhammad

**Medina** Muhammad's destination in Saudi Arabia after his flight (hijrah) from Mecca; a major Muslim pilgrimage site and regarded as the second holiest site in Islam

**Mosque** place of worship for Muslims, typically with a prayer hall and minarets

**Muhammad** born in the year 570 CE, in the town of Mecca on the Arabian peninsula. Muslims believe Muhammad was the last of the divinely ordained prophets whom God selected to impart his message to humankind

**Mufti** Islamic scholar of Sharia law, can issue a fatwa

**Millets** non-Muslim religious community of the Ottoman Empire, self-ruled under its own laws but under the overall supremacy of Ottoman administration; usually references Christians and Jews

**Mujahid** soldier of Islam engaged in jihad, especially guerrilla war

**Mujahideen** plural for Mujahid

**Mujtahid** a person who engages in the process of ijtihad

**Mullah** Islamic clergy

**Muslim** a follower of the religion of Islam

**Muslim Brotherhood** "The Society of Muslim Brothers"; a transnational Sunni Islamist organization founded in 1928 by the Egyptian scholar Hassan al-Banna

**Nabi** prophet—a man sent by God to give guidance to man

**NCCM** National Council of Canadian Muslims; formerly CAIR-CAN

**Niqab** another word for the veil for covering the face

**Orientalism** an academic term to describe Western (or European) knowledge and studies of language, literature, religion, philosophy, history, art, and law in the eighteenth and nineteenth centuries of the

Orient, of the cultures of the Middle East, North Africa, Southwest Asia, and Southeast Asia

**Organization of Islamic Cooperation (OIC)** an association of 56 Islamic states promoting Muslim solidarity in economic, political, and social issues. The OIC is often said to represent 57 states, to include Palestine as a state

**Ottoman Empire** also known as the Turkish Empire which spanned more than 600 years under Islamic rule and came to an end in 1922, when it was replaced by the Turkish Republic and various successor states in southeastern Europe and the Middle East

**Petrodollars** the primary source of government revenue in many Middle Eastern countries

**Prophet** one who receives revelation from Allah but is not required to spread it

**Rajm** Arabic word for "stoning" as punishment

**Ramadan** month of fasting to mark the revelation of the Koran to Muhammad

**Rasul** a messenger in Islam who receives revelation from Allah and is told to spread it

**Sabb** "abuse of the prophet," blashphemy, insulting Allah or Muhammad

**Salaf** ancestors, predecessors, first three generations of Muslims

**Salafi movement** ultra-conservative movement in Sunni Islam that developed in the eighteenth century, advocating a return to the "devout ancestors"—the salafis

**Salam** literally "peace"; also used as a general greeting

**Sharia** Islamic religious law, derived from the Koran and Hadith; traditional theory of Islamic jurisprudence recognizes four sources of Sharia: Koran, Sunnah, qiyas, and ijma

**Shia** second denomination of Islam; one of the two major groups in Islam, comprising approximately 15–20 percent of Muslims worldwide. Shiites believe that Ali, the cousin and son-in-law of the prophet Muhammad, was designated as Muhammad's successor.

**Stealth Islamists** one who advocates and/or advances political Islam covertly; an advocate of "soft jihad" and Sharia under the concealment of "tolerance" and "civil rights"

**Sufi** muslim mystic; the inner, spiritual dimension of Islam that relates to purification of the heart and involves devotional practices to bring one closer to God

**Sunni** largest denomination of Islam, from the Arabic word Sunnah, meaning words or actions based on Muhammad. The majority group of Islam, comprising about 80 percent of Muslims worldwide. Sunnis believe that the prophet's best friend, Abu Bakr, was selected by consensus of the majority to succeed him

**Sunni schools of law (thought)** the Hanafi, the Maliki, the Shafi'i, and the Hanbali

**Tajdid** to purify or reform society towards renewal of religious faith, practice, and strict adherence to the Koran

**Takfiri** a Muslim who excommunicates another Muslim or accuses him or her of apostasy

**Taqiyya** an Islamic juridical term which permits a Muslim under Sharia law to lie or dissimulate like "kitman," e.g., the denying of religious belief and practice in the face of persecution

**Ulema/Ulama** recognized scholars, leaders, and authorities of Islam; the guardians and judges of legal and religious tradition in Islam

**Umma** global community of Muslims

**Wahhabism** puritanical Islamist revivalist movement based on the teachings of Muhammad ibn Abd al-Wahhab. An oath between Ibn Abd al-Wahhab and Muhammad bin Saud led to the development of a powerful state based on Islamic principles: the kingdom of Saudi Arabia

**Young Turks** a political reform movement in the early twentieth century, which led a rebellion against the Ottomans

**Zakat** the practice of giving charity which is treated as a religious obligation like tax

# A TIMELINE HISTORY OF ISLAM

EARLY CALIPHS

| 570 | Birth of Muhammad |
|---|---|
| 610 | Muhammad's first vision of Angel Gabriel in cave near Mecca |
| 610–22 | Muhammad preaches in Mecca |
| 622 | First hijrah—Muhammad and followers flee to Medina |
| 624 | Muslims attack Meccan caravans at Badr |
| 625 | Muslims are defeated by Meccans at Uhud |
| 630 | Muslims capture Mecca |
| 632 | Death of Muhammad. Abu Bakr chosen as caliph (Rashidun caliphate) |
| 632–33 | Wars of Ridda (also known as Wars of Apostasy) against rebel Arabian Tribes |
| 634 | Umar ibn al-Khattab (Rashidun caliphate) |
| 633–42 | Muslim armies conquer Fertile Crescent |
| 636 | Battle of Yarmouk, which ends Byzantine rule in Syria and marks the first great wave of conquests since Muhammad's death |
| 642 | Battle of Nahavand. Persian conquered by Sasanian Arab forces, representing a great turning point in Iranian history |
| 644 | Third Caliph Uthman ibn Affan (Rashidun caliphate) |
| 656 | Ali ibn Abi-Talib becomes fourth caliph (Rashidun caliphate) |
| 661 | Al-Hasan ibn 'Ali, fifth Caliph (Rashidun caliphate), deemed first Imam of all Muslims as of the house of Muhammad in Shia view |
| 661 | Mu 'āwiyah ibn 'Abī Sufyān succeeds his father to |

|  | become caliph and establish the Umayyad Dynasty. (661–750). He is deemed second Imam of all Muslims in Shia view |
| 670 | Al-Husayn ibn 'Ali becomes Imam of Shiites after death of older brother Al- Hasan |
| 674–78 | First Arab siege of Constantinople and first expansion into Byzantine Empire |
| 680 | Death of Al-Husayn marks beginning of the Shia sect |
| 680 | Yazīd ibn Mu'awiya becomes second Caliph of the Umayyad Dynasty |

## CONTINUING SPREAD OF ISLAM

| 710 | Arab armies enter Spain from North Africa and India in the east. Eventually almost the entire Iberian Peninsula is under Islamic control |
| 732 | Muslims are defeated at Poitiers in France by Charles Martel |
| 750 | Abbasid Dynasty overthrows Umayyad Caliphate, shifting the seat of power to Baghdad. Abu al-Abbas al-Saffah becomes caliph in Iraq. Abbasids descended from an uncle of Muhammad and were cousins to the ruling Umayyad Dynasty. The commonly referenced Golden Age of Islam was during the reign of the Abbasid Caliphate |
| 754 | Abu Ja'far Abdallah ibn Muhammad al-Mansur becomes second Caliph and Baghdad becomes the new capital of the Abbasid Empire |
| 765 | Division among Shiites; majority are Imamiyya (Twelvers) who co-exist with Abbasid caliphs; minority are Ismailiya (Seveners) |
| 800 | Written collections of Hadith (sayings of the Prophet) are compiled. Sicily comes under Muslim rule |
| 813–33 | Reign of seventh Caliph Abū Ja 'far Abdullāh al-Ma'mūn ibn Hārūn al-Rashīd Ma'mun of the Abbasid Caliphate. Theological controversy (Mu'tazila controversy) over whether the Koran is created or uncreated and eternal. Center for translation of texts from Greek to Arabic founded in Baghdad |

| | |
|---|---|
| 869 | Uprising of black slaves (Zanj) against Abbasid Empire. Zanj forces grew rapidly in numbers and power, absorbing the well-trained black contingents that defected from defeated caliph armies but the Zanj rebellion was crushed in 883 |
| 908 | First Fatimid Caliph in Tunisia |
| 928 | Umayyad Abd ar-Rahman III declares himself caliph in Cordoba |
| 940 | Muhammad al-Mahdi, the twelfth Imam, disappears. Twelvers still await the future return of the "Hidden Imam" |
| 945 | The Buyids (Persian) invade Baghdad and take power from caliph to become the Buyid Shia Dynasty which represents the period in Iranian history sometimes called the "Iranian Intermezzo" |
| 969 | The Fatimid Ismaili Shia Caliphate seize power in Egypt and attack Palestine, Syria, and Arabia. Cairo (Al-Qahira, "the victorious city") is founded |
| 1000 | Islam continues to spread through the continent of Africa, including Nigeria, which served as a trading liaison between the northern and central regions of Africa |
| 996–1021 | Al-Hakim bi-Amr Allah, caliph of the Fatimid Caliphate, 16th Ismaili Imam. He and Hamza ibn 'Ali ibn Ahmad establish the Druze sect |
| 1030 | Umayyad Caliphate in Cordoba defeated by the Christian Reconquista |
| 1055 | Seljuk Turks conquer Baghdad; Abbasids now only nominal rulers |
| 1061–91 | Sicily which was under Arab control falls to the Normans |
| 1071 | Seljuk Turks defeat Byzantines at Battle of Manzikert. |
| 1078–1166 | Sufi orders founded by the Hanbalī theologian 'Abd al-Qādir al-Jīlānī |
| 1099 | Christian Crusaders take Jerusalem from Muslims. |
| 1120 | Islam continues to spread throughout Asia. |
| 1171 | Saladin ends Fatimid Caliphate in Egypt and Fatimid brought under Abbasid Caliphate |

| 1174 | Saladin—Sunni founder of Ayyubid Dynasty—declares himself first sultan of Egypt and Syria |
|------|------|
| 1179 | Final Reconquista of Spain (Valencia) from the Moors |
| 1187 | Saladin captures Jerusalem away from the Franks, the most powerful Christian kingdom of early medieval Western Europe |
| 1193 | Death of Saladin; most of Crusader states have been conquered and returned to Islam |
| 1200s | Assassins (Nizari Ismailis) wiped out by the Mongols. Indian rulers in Delhi take the title of Sultan |
| 1221 | Genghis Khan (founder and emperor of the Mongol Empire) and the Mongols enter Persia |
| 1241 | Mongols conquer the Punjab |
| 1258 | Mongols capture Baghdad; kill Caliph Al-Musta'sim Billah which ends Abbasid Caliphate |
| 1299 | The earliest Ottoman state is formed in Anatolia, Turkey. |
| 1281–1324 | Reign of Uthman (Osman), who founded the Ottoman Empire. Muslim merchants and Sufis settle in SE Asia |
| mid-1300s | Ottomans expand into Europe |
| late 1300s | Ottomans take control of the Balkans |
| 1400s | Islam spreads to the Philippines |
| 1453 | Mehmet Fatih (rules 1451–81) and the Ottomans conquer the Byzantine seat of Constantinople and change its name to Istanbul |
| 1501 | Ismail (1487–1524) claims to be the Hidden Imam and is proclaimed Shah (king) of Persia (Iran). Twelver Shi'ism becomes official religion of Persia |
| 1516 | Ottomans conquer Syria and Egypt |
| 1517 | Ottomans control Mecca and Medina |
| 1520–66 | Reign of Suleiman the Magnificent—the longest ruling Sultan of the Ottoman Empire Hungary and coastlands of Algeria and Tunisia come under Ottoman rule |

## THE COLLAPSE OF THE OTTOMAN EMPIRE

1566–1807 The decline of the Ottoman Empire was steady due to tired campaigns, declining military power, failed administration, inflation, corruption and economic difficulty, social unrest, weakness of central government, and resistance to change.

1683   The siege at Vienna—Ottoman army defeated by Polish King Jan III Sobieski and Ottoman expansion into Europe stymied

1882–1952 British domination of Egypt

1839–76 Rise of nationalistic "Young Turks," who favored constitutional government over monarchy rule, leading to a revolutionary reform movement against the regime of Ottoman sultan Abdulhamid II which culminated in the First Constitutional Era in 1876 (Tanzimat)

1877   Following war with Russia, Abdulhamid II suspends constitution and adopts Pan-Islamism as a policy to oppose Western expansion in Ottoman affairs

1870–1924 Muslim immigrants from the Arab world immigrate to America

1914   Britain and France declare war on Ottomans.

1918   Collapse and dissolution of the Ottoman Empire with the end of World War I. League of Nations grants Britain mandatory administrative control over Palestine and Iraq, and France over Lebanon and Syria

## POST-OTTOMANS

1923   Republic of Turkey established with Mustafa Kemal (Atatürk) is first president

1928   Ikhwan al-Muslimun (Muslim Brothers) founded in Egypt by Hassan al-Banna

1932   Kingdom of Saudi Arabia founded by Abdulaziz 'Ibn Saud'

1941   Jamaat-e-Islami Islamist movement founded in Lahore, India

1945   Indonesia becomes an independent republic

1945–60s Islam spreads to the West with mass migrations from Asia, Africa, and India

1947   Pakistan founded as an Islamic nation while Islam becomes a minority religion in India

1979       Shah of Iran is overthrown by Ayatollah Ruhollah Mūsavi Khomeini who establishes strict Shia political rule

late 1990s    Taliban rises to power in Afghanistan

# ACKNOWLEDGMENTS

There are many individuals who directly impacted the creation of this book, *The Challenge of Modernizing Islam*, those who influenced me personally and others who helped shape the work years before its inception. My hope is that I did not leave anyone out of my list of acknowledgements. I also extend much gratitude to those who were peripheral to this project but made significant and meaningful contributions in their thoughts and support.

I thank Dr. Daniel Pipes and the Middle East Forum Education Fund for commissioning this book project and for Dr. Pipes's belief in my work when I grew weary of its immensity and intricacy. I thank Robert Spencer, the first subject matter expert and academic skeptic to appraise this book upon its completion. His feedback was refreshingly relieving and appreciated, as was his support.

I would also like to thank those who supported me and my work on a deep personal level: my love Vincent Paul, Natasha Leigh Williams for her deep inspiration, encouragement, and permanent influence in my life and work; also, Michelle Lee, Phillip Matthew, Wilma Kay, Kenneth Hugh Francis, and my late friend Rebecca Moulds, whom I miss.

I owe much gratitude to the interviewees in this book who were warm and engaging, and who gave their time to enable this work to come to fruition. I would like to also extend a special thank you to Raheel Raza, Tarek Fatah, and Farzana Hassan whom I regularly interviewed during my nine years of daily, live TV shows, who are often spicy with their opening lines. These were the three individuals who first opened my eyes to the immense struggle of Islamist incursions in our midst. Their brevity and opposition were distinct on our programs, as was the challenge before them, which inspired me to follow this path. Another inspiration was the founder of Crossroads Christian

Communications Incorporated in Canada, Reverend David Mainse, who courageously recognized early on the grave danger of Islamist incursions into religious freedoms and Western civil and political rights. Reverend Mainse supported my efforts in its emergent stages and for this I am greatly appreciative.

I thank Roger Kimball, publisher of Encounter Books, whose thrilling reply to my book proposal still rings loudly: "I like your book proposal and would like to publish the book." I also thank Maura Moynihan, my editor, who was most helpful and encouraging through the editing process. I thank her legendary dad, Senator Daniel Patrick Moynihan, who imparted to her an invaluable sense of cogent creativity, harnessed in presentation, which I benefited from. I send my gratitude to Heather Ohle, Katherine Wong, Lauren Miklos, Sam Schneider, and the rest of the team at Encounter who also worked toward the publication of my book and whose talents and insights contribute to Encounter's superb quality and high standards.

I would also like to acknowledge Nina Rosenwald, editor and founder of the Gatestone Institute, who helped shape my writings about Islamism, and the David Horowitz Freedom Center for its vast, commendable work as a leader in the counter-Jihad movement, and for allowing me the opportunity to write about Islam since 2008 through *FrontPage Magazine*; the former *NewsReal Blog*; a personal interview with me by editor Jamie Glazov, as well as Glazov's online symposium about homegrown Jihadis, which collectively shaped my developing interests; and currently, Robert Spencer's *Jihad Watch*.

# NOTES

## PREFACE TO THE PAPERBACK EDITION

1  Jennifer Yang, "Board member of anti-racism agency fired amid accusations of Islamophobic commentary," *Toronto Star,* December 21, 2017.

2  "Iqra Khalid – Private Members' Motions – Current Session," House of Commons, Government of Canada, March 23, 2017. http://www.ourcommons.ca/Parliamentarians/en/members/Iqra-Khalid(88849)/Motions?document Id=8661986%2520

3  "Tenth OIC Observatory Report on Islamophobia" Presented to the 44th Council of Foreign Ministers, July 10–11, 2017.

4  Barbara Kay, "Liberals left reeling by clear, rational criticisms of M-103," *National Post,* October 4, 2017.

5  Michael Mostyn, "By discouraging criticism of Islam, M103 could make it harder to combat anti-Semitism," *National Post,* October 16, 2017.

6  Ibid.

7  Ibid.

8  Shawn Jeffords, "Toronto District School Board revises Islamic guide," The Canadian Press, October 2, 2017.

9  "Underlying Trends in Research and Consultation, Islamophobia," Ontario Human Rights Commission, accessed July 20, 2018. http://www.ohrc.on.ca/en/3-current-discrimination-trends/32-underlying-trends-research-and-consultation

10  Christine Douglass-Williams, "Canadian human rights lawyer: 'Fear of some elements of Islam is mere prudence,'" *Jihad Watch,* October 20, 2017.

11  Muslim Students Association (MSA), Clarion Project, February 3, 2018.

12  Christine Douglass-Williams, "Canadians Duped: A Victorious Day for Islamic Supremacists," *Jihad Watch,* March 25, 2017.

13  Ibid.

14  "Taking Action Against Systemic Racism and Religious Discrimination Including Islamophobia," Government Response to the 10th Report of the Standing Committee on Canadian Heritage, June 1, 2018.

15  Ibid.

16  "MP Iqra Khalid Announces Liberal Government Response of $23 M Funding Initiatives in context of M103," TAG TV, June 29, 2018.

17  Brian Daly, "RCMP probe into Islamist financing didn't end with IRFAN," *Toronto Sun,* February 10, 2015.

18  Ibid.

19  "Taking Action Against Systemic Racism and Religious Discrimination

Including Islamophobia," Government Response to the 10th Report of the Standing Committee on Canadian Heritage, June 1, 2018.

20  "Training and Workshops," National Council of Canadian Muslims. https://www.nccm.ca/connect/training/

21  Jennifer Yang, "Board member of anti-racism agency fired amid accusations of Islamophobic commentary," *Toronto Star,* December 21, 2017.

## FOREWORD BY ROBERT SPENCER

1  Caroline Fourest, *Brother Tariq: The Doublespeak of Tariq Ramadan,* (New York: Encounter Books, 2007), 233.

## INTRODUCTION

1  Daniel Greenfield, "Moderate Islam Is Multiculturalism Misspelled," *FrontPage Magazine,* September 1, 2014.

2  Bernard Lewis, "The Roots of Muslim Rage," *The Atlantic,* September 1990.

3  Stephen Ulph & Patrick Sookhdeo, eds., *Reforming Islam: Progressive Voices From the Arab Muslim World* (Virginia: Almuslih Publications, 2014), 2.

4  Ibid., 2.

5  Ibid.

6  Ibid.

7  Ibid., 5, 10.

8  Ibid., 6.

9  Ibid., 345.

10  Ibid., 422.

11  Ibid., 131.

12  Robert Joyce and Asma Smadhi, "Tunisia's Arab Spring: Three years on," *Aljazeera Media Network,* January 14, 2014.

13  Fouad Ajami, "Iran: The Impossible Revolution," *Foreign Affairs,* Winter 1988/89.

14  Robert Tait, "Khamenei Praises Arab Revolts As Iran Crushes Its Own Protests," *Radio Free Europe/Radio Liberty,* February 21, 2011.

15  "Iran's Ayatollah to Arab World: Don't Let West, Israel 'Confiscate' Arab Spring," *Haaretz (Associated Press),* August 31, 2011.

16  Elaine Sciolino, "Director Admits C.I.A. Fell Short In Predicting the Soviet Collapse," *The New York Times,* May 21, 1992.

17  Kirsten Lundberg, "CIA and the Fall of the Soviet Empire: The Politics of 'Getting It Right,'" accessed February 2017, https://www.cia.gov/library/readingroom/docs/DOC_0005302423.pdf.

18  Ayaan Hirsi Ali, "Here's What I Would Have Said at Brandeis," *The Wall Street Journal,* April 10, 2014.

19  Susan Dominus, "Ayaan Hirsi Ali's 'Heretic,'" *The New York Times,* April 1, 2015.

20  Karen Kleiss, "Muslims pray at Alberta legislature for victims of Ottawa, Montreal attacks," *Edmonton Journal,* November 1, 2014.

21  "About MAC," Muslim Association of Canada, accessed June 14, 2016, www.macnet.ca/.

22  "CAIR Condemns 'Barbaric Murder' of U.S. Aid Worker Peter Kassig by ISIS," *PR Newswire,* November 16, 2014.

23  "Vision, Mission, Core Principles," Council on American–Islamic Relations, October 1, 2015.

24  Josh Gerstein, "Islamic Groups Named in Hamas Funding Case," *The New York Sun,* June 4, 2007.

25  "UAE blacklists 82 groups as 'terrorist,'" *Al Arabiya Network*, November 15, 2014. Daniel Pipes, "Is CAIR a Terror Group?," Middle East Forum, November 28, 2014.

26  Bernard Lewis, "The Roots of Muslim Rage," *The Atlantic,* September 1990.

27  "Moderate Muslims Speak Out on Capitol Hill," The Investigative Project on Terrorism, October 1, 2010.

28  Daniel Pipes, "Canada's Muslims, Not of One Mind," Middle East Forum, November 2011.

29  Kathryn Blaze Carlson, "New moderate Muslim group aims anti-extremism message at youth," *National Post*, September 11, 2012.

30  "Moderate Muslims Speak Out on Capitol Hill," The Investigative Project on Terrorism, October 1, 2010.

31  Robert S. Wistrich, "Muslim Anti-Semitism: A Clear and Present Danger," The American Jewish Committee, 2002, v.

32  Bernard Lewis, *Semites and Anti-Semites: An Inquiry into Conflict and Prejudice* (New York: W.W. Norton & Company, May 17, 1999), 256.

## CHAPTER ONE

1  "Leading the Movement: Engaging in the war of ideas against the ideology of political Islam," American Islamic Forum for Democracy, 2016.

2  Ibid.

3  Ibid.

4  Ibid.

5  Ibid.

## CHAPTER TWO

1  Raheel Raza, "About Raheel Raza," Raheel Raza Diversity Inc., accessed August 2013, http://www.raheelraza.com/about.htm.

2  Ibid.

3  Raheel Raza, "The Danger In Our Midst," Gatestone Institute, September 25, 2013.

4  Ibid.

## CHAPTER THREE

1  Meira Svirsky, "Dr. Ahmed Mansour: Human Rights Need to Be Islamic Law," Clarion Project, May 9, 2013.

2  Ibid.

## CHAPTER FOUR

1  Tawfik Hamid, "Tawfik Hamid – Biography," *Newsmax*, April 2, 2017.

2  Meira Svirsky, "Dr. Tawfik Hamid: Islam Needs Modern Interpretation," Clarion Project, December 4, 2012.

3  Ibid.

## CHAPTER FIVE

1  Salim Mansur, "About Salim Mansur," *ProudToBeCanadian*, November 24, 2012.

2  Ibid.

3  Ibid.

4 Robert Fulford, "Canada's angriest 'moderate,'" *The National Post*, November 21, 2009.

## CHAPTER SIX

1 Qanta Ahmed, *In the Land of Invisible Women: A Female Doctor's Journey in the Saudi Kingdom* (Sourcebooks, 2008).
2 Ibid.
3 Ibid.
4 Ibid.
5 Ibid.

## CHAPTER SEVEN

1 Jalal Zuberi, "Bollywood Perpetuating Myths of Muslims Victimized in the West?," Gatestone Institute, April 9, 2010.

## CHAPTER NINE

1 Daniel Pipes, "Distinguishing between Islam and Islamism," Center For Strategic and International Studies, June 30, 1998.
2 Ibid.
3 John M. Broder, "For Muslim Who Says Violence Destroys Islam, Violent Threats," *The New York Times*, March 11, 2006.
4 Ibid.
5 Ibid.
6 Ibid.
7 Ibid.
8 Asra Q. Nomani, "Heroes & Pioneers: Wafa Sultan," *Time*, May 8, 2006.
9 John M. Broder, "The Saturday Profile: For Muslim Who Says Violence Destroys Islam, Violent Threats," *The New York Times*, March 11, 2006.
10 "Report: Dr. Wafa Sultan in Hiding," *Arutz Sheva: Israel National News*, March 31, 2008.
11 Ned May, "Expert Testimony at the Trial of Geert Wilders, Part 2: Wafa Sultan," *Breitbart*, October 23, 2010.
12 Ibid.
13 Robert Spencer, "Geert Wilders: The Specter of Islam Is Haunting the Free World," *Jihad Watch,* October 8, 2013.
14 Christine Williams, "Fighting for Freedom While Losing His Own: An Interview with Geert Wilders," *Europe News* (David Horowitz *NewsReal*), May 17, 2011.
15 Ahmed Subhy Mansour, "Ahl-Al Quran's Beliefs," *Ahl AlQuran*, December 28, 2013.
16 Ibid.
17 Ibid.
18 "United Against Terrorism handbook released at Winnipeg mosque," *CBC News*, September 29, 2014.
19 "DOJ: CAIR's Unindicted Co-Conspirator Status Legit," The Investigative Project on Terrorism, March 12, 2010.
20 "United Against Terrorism handbook released at Winnipeg mosque," *CBC News,* September 29, 2014.
21 Part 1, Chapter 3, Dr. Sheikh Subhy Mansour.

22 Rowan Scarborough, "Obama's scrub of Muslim terms under question; common links in attacks," *The Washington Times*, April 25, 2013.

23 Ibid.

24 Luke Harding, "Charlie Hebdo timeline: how events have unfolded," *The Guardian*, January 9, 2015.

25 Ibid.

26 Ibid.

27 Kevin Rawlinson, "Charlie Hebdo: 'Islamist cyber attacks' hit France," *BBC News*, January 16, 2015.

28 "Pakistan clashes over Charlie Hebdo cartoon," *BBC News*, January 16, 2015.

29 "Bill O'Reilly: Another terror attack by Muslim killers," *Fox News*, January 8, 2015.

30 Ibid.

31 Ibid.

32 Mendeleyeev, "Russian Muslim Leaders Condemn Both Terrorists and Newspaper," *The Mendeleyev Journal – Live From Moscow*, January 8, 2015.

33 "Watch: Jimmy Carter Says Israeli–Palestinian Conflict 'One of the Origins' of Islamist Violence," *Jerusalem Post*, January 13, 2015.

34 Loulla-Mae Eleftheriou-Smith, "Paris attacks: US politician Jack Lindblad claims Charlie Hebdo killings were by 'US and Mossad' to keep Israel's Netanyahu in power," *UK Independent,* January 15, 2015.

35 Sara Malm, "Turkish president accuses 'the West' of being behind Charlie Hebdo attacks and deliberately 'blaming Muslims' as conspiracy theories sweep the Internet accusing Israel of orchestrating it," *UK Daily Mail*, January 13, 2015.

36 "Terror and Islam: After the atrocities," *The Economist*, January 15, 2015.

37 Josh Feldman, "French PM: We're at War Against 'Radical Islamism,' Not Islam," *Mediaite*, January 13, 2015.

38 Ibid.

39 Daniel Pipes interview with author, March 2013.

40 Daniel Pipes, "PIPES: Islam and its infidels," *The Washington Times*, May 13, 2013.

41 Ayaan Hirsi Ali, "Here's What I Would Have Said at Brandeis,*" The Wall Street Journal*, April 10, 2014.

42 Ibid.

43 Susan Dominus, "Ayaan Hirsi Ali's 'Heretic,'" *The New York Times*, April 1, 2015.

44 Ibid.

45 Daniel Pipes interview with author, March 2013.

46 Ibid.

47 Ibid.

48 Koran 16:97.

49 Koran 3:56.

50 Daniel Pipes interview with author, March 2013.

51 Ibid.

52 Jonathan Schanzer, "At War With Whom? A short history of radical Islam," Middle East Forum, Spring 2002.

53 Ibid.

54 Ibid.

55 Karen Kleiss, "Muslims pray at Alberta legislature for victims of Ottawa, Montreal attacks," *Edmonton Journal*, November 1, 2014.

56 Ibid.

57 "About MAC," Muslim Association of Canada, accessed June 14, 2016, www.macnet.ca/.

58 Ambassador Professor Dumitru Chican, "THE PROJECT – A Project of the Cultural Jihad," *World Security Network*, November 10, 2014.

59 Zhyntativ, "Hasan Al-Banna and His Political Thought of Islamic Brotherhood," *Ikhwanweb*, May 13, 2008.

60 Ibid.

61 Ibid.

62 Ambassador Professor Dumitru Chican, "THE PROJECT – A Project of the Cultural Jihad," *World Security Network*, November 10, 2014.

63 Jonathan D. Halevi, "Where is The Muslim Brotherhood Headed?," Jerusalem Center for Public Affairs, June 20, 2012.

64 Stephen Lendman, "More Evidence of Turkey's Support of the Islamic State (ISIS), in Liaison with US and NATO," Global Research, January 12, 2016.

65 Nick Paton Walsh, "The secret jihadi smuggling route through Turkey," *CNN*, November 5, 2013, http://edition.cnn.com/2013/11/04/world/europe/isis-gaining-strength-on-syria-turkey-border/.

66 Ibid.

67 "Turkey's Erdogan accuses West of hypocrisy over Paris attacks," *Reuters*, January 12, 2015.

68 Sara Malm, "Turkish president accuses 'the West' of being behind Charlie Hebdo attacks and deliberately 'blaming Muslims' as conspiracy theories sweep the Internet accusing Israel of orchestrating it," *UK Daily Mail*, January 13, 2015.

69 Haeyoun Park, Sergio Peçanha, and Tom Giratikanon, "Charlie Hebdo Attackers' Path to Radicalization," *The New York Times*, January 17, 2015.

70 Gunnar Heinsohn and Daniel Pipes, "Arab-Israeli Fatalities Rank 49th," Middle East Forum, October 8, 2007.

## CHAPTER TEN

1 Carol E.B. Choksy and Jamsheed K. Choksy, "The Saudi Connection: Wahhabism and Global Jihad," *World Affairs Journal*, May/June 2015.

2 Ibid.

3 Christopher M. Blanchard, "The Islamic Traditions of Wahhabism and Salafiyya," Congressional Research Service Report, January 25, 2006.

4 Ibid.

5 Ibid.

6 Raymond Ibrahim, "Obey The Prophet, Even If He Tells You To Kill," Gatestone Institute, November 26, 2012.

7 Jonathan Schanzer, "At War With Whom? A short history of radical Islam," Middle East Forum, Spring 2002.

8 Ibid.

9 Ibid.

10 "Hassan Nasrallah: In His Own Words," Committee for Accuracy In Middle East Reporting in America, July 26, 2006.

11 Daniel Pipes, "Distinguishing between Islam and Islamism," Middle East Forum, June 30, 1998.

12 Stephen Ulph and Patrick Sookhdeo, *Reforming Islam: Progressive Voices from the Arab Muslim World*, Reviewed by Christine Williams, *Middle East Quarterly*, Summer 2015.

13 William Kilpatrick, "Stealth Jihad Meets PC America," *FrontPage Magazine*, June 19, 2014.

14 Ibid.

15 Ibid.

16 AFP, "Islamic State recruiting in Canada, local imam warns," *The Telegraph*, August 23, 2014.

17 "ISIS 'betraying' Muslims, says Calgary imam before hunger strike," *CBC News*, August 22, 2014.

18 Dylan Robertson, "Updated: Calgary imam declares 'fatwa' on ISIL," *Calgary Herald*, March 11, 2015.

19 Graeme Morton, "Muslim leader drops Ezra Levant cartoon complaint," *National Post*, February 12, 2008.

20 Ibid.

21 Ibid.

22 Ibid.

23 Ibid.

24 Ibid.

25 Stephen Schwartz email message to author, January 9, 2012.

26 Stephen Ulph and Patrick Sookhdeo, *Reforming Islam: Progressive Voices from the Arab Muslim World*, Reviewed by Christine Williams, *Middle East Quarterly*, Summer 2015.

27 Stephen Schwartz, "The Terrorist War Against Islam: Clarifying Academic Confusions," Center For Islamic Pluralism, January 28, 2011.

28 Stephen Schwartz, "Wahhabi Monopoly," *Islam Daily*, July 1, 2005.

29 Tarek Heggy, "Political Islam vs Modernity," Almuslih.org, 2012.

30 Irshad Manji, *Allah, Liberty and Love: The Courage to Reconcile Faith and Freedom* (Toronto: Random House, 2011), 9.

31 Ibid., inside cover.

32 Ibid., 218.

33 Ibid., 197-199.

34 Ibid., 219.

35 Sura 9:5.

36 Irshad Manji, *Allah, Liberty and Love: The Courage to Reconcile Faith and Freedom* (Toronto: Random House, 2011), 219.

37 Ibid.

38 Ibid., 220.

39 Ibid., 222.

40 Ibid.

41 Ibid.

42 Ibid., 18, 19.

43 Ibid., 19.

44 Ibid.

45 Irshad Manji, "Islam Needs Reformists, Not 'Moderates,'" *The Wall Street Journal*, May 7, 2011.

46 Meira Svirsky, "Dr. Tawfik Hamid: Islam Needs Modern Interpretation," Clarion Project, December 4, 2012.

47 Harold Rhode, "Can Muslims Reopen the Gates of Ijtihad?," Gatestone Institute, June 15, 2012.

48 Ibid.

49 Ibid.

50 Stephen Ulph and Patrick Sookhdeo, *Reforming Islam: Progressive Voices from the Arab Muslim World* (Virginia: Almuslih Publications, 2014), 76.
51 Ibid.
52 Ibid., 14.
53 "Together We Came," Arab American Institute, June 25, 2014.
54 Joshua Muravchik, "Enough Said: The False Scholarship of Edward Said," *World Affairs*, March/April 2013.
55 Bernard Lewis, *The Political Language of Islam* (Chicago: University of Chicago Press, 1988), 72.

## CHAPTER ELEVEN

1 "Islamist Terrorism From 1945 to the Rise of ISIS," Constitutional Rights Foundation, Spring 2017.
2 "Jihad Against Jews and Crusaders," Federation of American Scientists Intelligence Resource Program, February 23, 1998.
3 Stephen Ulph and Patrick Sookhdeo, eds., *Reforming Islam: Progressive Voices from the Arab Muslim World* (Virginia: Almuslih Publications, 2014), 2.
4 Ibid., 3.
5 Gregory M. Davis, "Islam 101," *Jihad Watch*, accessed June 2016.
6 Stephen Ulph and Patrick Sookhdeo, eds., *Reforming Islam: Progressive Voices from the Arab Muslim World* (Virginia: Almuslih Publications, 2014), 31.
7 Bukhari Volume 4, Book 52, Number 53.
8 Bukhari Volume 1, Book 3, Number 125.
9 Bukhari, Book 31, Number 5917.
10 Koran 9:5.
11 Efraim Karsh, "It's Anti-Semitism, Stupid," *The Jerusalem Post*, August 11, 2014.
12 Jeffrey Goldberg, "New Chapter, Old Story," review of *The Devil That Never Dies*, by Daniel Jonah Goldhagen, *The New York Times*, October 11, 2013, Sunday Book Review.
13 "WCC Invites Israel-Hating Conspiracy Theorist to Interfaith Event in Switzerland," Committee for Accuracy in Middle East Reporting in America, September 27, 2016.
14 Andrew E. Harrod, "Georgetown University's One-Way Street of Christian-Muslim Understanding," *Family Security Matters*, December 5, 2013.
15 Andrea Bistrich, "Discovering the common ground of world religions," *Share International,* Vol. 26, No. 7, September 2007, 21–22.
16 Robert R. Reilly, "Exterminating Christians in the Middle East," *The Wall Street Journal,* August 20, 2015.
17 Thomas F. Madden, "The Real History of the Crusades," *Christianity Today*, May 6, 2005.
18 Gunnar Heinsohn and Daniel Pipes, "Arab–Israeli Fatalities Rank 49th," Middle East Forum, October 8, 2007.
19 "Isis rebels declare 'Islamic state' in Iraq and Syria," *BBC News*, June 30, 2014.
20 Cole Bunzel, "From Paper State to Caliphate: The Ideology of the Islamic State," The Brookings Project on U.S. Relations with the Islamic World, Analysis Paper, No. 19, March 2015.
21 John Hall, "The ISIS map of the world: Militants outline chilling five-year plan for global domination as they declare formation of caliphate - and change their name to the Islamic State," *UK Daily Mail,* June 30, 2014.
22 Devadmin, "The Islamic State (ISIS, ISIL)," Clarion Project, August 23, 2016.

23  *Associated Press*, "ISIS is recruiting all sorts of people, not just male fighters," *New York Post*, December 16, 2014.

24  Devadmin, "The Islamic State (ISIS, ISIL)," Clarion Project, August 23, 2016.

25  Ibid.

26  Alex Thurston, "'The disease is unbelief': Boko Haram's religious and political worldview," The Brookings Project on U.S. Relations with the Islamic World, Analysis Paper, No. 22, January 2016, 8.

27  Ibid.

28  Monica Mark, "Boko Haram's 'deadliest massacre': 2,000 feared dead in Nigeria," *The UK Guardian*, January 10, 2015.

29  Efraim Karsh, *Islamic Imperialism: A History* (New Haven and London: Yale University Press, 2007), 67.

30  Raymond Ibrahim, "Are Judaism and Christianity as Violent as Islam?," Middle East Forum, Summer 2009.

31  Majid Khadduri, *War and Peace in the Law of Islam* (London: Oxford University Press, 1955), 60.

32  Daniel Pipes interview with author, March 2013.

33  "Sunnah" from "The Islamic World: Past and Present," *Oxford Islamic Studies Online* (Oxford University Press, 2017).

34  Stephen Ulph and Patrick Sookhdeo, eds., *Reforming Islam: Progressive Voices from the Arab Muslim World* (Virginia: Almuslih Publications, 2014), 393.

35  Ibid., 395.

36  Ibid., 420–422.

37  Ibid., 130–132.

38  Ibid.

39  Ayaan Hirsi Ali, "Islam Is a Religion of Violence," *Foreign Policy*, November 9, 2015.

40  Bat Ye'or, *The Dhimmi: Jews and Christians Under Islam* (NJ: Fairleigh Dickinson University Press, 1985), 43-44.

41  "Constitution of Medina," *Oxford Islamic Studies Online* (Oxford University Press, 2017).

42  David Bukay, "Peace or Jihad? Abrogation in Islam," Middle East Forum, Fall 2007.

43  Ibid.

44  Daniel Pipes interview with author, March 2013.

45  David Bukay, "Peace or Jihad? Abrogation in Islam," Middle East Forum, Fall 2007.

46  Harold Rhode, "Can Muslims Reopen the Gates of Ijtihad?," Gatestone Institute, June 15, 2012.

47  Meira Svirsky, "Dr. Tawfik Hamid: Islam Needs Modern Interpretation," Clarion Project, December 4, 2012.

48  Ibid.

49  Ibid.

50  Ahmed Subhy Mansour, "Constitution of Quranists," *Ahl AlQuran*, accessed March 2017.

51  Ibid.

52  Ahmed Subhy Mansour, "Egypt persecutes Muslim moderates," *The New York Times*, February 3, 2009.

53  Ibid.

54  Ibid.

55 Dr. Abdulkhaliq Hussein, "Who Is Benefiting From The Attack On The Quranists In Egypt?," *Ahl AlQuran*, 2006.

56 Ibid.

57 Ibid.

58 Ibid.

59 Robert Spencer, *The Complete Infidels Guide to the Koran* (Washington D.C.: Regnery Publishing, 2009), 18.

60 Ibid.

61 Nabil Abu, "Meeting with Shaykh Al-Albani," *Sunnahonline.com*, accessed March 2016.

62 Ibid.

63 Ibid.

64 Ibid.

65 Ibid.

66 "Hadith & Sunnah," *Islam Unraveled*, 1997–2017.

67 Ibid.

68 Ibid.

69 Stephen Schwartz, "The Terrorist War Against Islam: Clarifying Academic Confusions," Center for Islamic Pluralism, January 28, 2011.

70 Khaleel Mohammed, "Assessing English Translations of the Qur'an," Middle East Forum, Spring 2005.

71 Tawfik Hamid, "Underlying Factors Behind Muslim Riots," *Newsmax*, September 21, 2012.

72 Ibid.

73 Khaleel Mohammed, "Assessing English Translations of the Qur'an," Middle East Forum, Spring 2005.

74 Barry Hoberman, "The First Muezzin," *Aramco World*, July/August 1983.

75 Khaleel Mohammed, "Assessing English Translations of the Qur'an," Middle East Forum, Spring 2005.

## CHAPER TWELVE

1 "Race, religion, immigration: the Rotherham sex abuse scandal consumes UK," *The Sydney Morning Herald*, August 28, 2014.

2 "Independent Inquiry into Child Sexual Exploitation in Rotherham," Rotherham Metropolitan Borough Council, 1997–2013.

3 Paul Peachey, "Rotherham child abuse report: 1,400 children subjected to 'appalling' sexual exploitation over 16-years," *UK Independent*, August 26, 2014.

4 "Rotherham child abuse scandal: 1,400 children exploited, report finds," *BBC News*, August 26, 2014.

5 John Bingham, "Rotherham: politics 'imported from Pakistan' fuelled sex abuse cover-up – MP," *The Telegraph*, August 31, 2014.

6 Mia De Graaf and Amanda Williams, "Revealed: How fear of being seen as racist stopped social workers saving up to 1,400 children from sexual exploitation at the hands of Asian men in just ONE TOWN," *UK Daily Mail*, August 26, 2014.

7 Ibid.

8 Brian Lilley, "Mounties apologized for Ramadan terror arrests," *Toronto Sun*, January 5, 2011.

9 Ibid.

10  Ibid.

11  Ibid.

12  Brian Lilley, "PM on Ramadan Apology: Law Should Apply Every Day," *Toronto Sun*, January 6, 2011.

13  Ibid.

14  Ibid.

15  Robert Sibley, "Cops Criticized For Apologizing to Ottawa Muslims: Arrests Made During Ramadan," *Windsor Star*, January 7, 2011.

16  Ibid.

17  "Al-Taqiyya, Dissimulation Part 1," al-Islam, *A Shi-ite Encylopedia*, accessed July 2016.

18  Ibid.

19  "Narrated Jabir bin 'Abdullah: The Prophet said 'War is deceit,'" Mervyn Hiskett, *Some to Mecca Turn to Pray: Islamic Values and the Modern World*, 101, Volume 4, Book 52, Number 269.

20  Raymond Ibrahim, "How Taqiyya Alters Islam's Rules of War: Defeating Jihadist Terrorism," Middle East Forum, Winter 2010, pp. 3–13.

21  Walid Phares, "U.S. Must Address Homegrown Terror Threat," *Newsmax*, July 30, 2009.

22  Christine Williams, "The 'Victimology' Subterfuge," Gatestone Institute, January 15, 2013.

23  Ibid.

24  Caroline May, "8 questions with Dr. Zuhdi Jasser of the American Islamic Forum for Democracy," *The Daily Caller*, August 9, 2010.

25  Ibid.

26  Patrick Strickland, "Islamophobia seen as US states shun Syrians," *Al Jazeera*, November 17, 2015.

27  Ishaan Tharoor, "Were Syrian refugees involved in the Paris attacks? What we know and don't know," *The Washington Post*, November 17, 2015.

28  Gardiner Harris, David E. Sanger, and David M. Herszenhorn, "Obama Increases Number of Syrian Refugees for U.S. Resettlement to 10,000," *The New York Times*, September 10, 2015.

29  Patrick Strickland, "Islamophobia seen as US states shun Syrians," *Al Jazeera*, November 17, 2015.

30  Aaron Brown, "'Just wait…' Islamic State reveals it has smuggled THOUSANDS of extremists into Europe," *Sunday Express*, November 18, 2015.

31  "Legislating Fear: Islamophobia and its Impact in the United States," Council on American–Islamic Relations, Report 2013.

32  Ibid.

33  Ibid.

34  Ibid.

35  Meira Svirsky, "CAIR, a Muslim Brotherhood Front, Praises Chris Christie," Clarion Project, September 20, 2013.

36  "Muneer Awad v. Paul Ziriax, Oklahoma State Board of Elections, et al.," American Civil Liberties Union, August 15, 2013.

37  Ibid.

38  Ariane De Vogue, "Federal Appeals Court Considers Sharia Law," *ABC News*, September 12, 2011.

39  Harvey Simmons, "'One law for all Ontarians,'" *Toronto Star*, September 14, 2010.
40  Ibid.
41  Ibid.
42  Tarek Fatah, "Muslim Group Opposes Sharia Law," Muslim Canadian Congress, August 28, 2004.
43  Harvey Simmons, "'One law for all Ontarians,'" *Toronto Star*, September 14, 2010.
44  Ibid.
45  Daniel Pipes and Sharon Chadha, "CAIR: Islamists Fooling the Establishment," Middle East Forum, Spring 2006.
46  Ibid.
47  Meira Svirsky, "Chris Christie Bent on Including Islamists in Security Forums," Clarion Project, September 2, 2013.
48  Ibid.
49  Ibid.
50  Ibid.
51  Meira Svirsky, "Gov. Christie Appoints Islamist-Friendly AG to Be New Senator," Clarion Project, June 9, 2013.
52  Meira Svirsky, "CAIR, a Muslim Brotherhood Front, Praises Chris Christie," Clarion Project, September 20, 2013.
53  Meira Svirsky, "Chris Christie Bent on Including Islamists in Security Forums," Clarion Project, September 2, 2013.
54  Meira Svirsky, "Christie Responds to Critics About His Ties to Radical Islamists," Clarion Project, August 7, 2012.
55  "Legislating Fear: Islamophobia and its Impact in the United States," Council on American–Islamic Relations, Report 2013.
56  Daniel Burke, "Senate hearing focuses on U.S. Muslims' rights, not radical ties," *USA Today*, March 30, 2011.
57  "The Muslim Brotherhood's Strategic Plan For America – Court Document," Clarion Project, accessed April 2014.
58  "Islamic Association of Palestine: Now-defunct Illinois-based front group for the terrorist organization Hamas," *Discover The Networks*, March 2017.
59  Qanta Ahmed, "Moderate Muslims must confront the threat that Islamism poses to countries like Iraq, Syria and Egypt," *USA Today*, September 4, 2013.
60  Ibid.
61  Ibid.
62  Ibid.
63  Ibid.
64  Jessica Murphy, "West should do more to fight Islamophobia: Turkish minister," *Canoe News*, September 20, 2012.
65  Ibid.
66  Ibid.
67  Ibid.
68  Terence P. Jeffrey, "U.S. President Speaks to U.N. About YouTube Video Posted in June," *CNS News*, September 25, 2012.
69  Christine Williams, "The 'Victimology' Subterfuge," Gatestone Institute, January 15, 2013.
70  Ibid.

71 Michael Shields, "Danish Mohammad cartoonist rejects censorship," *Reuters*, September 20, 2012.

72 Lisa Daftari, "Islamophobia in action? 'Honor Diaries' screening shut down by CAIR," *Fox News Opinion*, March 31, 2014.

73 Ibid.

74 David Horowitz and Robert Spencer, "Islamophobia: Thought Crime of The Totalitarian Failure," David Horowitz Freedom Center, 2011.

75 Ibid.

76 Abdur-Rahman Muhammad, "Whether or not Ground Zero mosque is built, U.S. Muslims have access to the American Dream," *NY Daily News*, September 5, 2010.

77 Bulent Senay, "Islamophobia: Europe's Identity Crisis," Dutch Islamic Foundation, OSCE Review Conference – WARSAW, October 8, 2010.

78 "MCC shocked at OHRC decision to trumpet Islamist cause," Muslim Canadian Congress, April 9, 2008.

79 Ibid.

80 "2013 Hate Crime Statistics," U.S. Department of Justice, Federal Bureau of Investigation, Criminal Justice Information Services Division, 2013.

81 Private Member's Bill, 41st Parliament, 1st Session, Parliament of Canada, June 12, 2011–September 13, 2013.

82 "Bill C-304 - An Act to amend the Canadian Human Rights Act (protecting freedom)," *The FreedomSite Blog*, September 30, 2011

83 "Bill C-304 (Historical): An Act to amend the Canadian Human Rights Act (protecting freedom)," Open Parliament, Library of Parliament, September 2013.

84 Bruce Bawer, *While Europe Slept* (New York: Doubleday, 2006), 248.

85 Ibid.

86 Baptist Press, "NINA SHEA: The fatwa against free speech," *Townhall*, October 5, 2012.

87 "Blasphemy Laws and Censorship by States and Non-State Actors," Statement of Nina Shea, Director, Hudson Institute's Center for Religious Freedom Before the Tom Lantos Human Rights Commission, July 14, 2016.

88 Baptist Press, "NINA SHEA: The fatwa against free speech," *Townhall*, October 5, 2012.

89 "Military investigates video of racially charged skit," *CBC News*, November 8, 2012.

90 Ibid.

91 Ibid.

92 Dakshana Bascaramurty, "Controversial Muslim writer says multiculturalism isn't what it once was," *The Globe and Mail*, March 7, 2014.

93 Dr. Hatem Bazian, "Islamophobia Research & Documentation Project," Center for Race & Gender, University of California, Berkeley, accessed March 2017.

94 Ibid.

95 Ibid.

## CHAPTER THIRTEEN

1 Meira Svirsky, "Dr. Tawfik Hamid: Islam Needs Modern Interpretation," Clarion Project, December 4, 2012.

2 "How Central Is Muslim Anti-Semitism?" *Fox News: On the Record with Greta Van Susteren,* June 24, 2002.

3   Nonie Darwish, "Why Muslims Must Hate Jews," *Jihad Watch*, August 2, 2012.

4   Ibid.

5   Ibid.

6   Ibid.

7   "Muhammad: Legacy of a Prophet," *PBS*, 2002, http://www.pbs.org/muhammad/ma_otherrel.shtml.

8   Ibid.

9   "Muhammad," *PBS*, accessed May 2016, http://www.pbs.org/empires/islam/profilesmuhammed.html.

10  Ibid.

11  Nonie Darwish, "Why Muslims Must Hate Jews," *Jihad Watch*, August 2, 2012.

12  Ibid.

13  Mitchell G. Bard, "Chapter 11: Treatment of Jews in the Arab World," Jewish Virtual Library, 2016.

14  Ibid.

15  "The Nuremberg Laws: Background and Overview," Jewish Virtual Library, 2016.

16  Ibid.

17  Ibid.

18  Sean O'Neill and John Steele, "Mein Kampf for sale, in Arabic," *The Telegraph*, March 19, 2002.

19  Aaron Klein, "Abbas Publishes Anti-Semitic Screed," *World Net Daily*, May 21, 2005.

20  Itamar Marcus and Barbara Crook, "The Protocols of the Elders of Zion: An authentic document in Palestinian Authority ideology," *Palestinian Media Watch*, May 2015.

21  Ibid.

22  Andrea Levin, "Palestinian Textbooks Teach Anti-Israel Hate," Committee for Accuracy in Middle East Reporting in America, June 1, 1999.

23  Ibid.

24  Ibid.

25  Ibid.

26  Ibid.

27  Ibid.

28  Ibid.

29  Joshua A. Dalva, "Antisemitism in the Arab World," Boston University, accessed September 2016.

30  Mitchell G. Bard, "Chapter 11: Treatment of Jews in the Arab World," Jewish Virtual Library, 1998–2017.

31  Ibid.

32  Sarah Honig, "Another Tack: The Poison In The Well," *Jerusalem Post*, December 16, 2011.

33  Ibid.

34  "Arab Media Review: Anti-Semitism And Other Trends," Anti-Defamation League, January–June, 2012.

35  "South Sudan and Israel - unlikely allies?," Inside Story, *Al Jazeera*, December 22, 2011.

36  Robert S. Wistrich, "Islamic Judeophobia: An Existential Threat," in *Muhammad's Monsters*, edited by David Bukay (Balfour Books, 2004).

37 Ibid.

38 Ibid.

39 "Hassan Nasrallah: In His Own Words," Committee for Accuracy in Middle East Reporting in America, July 26, 2006.

40 David Meir-Levi, "'They Stole Our Land' vs. The Grand Mufti of Jerusalem," *FrontPage Magazine*, November 24, 2011.

41 "More Baseless Israel Vilification From CAIR Rep," The Investigative Project on Terrorism, December 28, 2012.

42 Yaakov Lappin, "Muslim Brotherhood: 'Prepare Egyptians For War With Israel,'" *Jerusalem Post*, February 1, 2011.

43 Natasha Mozgovaya, "U.S.: Muslim Brotherhood Gave Assurances on Egypt-Israel Peace Treaty," *Haaretz*, January 6, 2012.

44 Ibid.

45 "Hamas Covenant 1988: The Covenant of the Islamic Resistance Movement," The Avalon Project, Yale Law School, August 18, 1988.

46 Morton A. Klein, "Abbas' Fatah Praises Hamas' Call For Israel's Demise," *Algemeiner*, December 11, 2012.

47 Ibid.

48 "Hamas Leader Khaled Mash'al at a Damascus Mosque: The Nation of Islam Will Sit at the Throne of the World and the West Will Be Full of Remorse – When It's Too Late," Middle East Media Research Institute, February 7, 2006.

49 Ari Yashar, "PA Live TV Event Glorifies Terror, Murder, Hatred," *Arutz Sheva*, December 20, 2013.

50 Ibid.

51 Ibid.

52 David Matas, B'nai B'rith International Mission to the 25th session of the United Nations Human Rights Council, March 2014.

53 Ibid.

54 Ibid.

55 Jeffrey Goldberg, "New Chapter, Old Story," review of *The Devil That Never Dies*, by Daniel Jonah Goldhagen, *The New York Times*, October 11, 2013, Sunday Book Review.

## CHAPTER FOURTEEN

1 "Vision, Mission, Core Principles," Council on American–Islamic Relations, October 1, 2015.

2 Daniel Pipes, "CAIR: 'Moderate' friends of terror," *New York Post*, April 22, 2002.

3 Josh Gerstein, "Islamic Groups Named in Hamas Funding Case," *The New York Sun*, June 4, 2007.

4 Ibid.

5 "Moderate Muslims Speak Out on Capitol Hill," The Investigative Project on Terrorism, October 1, 2010.

6 Clare M. Lopez, "History of the Muslim Brotherhood Penetration of the U.S. Government," Gatestone Institute, April 15, 2013.

7 Ibid.

8 Ibid.

9 John Rossomando, "Egyptian Magazine: Muslim Brotherhood Infiltrates Obama Administration," The Investigative Project on Terrorism, January 3, 2013.

10 Ibid.

11   Chris Stephen, Eileen Byrne, and Peter Beaumont, "Controversial film sparks protests and violence across the Muslim world," *The Guardian*, September 14, 2012.

12   Michael J. Totten, "Radical Islam's Global Reaction: The Push for Blasphemy Laws," *World Affairs*, January/February 2013.

13   Christopher Williams, "Anti-Islam film prompts Saudi call for net censorship body," *The Telegraph*, October 11, 2012.

14   David Martosko, "Hillary hammers 'obsession' with the words 'radical Islamic terrorism' as she insists 'Muslims... have nothing whatsoever to do with terrorism,'" *UK Daily Mail*, November 19, 2015.

15   Suzan Fraser and Matthew Lee, "Islamophobia should be a crime against humanity, 'just like Zionism': Turkey's PM draws fire for 'offensive' comment," *National Post*, March 1, 2013.

16   "If EU opposes Islamophobia, it must accept Turkey as member: Erdoğan," *Hurriyet Daily News*, January 24, 2015.

17   "Saudi Publications on Hate Ideology Invade American Mosques," Center for Religious Freedom, Freedom House, 2005.

18   Dave Gaubatz, "Muslim Children in America are Being Taught to Hate," *Family Security Matters*, January 18, 2012.

19   Meira Svirsky, "Exclusive: Islamist Terror Enclave Discovered in Texas," Clarion Project, February 18, 2014.

20   Meira Svirsky, "Muslims of the Americas (MOA)," Clarion Project, February 12, 2013.

21   Ibid.

22   Ibid.

23   Meira Svirsky, "American Muslims Stone Christians in Dearborn, Michigan," Clarion Project, June 27, 2012.

24   John Perazzo, "The Muslim Students Association and the Jihad Network: A Report by the Terrorist Awareness Project," David Horowitz Freedom Center, 2008.

25   Daniel Pipes, "Niqab Security Outrages at Airports," Middle East Forum, August 3, 2010.

26   "U.S. Immigration Policy Aided Boston Marathon Terrorists," USBC, *National Security/Immigration News*, 2013.

27   Peter Finn, Carol D. Leonnig, and Will Englund, "Tsarnaev brothers' homeland was war-torn Chechnya," *The Washington Post*, April 19, 2013.

28   "Boston Marathon Terror Attack Fast Facts," *CNN Library*, March 29, 2017.

29   "U.S. Immigration Policy Aided Boston Marathon Terrorists," USBC, *National Security/Immigration News*, 2013.

30   Aaron Brown, "'Just wait...' Islamic State reveals it has smuggled THOUSANDS of extremists into Europe," *UK Express*, November 18, 2015.

31   Koran 4:100.

32   Christine Williams, "Shut Down Iran's Embassy in Canada," Gatestone Institute, August 9, 2012.

33   Ibid.

34   Tom Godfrey, "Muslims claiming cash for numerous wives," *Canoe News*, October 5, 2015.

35   Oren Dorell, "Some say schools giving Muslims special treatment," *USA Today*, 2011.

36 Emma Teitel, "Opposing prayer in Toronto public schools, with dignity," *Maclean's*, July 27, 2011.

37 Ibid.

38 *UK Daily Mail* reporter, "Nicolas Sarkozy joins David Cameron and Angela Merkel view that multiculturalism has failed," *UK Daily Mail*, February 11, 2011.

39 Ibid.

40 Hannah Roberts, "ISIS threatens to send 500,000 migrants to Europe as a 'psychological weapon' in chilling echo of Gaddafi's prophecy that the Mediterranean 'will become a sea of chaos,'" *UK Daily Mail*, February 18, 2015.

41 Aaron Brown, "'Just wait…' Islamic State reveals it has smuggled THOUSANDS of extremists into Europe," *UK Express*, November 18, 2015.

42 John Irish, "French security chief warns Islamic State plans wave of attacks in France," *Reuters*, May 19, 2016.

43 Manasi Gopalakrishnan, "'Islamic State' reportedly training terrorists to enter Europe as asylum seekers," *Deutsche Welle*, November 14, 2016.

44 Belinda Robinson, "'There are big problems' Outrage as migrant rapes soar by 133% – in just ONE YEAR," *UK Express*, December 9, 2016.

45 Virginia Hale, "Islam Academic: Migrants Want Eurabia, Globalists Using Migrants to Destroy the West," *Breitbart*, August 14, 2016.

46 "Canadian Multiculturalism Act," Government of Canada, Justice Laws Website, R.S.C., 1985, c. 24 (4th Supp.), http://laws-lois.justice.gc.ca/eng/acts/C-18.7/page-1.html.

47 Stewart Bell, "Justin Trudeau defends his decision to attend Islamic conference sponsored by organization linked to Hamas," *National Post,* December 12, 2012.

48 Ibid.

49 Ibid.

50 Tarek Fatah, "Trudeau in hot seat with Muslims," *London Free Press*, December 21, 2012.

51 "CAIR-CAN condemns anti-Muslim website for slandering conference participants and guests," *Cair-Can News*, December 12, 2012.

52 Stewart Bell, "Justin Trudeau defends his decision to attend Islamic conference sponsored by organization linked to Hamas," *National Post,* December 12, 2012.

53 "The Muslim Brotherhood's 'General Strategic Goal' For North America," *Discover The Networks*, 2005.

54 "United Against Terrorism: A Collaborative Effect Towards a Secure, Inclusive and Just Canada," National Council of Canadian Muslims/Royal Canadian Mounted Police, 2014.

55 Douglas Quan, "RCMP took issue with 'adversarial' tone of Muslim groups' counter-radicalization handbook," *Canada.com*, 2014, http://o.canada.com/news/national/rcmp-took-issue-with-adversarial-tone-of-muslim-groups-counter-radicalization-handbook.

56 "United Against Terrorism: A Collaborative Effect Towards a Secure, Inclusive and Just Canada," National Council of Canadian Muslims/Royal Canadian Mounted Police, 2014.

57 Ibid.

58 Ibid.

59 Sarah Ahmad, "The True Spirit of Jihad," *Ahmadiyya Anjuman Isha 'at Islam Lahore Inc. U.S.A.*, accessed March 2017.

60  Douglas E. Streusand, "What Does Jihad Mean?," Middle East Forum, September 1997.

61  Robert Sibley, "Muslim group indulging in 'lawfare jihad'?," *Ottawa Citizen*, January 29, 2014.

62  "Notice of Libel, Ontario Superior Court of Justice Between National Council of Canadian Muslims (NCCM) and The Right Honourable Stephen Harper, Jason Macdonald, and Her Majesty the Queen in Right of Canada," 2014.

63  "Proceedings of the Standing Senate Committee on Social Affairs, Science and Technology," Senate of Canada, Issue 18, February 3, 2011.

64  Ibid.

65  "P.M. Harper tells Muslims: No Special Treatment," *Live Leak*, January 6, 2011.

66  Jake Flanagin, "The Dangerous Logic of Quebec's 'Charter of Values,'" *The Atlantic*, January 23, 2014.

67  Benjamin Shingler, "Amnesty International warns Quebec values charter would violate 'fundamental rights,'" *National Post*, September 21, 2013.

68  Jonathan D. Halevi, "MP Iqra Khalid suggests that terrorism carried out by Muslims 'has no religion,' *CIJnews*, May 2, 2016.

69  *CIJnews* Staff, "Liberal MP Iqra Khalid tables second anti-Islamophobia motion," *CIJ News*, December 9, 2016.

70  Petition e-411 (Islam), 42nd Parliament, House of Commons, Parliament of Canada, initiated by Samer Majzoub from Pierrefonds, Quebec, on June 8, 2016.

71  Althia Raj, "Tory MPs Oppose NDP Motion Condemning All Forms Of Islamophobia," *The Huffington Post*, October 6, 2016.

72  Nurbanu Kizil, "Canadian parliament passes anti-Islamophobia motion," *Daily Sabah*, November 3, 2016.

73  Jonathan D. Halevi, "MP Iqra Khalid meets with board members of the pro intifada Palestine House," *CIJnews*, January 22, 2016.

74  Rhonda Spivak, "Will Palestine House, De-funded Under Harper Gov't For Pattern of Extremism, Be Involved In Resettlement of Syrian Refugees?," *Winnipeg Jewish Review*, December 20, 2015.

75  Jonathan D. Halevi, "Toronto-based Palestine House mourns Palestinian terrorists," *CIJnews*, March 2, 2016.

76  Jonathan D. Halevi, "MP Iqra Khalid meets with board members of the pro intifada Palestine House," *CIJnews*, January 22, 2016.

77  Iqra Khalid - Private Members' Motions, M-103, Parliament of Canada, March 2017, http://www.parl.gc.ca/Parliamentarians/en/members/Iqra-Khalid(88849)/Motions.

78  "Protecting Canadian Free Speech Rights from Allegations of 'Islamophobia,'" Act! for Canada, December 15, 2016.

79  Lorenzo Vidino, "The Tripartite Threat of Radical Islam to Europe," Jewish Policy Center, Winter 2007.

80  Ibid.

81  Ibid.

82  "ANALYSIS: Holy Land Documents Point to Covert Muslim Brotherhood Structure In The U.S.," *The Global Muslim Brotherhood Daily Watch*, August 29, 2007.

83  Leslie Eaton, "Prosecutors Say a Charity Aided Terrorists Indirectly," *The New York Times*, September 18, 2007.

84  Ibid.

85 "An Explanatory Memorandum on the General Strategic Goal For The Group In North America," From the Archives of the Muslim Brotherhood in America, Center for Security Policy, May 25, 2013.

86 Ibid.

87 Ibid.

88 "ANALYSIS: Holy Land Documents Point to Covert Muslim Brotherhood Structure In The U.S.," *Global MB Watch*, August 29, 2007.

89 "An Explanatory Memorandum on the General Strategic Goal For The Group In North America," From the Archives of the Muslim Brotherhood in America, Center for Security Policy, May 25, 2013.

90 Ambassador Professor Dumitru Chican, "THE PROJECT – A Project of the Cultural Jihad," *Word Security Network*, November 10, 2014.

91 Ibid.

92 "Former Al-Taqwa Bank Employee Featured In Swiss Seminar," *The Global Muslim Brotherhood Daily Watch*, September 16, 2007.

93 "Profile: Yusuf al-Qaradawi," The Investigative Project on Terrorism, accessed August 2015.

94 Ibid.

95 Ambassador Professor Dumitru Chican, "THE PROJECT – A Project of the Cultural Jihad," *World Security Network*, November 10, 2014.

96 Ibid.

97 Ibid.

98 Ibid.

99 Ibid.

100 Ibid.

101 Liz Sly and Ahmed Ramadan, "Insurgents seize Iraqi city of Mosul as security forces flee," *The Washington Post*, June 10, 2014,

102 Ibid.

103 Daniel Pipes, "ISIS Rampages, the Middle East Shakes," Middle East Forum, June 12, 2014.

104 Cassandra Vinograd, "What Does Boko Haram's Pledge of Allegiance to ISIS Really Mean?," *NBC News*, March 9, 2015.

105 Pascale Combelles Siegel, AQIM's Playbook in Mali, Combating Terrorism Center, March 27, 2013.

106 Ibid.

105 Ibid.

106 Ibid.

107 Ibid.

108 Ibid.

109 Ibid.

110 Ibid.

111 Ibid.

112 Daniel Pipes interview with author, March 2013.

## CONCLUSION

1 Bernard Lewis, *What Went Wrong?: The Clash Between Islam and Modernity in the Middle East* (New York, London: Harper Perennial, January 2003).

2 Yevgeniya Baraz, "The Position of Jews and Christians in the Ottoman Empire," *Inquiries Journal*, Vol. 2 No. 05, 2010.

3 Efraim Karsh, "Efraim Karsh on the Ottoman Catastrophe: A review of Eugene

Rogan's 'The Fall of the Ottomans.' From the May 13, 2015, issue of the Times Literary Supplement," The Wall Street Journal, May 13, 2015.

4  Ibid.

5  "The Origins of Sufism," Open Path/Sufi Way, accessed March 2017.

6  Stephen Schwartz, "How Many Sufis Are There in Islam?," *The Huffington Post*, September 19, 2011.

7  Bernard Lewis, "'The Crisis of Islam,'" *The New York Times*, April 6, 2003.

8  Ibid.

# INDEX